0903845

796.357
Sulli
Sullivan, Neil

ON LINE

The Diamond in the Bronx

THE
DIAMOND
IN THE BRONX

YANKEE STADIUM AND
THE POLITICS OF NEW YORK

With a New Epilogue

NEIL J. SULLIVAN

OXFORD
UNIVERSITY PRESS

OXFORD
UNIVERSITY PRESS

Oxford University Press, Inc., publishes works that further
Oxford University's objective of excellence
in research, scholarship, and education.

Oxford New York
Auckland   Cape Town   Dar es Salaam   Hong Kong   Karachi
Kuala Lumpur   Madrid   Melbourne   Mexico City   Nairobi
New Delhi   Shanghai   Taipei   Toronto

With offices in
Argentina   Austria   Brazil   Chile   Czech Republic   France   Greece
Guatemala   Hungary   Italy   Japan   Poland   Portugal   Singapore
South Korea   Switzerland   Thailand   Turkey   Ukraine   Vietnam

Copyright © 2001, 2008 by Oxford University Press, Inc.

First published by Oxford University Press, Inc., 2001
198 Madison Avenue, New York, NY 10016
www.oup.com

Issued as an Oxford University Press paperback, 2002, 2008

Oxford is a registered trademark of Oxford University Press

Library of Congress Cataloging-in-Publication Data is available.
Library of Congress Control Number 2001269770
ISBN 978-0-19-533183-7 (pbk.)

1 3 5 7 9 8 6 4 2
Printed in the United States of America

For Carol Murray
and
In loving memory of Tom Murray

Contents

Acknowledgments

The idea for this book was the product of countless conversations about baseball and politics with many friends over many years. Much of the material was made available by the staffs at the Bronx Municipal Building, the New York City Municipal Archives, and the New York Public Library. Their patient and professional efforts belie the easy and erroneous remarks sometimes made about public employees. Mario Charles and Jerry Bornstein were especially helpful at the Newman Library at Baruch College. Susan Freedman provided extremely useful research assistance as well as many thoughtful suggestions. The Bronx Historical Society has an invaluable collection for any work on that borough.

Peter Ginna, Rudy Faust, and Aimee Chevrette at Oxford University Press have been encouraging throughout the project, and invaluable in keeping me on track. Jane Dystel has continued to be a valued friend as well as agent.

Bill Agee and Jerry Mitchell are friends and fellow academics who have not yet mastered the art of passing off baseball as scholarship. Dan Fenn's extensive knowledge of business and government has been particularly thought provoking. Peter Woll was my mentor at Brandeis University, and he continues to be a cherished friend and teacher. Joseph Cianciulli and my colleagues on the Yonkers Zoning Board of Appeals offer inspired instruction on balancing economic development with other aspects of the public interest. Tom Vilante generously offered his own insights on Yankee Stadium as well as considerable help in securing interviews.

I am grateful to Roger Hannon and Father Walt Modrys, S.J.—Yankee fans who have been gracious these past few years to a suffering Dodger fan. Patricia Flynn has been a dear friend and steadfast help to my family. From his tonsorial parlor, Emile Vaessen dispenses unparalleled wisdom and makes the Sullivan boys look as good as the gene pool allows. Bob Fitzpatrick was very encouraging about this book, and it renews a terrible loss that he is not here to read the finished product. Greg Shuker is another absent friend who would have offered an early and honest review.

Authors often thank their families for being patient during the research and writing. Neither Kate nor Tim ever displayed such patience, but I love them anyway. To their great fortune and mine, their mother Joyce has enough patience and love for all of us, and it is to her parents that this book is gratefully dedicated.

Y ankee Stadium is an incomparable theater in American sports. The World Series visits other ballparks, but its home is Yankee Stadium, where the championship flag has been raised twenty-six times. Since 1923, a few dreary seasons aside, any fan visiting the Stadium would see at least one future Hall of Famer in pinstripes. Babe Ruth, Lou Gehrig, and Joe DiMaggio are just some of the Yankees who have been legendary in American culture for more than the records they made playing baseball.

Other sports have borrowed the Stadium for great moments of their own. Joe Louis destroyed Max Schmeling in the first round of a heavy-weight championship fight in 1938, and kept his title with an even more gallant win against Billy Conn in 1946. Notre Dame and Army played memorable games there, including a scoreless tie in 1946 when both teams had undefeated seasons. The National Football League began its hold on the public imagination when the Baltimore Colts beat the New York Giants in a 1958 overtime championship game.

When popes say Mass in New York, Yankee Stadium can become a church. At a mass on October 2, 1979, John Paul II urged the faithful to meet their obligations to the poor and all those in need—a poignant appeal at a time when the Yankees thrived and the Bronx suffered.

In a rare mistake, the Beatles played Shea, but Pink Floyd rocked the Stadium. Billy Graham and Nelson Mandela have packed the place.

As riveting, popular, or significant as these other moments have been, they are grace notes to baseball. Yankee Stadium, more than anything else, is a baseball stadium and the home of the most successful team in professional sports. The National Football League and the National Basketball Association have taken runs at becoming the dominant sport in America, but they both have risen on television, with neither sport having a facility that compares in importance to Yankee Stadium. Baseball has its old lovables—Fenway Park and Wrigley Field—and the ghost of Ebbets Field can be seen again in new ballparks from Baltimore to the San Francisco Bay, but Yankee Stadium remains unique as a home of championships.

For all this remarkable history, Yankee Stadium has a very uncertain future because, by the standards of the sports industry, the Stadium is a relic. Within a few years, it could be replaced entirely or renovated in a way that puts the price of a seat beyond the financial reach of many fans.

The fate of the Stadium will be determined by George Steinbrenner, the Yankees' principal owner, and various public officials in New York. Their decision will reflect Steinbrenner's interests balanced against competing claims from other New Yorkers. In other words, it will be inevitably political, and it will almost certainly include a substantial public subsidy from the city treasury to the Yankees.

Politics and Yankee Stadium have been linked from the time Jacob Ruppert and Tillinghast Huston bought a sawmill on the Harlem River from the Astor family and built the house for which Babe Ruth gets credit. Ruppert and Huston had purchased the Yankees in 1915 when the team played in the Polo Grounds as tenants of the New York Giants. At that time, the sawmill's location was unpromising on its face, but, in a few years, subway lines provided access and the Bronx Terminal Market became a commercial anchor for the area. Jake Ruppert had been a four-term congressman connected politically through Tammany Hall, the machine that dominated New York City politics in the late nineteenth and early twentieth centuries; these projects and Ruppert's opportunity to know about them exemplified the kind of "honest graft" for which Tammany was notorious.

Most remarkable about the Stadium's construction, from our own perspective, was the financing. The effort was entirely the responsibility of the Yankee owners even though Ruppert's fortune rested on the family brewery and the Stadium was built while the country was in the middle of Prohibition. In an age when political connections made as many fortunes as new industrial technologies, no one suggested that city taxpayers should assume the cost of the Yankees' new facility.

Fifty years later, the Yankees were owned by the Columbia Broadcasting System (CBS), one of the most prosperous companies in America. The aging Stadium had been sold in the 1950s to a private party who had bequeathed the property to Rice University with the land beneath going to the Knights of Columbus. Despite financial forces that were driving the city to bankruptcy in the early 1970s, Mayor John Lindsay successfully pressed to have New York assume ownership of the Stadium along with the costs of renovation.

Other cities across America were building stadiums to attract or to keep their sports teams and Lindsay seemed to take those ventures as challenges to his own administration. All the resources of modern urban government—the professional structures that had swept aside the machines like Tammany—were brought to bear on the problem of how to provide an adequate baseball stadium for the Yankees. If no one thought to offer Ruppert public money to build the Stadium, the use of the public purse to pay over $100 million for the renovation was a foregone conclusion to Lindsay and the Yankee owners.

The deal cut between the city and the ball club secured the Yankees' future in New York for thirty years. The lease is up at the end of 2002, and the next relationship between the city and its legendary ball club is yet to be defined. Public money has been dedicated to minor league stadiums for the Yankees and Mets on Staten Island and in Brooklyn, but a proposal to build a new facility for the Yankees on the West Side of Manhattan collapsed despite the enthusiastic support of Mayor Rudolph Giuliani.

Giuliani is one of a number of public officials in recent years who have enjoyed considerable popularity by insisting that individual responsibility be an essential component of public policy. He has demanded that public spending meet clear standards of need, efficiency, and effectiveness when it has been directed to public health, education, shelter, and other civic responsibilities. He applies a different standard for spending public money on the Yankees.

New York is a city with an array of compelling demands. In its bleakest corners, thousands of children suffer and the question must be asked how those cries can be ignored while the city attends to the Yankees. In less urgent areas of public policy, the spending on professional sports stadiums can be examined against the needs of public recreation and scholastic athletics. Many neighborhoods and schools lack basic equipment and facilities for active popular participation in sports, yet the minimal public investment now proposed for the Yankees comes in at several hundred million dollars.

The stadium game in New York is not only an issue of public policy. It is a challenge as well for the business of major league baseball. A recent so-called Blue Ribbon Commission has issued a report on the commercial state of the business, and it finds grave problems of competitive imbalance. Implicit in the report is the question: How can the Yankees be reined in?

Competitive imbalance is troubling to many fans whose teams seem to have no chance even during the heady days of spring training. Some of these fans express exasperation when salaries reach new levels, but anyone concerned with this issue should consider the source of the players' new wealth. In the modern stadium game, the players are, in some respects, public employees. Taxpayers have relieved the clubs of the burden of paying for stadiums, so the owners have millions of dollars available to spend on players who may bring home a championship. Imagine the salaries of the best baby sitters and gardeners if the state picked up the payment of home mortgages.

The Basic Agreement between players and owners expires at the end of the 2001 season and the distress of many of the owners over the current contract raises the unsettling prospect that another strike or lock-out is possible. Complicating these negotiations is a new Stadium deal that will likely transfer millions of dollars from the taxpayers of New York to the Yankees. We can hardly calculate the impact throughout major league baseball of such a subsidy to a franchise that already operates in a commercial league of its own.

More important for New York, the city needs to determine its public interest in the context of professional sports. What support should it offer to its baseball teams and other entertainment firms that are both established and prosperous? Does a stadium subsidy take money from public safety, transportation, housing, health care, and other essential services that, among other effects, are necessary to attract other businesses? Does a new or renovated stadium price the average fan out of the building? What benefits accrue to New Yorkers who are not baseball fans? Do such subsidies contribute anything to the people in the city who most desperately need the help of the community?

These questions require decisions about complicated economic, social, and moral issues. Because those decisions reflect public choice, they will be made through the political institutions and processes of New York. To say that an issue is "political" invites some people to infer corruption, inefficiency, and neglect of their cherished interests. A critical premise of this book is that this dismal view of politics is legitimate only if New Yorkers allow it to be so.

The politics of a stadium deal refers to authorities in government who act on behalf of the public as well as the methods they use to determine the public interest. Several models have been used in the past regarding Yankee Stadium, and New Yorkers themselves will ultimately decide the nature of politics as the Stadium lease nears expiration. Public pressure on elected officials, a referendum, and lawsuits are just some of the tools at the public's disposal. Those devices can be abused if they serve only the narrow interests of a special few, so the representation of a wide array of New Yorkers actively participating in the politics of Yankee Stadium is indispensable in providing the surest determination of the city's public interest. This book is written to help New Yorkers in that effort.

1

OPENING DAY

In a decade that celebrated a mythical America, the opening of Yankee Stadium on April 18, 1923, was a high point of the party. Between noon and the 3:30 start, more than 60,000 fans packed the great structure while another 10,000 were turned away by the fire department.[1]

The day was blustery—cloudy with temperatures barely reaching fifty degrees, chilled further by a persistent breeze. Some fans wore straw hats with their overcoats, and that curious mix of fashion captured both the excitement for the summer game and the reality of the raw weather. Babe Ruth cooperated by hitting a home run in the third inning, so shivering fans could leave early without missing a classic moment. Those who stayed were rewarded with a 4–1 Yankee victory over the Boston Red Sox.

The crowd pressing into Yankee Stadium on Opening Day was not drawn to the kind of neighborhood ballpark that has reemerged as an architectural fashion in our own time. The Yankees had built the first true baseball *stadium*—a structure intended to accommodate massive crowds and make a progressive and confident statement about baseball's future:

Big was good; intimate was obsolete; and nostalgia had no warm memories yet to summon.

Fred Lieb, who coined the phrase "The House That Ruth Built," described the scene in the *New York Evening Telegram*. "Unlike the Polo Grounds, which is built in a hollow, the stadium can be seen for miles, as its triple decks grand stand majestically rises from the banks of the Harlem. Approaching it from the 150th Street viaduct one is impressed with its bigness. It looks only a short walk ahead, but as one approaches from Edgecombe Avenue he soon discovers it to be quite a hike."[2]

The *New York Times* praised the Stadium as "a skyscraper among baseball parks. Seen from the vantage point of the nearby subway structure, the mere height of the grandstand is tremendous."[3] The interior was equally impressive: "Once inside the grounds, the sweep of the big stand strikes the eye most forcibly. It throws its arms far out to each side, the grandstand ending away over where the bleachers begin. In the center of the vast pile of steel and concrete was the green spread of grass and diamond, and fewer ball fields are greener than that on which the teams played yesterday."[4]

The assembly that day was a snapshot of America in the Roaring Twenties, a country fashioning tranquility after tumultuous years of class, racial, and ethnic violence. By 1923, the turmoil seemed safely enough in the past for the country to enjoy its apparent peace and prosperity. The 1920s were a time to find comfort in American fables: a nation secure in splendid isolation; a land of opportunity for all; a place where heroes could rise from the most unlikely settings. Opening Day was a wonderful opportunity to profess this faith.

The pre-game festivities included a grand military display. The Superintendent of West Point, General F. W. Sladen, was featured, along with his aide, Captain Matthew Ridgway, later a hero of World War II and Korea. Representatives from the American Legion and the Veterans of Foreign Wars paraded on the field in a tribute to the doughboys who had recently fought in the Great War.

Music was provided by the Seventh Regiment Band under the baton of John Philip Sousa, "wearing only a few gross of his medals."[5] The

March King may have been overwhelmed by the Stadium. Robert F. Kelley of the *New York Post* wrote that "the best indication of the immensity of the new plant was furnished by the music of the Seventh Regiment Band, working hard in the corner of the left field stands, with only snatches of the tunes reaching the crowd near the home plate. It was like hearing the music of a parade on Fifth Avenue from an office window on a cross street."[6] Sousa led a parade of dignitaries to the center field flagpole where they played the National Anthem and raised the Yankees pennant from the championship season of 1922.

The notables then wound back to the area near home plate where the ceremonial first pitch was thrown. That honor went to Al Smith, New York's governor. The state's chief executive would have been an apt choice under most circumstances; but Smith was also a golden boy of Tammany Hall, and Tammany had played a central role in New York City baseball.[7]

Smith represented the bright side of the notorious Society of St. Tammany, an institution that had been around since the American Revolution. Whether in the hands of thieves or noble Sachems, Tammany reflected the hopes of New York's working class, and Al Smith personified those aspirations. With only a grade school education, Smith fit perfectly the legendary description George Washington Plunkitt's of a Tammany man: "They have all the education they need to whip the dudes who part their names in the middle."[8] No A. Emanuel Smith here. Al Smith was a New York original with a cocked derby, a cigar in the side of his mouth, and a voice like a bugle.

The governor's career is a great American story, but that was not enough to put the ball in his hand on Opening Day. The critical Tammany connection was Colonel Jacob Ruppert, who had bought the Yankees in a partnership in 1915. Ruppert was one of New York's high rollers who had inherited a family beer business and became a national spokesman for the industry. Beyond his wealth and social position, Ruppert had also been a four-term congressman representing the Upper East Side of Manhattan for Tammany.

These political ties were not casual associations. The inside information that a politically connected businessman could get concerning

3

pending transportation routes, housing patterns, and public works could be decisive in securing wealth.[9] Aside from public largesse, other policy issues affecting baseball included Sunday games and the use of the city police force to enforce order at the ballpark.

Success in the baseball business was almost inseparable from influence at City Hall, courtrooms, and the state capital. In New York, the early magnates of the Dodgers, Giants, or Yankees were generally either officeholders themselves or important figures within political clubs like Tammany.[10]

This connection between baseball and politics was one of the great examples of "honest graft." In Plunkitt's classic explanation, "dishonest graft" consisted of "blackmailin' gamblers, saloonkeepers, disorderly people etc."[11] Plunkitt argued that such extortion was unnecessary because of the ample opportunities to get rich from inside information:

> I'll tell you of one case. They were goin' to fix up a big park, no matter where. I got on to it, and went lookin' about for land in that neighborhood.
>
> I could get nothin' at a bargain but a big piece of swamp, but I took it fast enough and held on to it. What turned out was just what I counted on. They couldn't make the park complete without Plunkitt's swamp, and they had to pay a good price for it. Anything dishonest in that?"[12]

Ballparks required sizeable lots, located in densely populated neighborhoods or near transportation lines. Insider information gave public officials a great advantage in the baseball business. With an outlook like Plunkitt's, they could sleep the sleep of the just. The sermon on "honest graft" concludes, "If my worst enemy was given the job of writin' my epitaph when I'm gone, he couldn't do more than write: 'George W. Plunkitt. He Seen His Opportunities, and He Took 'Em.'"[13]

In those days, the purpose of American government was very unsettled. Arguments were advanced for public ownership, management, or regulation of some private enterprise, but fear of radicals and communists seriously complicated the discussion. Through the boisterous de-

4

bate, Tammany remained focused on helping its friends and punishing its enemies. This crude philosophy failed reformers' tests of efficiency, effectiveness, and equity, but it presented opportunities both to the poor such as Smith and the privileged such as Ruppert.

On Opening Day, at center stage in Ruppert's dream house, Smith threw the first pitch to Yankee catcher Wally Schang. On this day of grand possibilities, Governor Smith enjoyed an ovation that perhaps fueled his own aspirations of being the first Catholic president of the United States.

As the Yankees took the field to start the game, most eyes would have turned to the curious juxtaposition in right field. The minimal grounds were a mere 296 feet down the foul line, but they were occupied by the man who had transformed baseball into a game of brute power.

Al Smith represented the New Yorkers who were born in the city under tough circumstances, then battled to the top. Babe Ruth represented the millions who were born somewhere else, sometimes in unclear circumstances. These people had little reason to preserve the family lineage and every reason to look ahead at what they might accomplish in New York. Ann Douglas, including the Babe in her list of those who came to New York in the 1920s and defined an era, observed "the overwhelming majority of the artists and performers who became identified with what Fitzgerald christened 'the metropolitan spirit' were arrivistes, arrivistes filled with excitement and eager to escape their hometowns, the places F.P.A [journalist Franklin P. Adams] liked to refer to as 'Dullsboro.' "[14]

In New York, Ruth established that if living in the moment is a virtue, then he was a saint. The man was pure appetite, and he was another of the wonderful distractions that assured people that the physical and sensual were sufficient. He "epitomized," Douglas wrote "the 'Watch me—I'm a Wow!' ethos."[15] For a nation that had spent itself wrangling over war, civil liberties, Bolshevism, and the Klan, Ruth was both a respite and a tonic.

As Robert Creamer put it,

Ruth was made for New York. It has been said that where youth sees discovery, age sees coincidence, and perhaps the retrospect of years makes Ruth's arrival in Manhattan in 1920 seem only a fortuitous juxtaposition of man and place in time. Nonetheless, Ruth in that place at that time was discovery. And adventure. And excitement. And all the concomitant titillations.[16]

Ruth is sometimes accused of, or applauded for, ending "inside baseball." The game had been played through its first generations by scratching for a single run—using the sacrifice and the stolen base to get a runner around to third base where a single, another sacrifice, or an error could bring him home with the decisive run. The efforts of four or more batters to post that single run could now be matched in an instant by the most powerful swing in baseball.

Ruth's approach was certainly less complicated than Ty Cobb's or John McGraw's. To someone new to the game—children, perhaps a recently arrived immigrant, or a casual fan unfamiliar with the intricacies of baseball—learning the hit-and-run play took time and attention that may have been needed elsewhere. But, waiting for the Babe to come to bat, then enjoying either the home run or the strikeout—that was fairly accessible. Babe Ruth made it easier to be a baseball fan than it had ever been before.

He added something else that was important in the 1920s. He added fun. The change from inside baseball to the home run was more than a switch from a cerebral game to a purely physical one. The game of Cobb and McGraw was brutally physical. Spikes and fists were all part of the tactics to push that precious run across. Cobb and McGraw were also angry men who seemed to take a warlike approach to the ballpark. They reflected the turmoil of the time while Ruth offered an escape. He was quick with a comeback and a smile. He generally could take a joke, even those of opposing players that pushed the most sensitive sexual and racial themes far beyond the bounds of decorum. (Ruth mistakenly was thought, even by some players in the Negro Leagues, to be part African American.)

Ruth seemed to be unburdened by celebrity. He loved the attention that the public and press gave him, and they appreciated simply his presence.

On Opening Day in 1923, the veneer of this New York celebrity was showing some cracks. Ruth's first season in New York in 1920 was a sensation. He hit fifty-four home runs (no one before had hit even thirty), led the Yankees to their first pennant, and helped the club set an attendance mark by drawing a million fans to the Polo Grounds—all as news of the Black Sox scandal broke. He followed in 1921 by breaking his year-old record with fifty-nine home runs, another pennant, and another million through the gate.

Ruth's 1922 season was relatively disappointing. He had defied Commissioner Kenesaw Landis by going on a barnstorming tour after the previous season, and his offense earned him a six-week suspension in April and May 1922. The Babe started slowly when he returned, and the fans were hard on him. The frustrating slump and the catcalls from the stands provoked Ruth's temper, including one instance in which he went into the seats after a heckler.

He returned to form during the last four months of the season. He wound up with thirty-five home runs, but lost the title to Ken Williams of the St. Louis Browns, who hit thirty-nine. The Yankees again won the American League pennant, and again drew over a million; but some of the Babe's luster was gone.

The Yankees got the home runs, the brio, and the attendance, but they also got a self-indulgent young man who battled authority like a petulant adolescent. As long as the battles remained in the front office, the effects could be overlooked, but the 1922 season suggested to some fans and writers that, at the age of twenty-seven, the Babe's best days were behind him. The strong start in the new house allayed some of those fears. W. O. McGeehan of the *New York Herald* expressed a common concern. "It seems to me that the Babe got his results because he was a joyous and care-free youngster who walked to the plate with a laugh on his lips and a merry song in his heart and just batted the ball against the welkin [sky] with a careless swing."[17] McGeehan was anxious that the fans and press had taken that joy from Ruth with potentially disastrous effects on his career.

After cheering for the Babe, the inaugural crowd would have been delighted to see Yankee shortstop Everett Scott take his position in the field at the top of the first. Scott had recently turned an ankle, but he shook it off to maintain a consecutive game streak that now reached 987. He had a fine Opening Day with a double in two official at bats along with a sacrifice bunt and four infield assists, including the front end of a double play. His streak would continue until it reached 1307, ending in May 1925. And, a couple of weeks later on June 2, Lou Gehrig would begin the run that would eclipse Scott.[18]

We are warned by John Kieran of the *New York Tribune* that describing the game on Opening Day is "almost as pointless as noticing the bridegroom at a wedding."[19] Nonetheless, Bob Shawkey pitched for the Yankees, and "Bob the Gob," a nickname from his naval service in World War I, was quite a sight wearing a red, long-sleeved undershirt that caught the eye even as the shadows lengthened in the late afternoon. Shawkey allowed only two walks, and he hit a batter. The first hit in the Stadium was a single by George Burns, the Red Sox first baseman. Burns later walked in the seventh inning, and he scored on a triple by Sox second baseman Norman McMillan. That was the only run for Boston as Shawkey gave up but one other hit on his way to a complete game.

The Red Sox countered with Howard Ehmke, who himself pitched well. He got into a jam in the bottom of the third inning that second baseman Aaron Ward began with a single to left field. Scott's sacrifice moved him to second, but he was tagged out at third after Shawkey grounded back to Ehmke. Shawkey advanced to second while Ward was pursued in a rundown. Leadoff hitter Whitey Witt, the center fielder, worked Ehmke for a walk. Shawkey scored on a single by third baseman Joe Dugan.

With two on and two out, Ehmke made the most common mistake of the era. In Grantland Rice's account in the *New York Tribune*, "A white streak left Babe Ruth's 52 ounce bludgeon in the third inning of yesterday's opening game at the Yankee Stadium. On a low line it sailed, like a silver flame, through the gray, bleak April shadows, and into the right field bleachers, while the great slugger started on his jog around the towpaths for his first home run of the year."[20]

The three-run homer completed the Yankees' scoring for the day, and, with Shawkey's pitching, it secured the win. Before the game, the

Babe had declared that he would give a year of his life to hit a home run, and at least part of the bargain was honored.

W. O. McGeehan understood the importance of Ruth's performance even if he saw a maturity that is almost comical to imagine. "[H]ere we have the Babe, a grown up and a person of great seriousness doing what the Peter Pan sort of Ruth used to do. . . . That home run on the first day means much to the Babe, and consequently much in relation to the prosperity of baseball. When the Babe was hitting them loosely and freely the customers were happy and the clubs were gathering in the profits. If the Babe had started badly it might have tended to discourage' him. But on the first day, before the biggest crowd that ever saw a ball game, he sent out his first home run of the year."[21]

McGeehan's faith in the Babe's "great seriousness" would be tested many times in the years ahead, but his grasp of the importance of the home run to the prosperity of baseball was on the mark. The short porch in right field was designed to take advantage of Ruth's power for the fans' enjoyment, and this feature of the Stadium became one of its most distinctive as the right field stands quickly became known as "Ruthville."

Joe Vila of *The Sporting News* completely missed McGeehan's insight. He characterized the right field design as a flaw. Describing the contours of the field, Vila wrote, "I doubt if a fly ball ever will be driven into the left and center field bleachers, but the right field seats fairly yawn for the home run hitters. In due time, however, when home running becomes a farce, the right foul line may be considerably lengthened by cutting off the extreme lower corner of the grand stand and by tearing down a section of the wooden rookery."[22]

Vila was likely reflecting the purists' opinion that the home run was a cheap contrivance. His expectation that the Yankee owners would push back the right field stands to cut down the number of home runs ignored the explosion of attendance that had accompanied the Babe's home run barrage. Vila had failed to see the obvious: Home runs meant money, and no owner was going to tear down the source of his income.

The commercial significance of Yankee Stadium was evident from day one. Even the accurate count of 60,000 fans in attendance was far greater than any other ballpark drew for Opening Day in 1923. The Philadelphia Athletics hosted the Washington Senators before 21,000. The Cleveland Indians were home to the Chicago White Sox, and 20,372 turned out. The St. Louis Browns drew 20,000 to their opener with the Detroit Tigers. In other words, the first game at Yankee Stadium was roughly equivalent to all the other Opening Day crowds in the rest of the American League together.

The National League was only a little more competitive. Over 33,000 packed Wrigley Field to see the Cubs play the Pittsburgh Pirates. The Cincinnati Reds drew more than 30,000 in their opener against the St. Louis Cardinals. The Boston Braves managed to attract 15,000 to see their game with the New York Giants. And 12,000 passed up the festivities in the Bronx to attend Ebbets Field, where the Dodgers played host to the Philadelphia Phillies. The Cubs and Reds were able to draw about half of the Yankees' crowd, but Jake Ruppert's team had staked a position in the baseball business that almost no other franchise could hope to challenge.

Yankee Stadium reflected a conscious decision by Ruppert to take full advantage of being the owner of the most popular team in baseball. For three years, he had outdrawn the Giants in their own house and now he had built his own facility tailor-made to his ball club and its great star, but to call Yankee Stadium The House That Ruth Built is a serious exaggeration. The nickname endures to our own time, but it obscures the other elements that were also critical factors in the construction of this famous American building. If the Babe were the whole story, the Red Sox could have taken advantage of their 1918 championship and the Stadium would have risen in Boston. As it was, the grand party of Opening Day was very much of the Bronx, where it reflected both the triumph of a once forlorn franchise as well as a startling transformation of New York City.

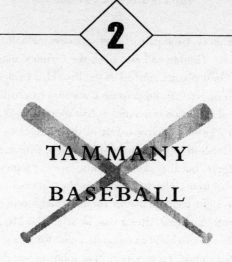

TAMMANY
BASEBALL

The young dynasty that took the field on Opening Day began its history as the bankrupt remnants of an old National League powerhouse. The Yankees were begat by the Baltimore Orioles of the 1890s, a team still familiar to serious baseball fans who know John McGraw, Ned Hanlon, Wee Willie Keeler, and Wilbert Robinson as the stars who led the Orioles to championships from 1894 to 1896.

Good as they were, the Orioles could not survive the commercial chaos of the time. After challenges in the 1880s from the American Association and the Players League in 1890, the National League reasserted its monopoly by inviting the best teams in those rival circuits to abandon their struggling partners for the more established major league. The tactic worked, but it swelled the National League to twelve teams, an awkward arrangement that sapped the game's popularity in many cities.

Interest in Baltimore collapsed as attendance fell from about 250,000 in 1897 to 123,000 the following year.[1] In February 1899, Orioles' owners Ned Hanlon and Harry von der Horst negotiated a syndicate deal, or joint ownership, with the Brooklyn Dodgers magnates Frederick Abell and Charles Ebbets. Each pair of partners became half owners of the other's franchise. Hanlon had also been the Orioles' manager, and he and the team's best players jumped to the Brooklyn Dodgers in the first of several raids by New York teams on Baltimore baseball.

McGraw and Robinson remained in Baltimore to look after business interests. They guided what was left of the Orioles to a remarkable fourth place finish in 1899—an 86–62 record, fifteen games behind Hanlon's Dodgers, but they still could not save the franchise. The Orioles were one of four clubs dropped from the National League when it returned to an eight-team format in 1900. McGraw remained a key figure for the proto-Yankees. After a year in St. Louis, McGraw returned to Baltimore in 1901 to build an expansion club for Ban Johnson's Western League, the minor league circuit that Johnson was developing into the American League. In Johnson's ambitious plan to establish a second major league, the Baltimore franchise was expected to move to New York as the American League's entrant in the nation's largest market.

The American League's invasion of Manhattan was helped by some important changes in local politics and government. The modern city of New York had been created through charter reform that consolidated five counties or boroughs in 1898. The most obvious effect was the fusing of Manhattan and Brooklyn, the nation's largest and fourth largest cities, to a single entity. Less dramatic, but ultimately of tremendous significance, the consolidation incorporated the less populous boroughs of the Bronx, Queens, and Staten Island into New York City. This redrawing of the city's boundaries created social and economic conditions that would drive much of the city's commerce, including the business of baseball.

The reform spirit also affected local politics when the municipal elections of 1901 put Seth Low in the mayor's office as part of an anti-Tammany tide. In the wake of their rout, bickering within the Wigwam, Tammany's headquarters on 14th Street, created the opening that Ban Johnson exploited.

The major obstacle to putting another team in New York City had been the opposition of Giants owner Andrew Freedman, a major power

within Tammany. Freedman used his connections to control land alloca-
tion, and was well positioned to block any other team's pursuit of a stadium site in the city. Freedman was one of Tammany Boss Richard
Croker's best friends, and he helped to steer city contracts to favored
firms who would then do right by Freedman and Croker.[2] These
arrangements led to several investigations during the 1890s that exposed the details of corruption and set the stage for a backlash.

Sensing that Freedman was vulnerable after Low's election, his foes
within baseball, led by Chicago's Albert Spalding, tried to drive the Giants owner from the game. Part of the antipathy to Freedman was personal: Most people in the game simply did not like the man. A clearly
frustrated Spalding characterized Freedman as "the incarnation of self-
ishness supreme" and possessed of "personal cussedness."[3] After supply-
ing some details about how Freedman fell short of the gentleman's
code, Spalding addressed the substantive issue that disturbed the owners. Even a century ago, the magnates of baseball were concerned about
the disparity between rich and richer franchises. Freedman owned the
wealthiest club in the game, and, by the lights of his foes, the Giants'
owner was eager to exploit his advantage with no regard for the reper-
cussions. Spalding charged that Freedman and his allies "were absolutely
devoid of sentiment, cared nothing for the integrity or perpetuity of the
game beyond the limits of their individual control thereof. With these
men it was simply a mercenary question of dollars and cents. Everything
must yield to the one consideration of inordinate greed."[4]

What Freedman had proposed that so disturbed many of his fellows
was to create a trust for professional baseball. Franchises would no
longer be owned individually but collectively. Owners would have a
number of shares in the clubs that would be owned in common. What
the Dodgers and Giants had done with the Baltimore teams would be
extended throughout baseball. "Syndicalism" was the term, and it
evoked terror in the owners unmatched until their heirs heard the
words "free agency."

One cause for concern about joint ownership involved the integrity
of the game. If all clubs were commonly owned, what was the incentive

for one team to beat another? The commercial interest might well favor the teams that could generate the greatest revenue—in other words, big city teams that could attract the most fans to the ballpark, specifically the New York Giants.

Freedman, in fact, was clear from the outset that the Giants would be the first among equals in the syndicate that he anticipated. Spalding cited the distribution of wealth that Freedman proposed, as published in the *New York Sun*. Preferred stock with a dividend of 7 percent would have been owned by the league as a whole. The Giants would have held 30 percent of the common stock with other teams owning from 6 to 12 percent.

Spalding coined the term "Freedmanism" to characterize this radically different kind of ownership. The syndicate plan threatened to turn every other owner into a minor partner of Andrew Freedman, and that prospect ensured the scheme's defeat. Freedman deflected Spalding's attempt to oust him, so he remained the owner of the Giants and an impediment to Johnson's ambition. As the 1902 season opened, the American League was a serious threat to the Nationals, but its future would be uncertain until it could gain a foothold in New York.

McGraw had initially assumed that he would manage the New York club when Johnson made his move, but the relationship between the two proved impossible. The rough, even brutal, play of McGraw's Orioles was exactly the kind of baseball that appalled Johnson, who intended the American League to display the grace of the game and leave the umpire-baiting, rowdy, brawling style to unpleasant memory.

Believing that he would be dropped as the team's manager when the new edition of the Orioles moved north, McGraw cut his own deal with Freedman. In another exercise of syndicalism, Freedman, with McGraw's help, acquired control of the Orioles on July 16, 1902, released most of the team's players, signed the best of them to contracts with the Giants, hired McGraw to manage the New Yorkers, and left Baltimore's American League franchise with an insufficient number of players to field a team.

The raid threatened the very existence of the American League, and Ban Johnson responded decisively. He took the Orioles into receivership, shifted players from other clubs to fill out Baltimore's roster, and the team, with Wilbert Robinson managing, lost only one game to forfeit. The American League was preserved, but the tense relationship between Johnson and McGraw deteriorated into a lifelong animosity.

Picking off McGraw and some star players from the Orioles was Freedman's last maneuver as Giants owner. He soon decided to sell the team to John Brush, who recently had sold the Cincinnati club. Freedman remained important in New York City politics, but his clout within baseball had been diminished.

Even without the kind of personal distrust that Freedman inspired, the American and National League owners had complicated one another's commercial lives to the point of distraction. Rival franchises in the same markets were vying for the top players in the game, and honest competition for players has always been a condition that baseball owners have hated like the capital gains tax. Lawsuits over alleged contract breaches, battles for stadium sites, and franchise shifts to new markets created additional incentives to find some kind of peace between the two leagues.

An agreement was reached on January 19, 1903. Its essence was to extend the National League monopoly to encompass Ban Johnson's American League. The two circuits shared the privilege that the Nationals had been unable to wield successfully alone. This odd arrangement of partnership and competition has remained the fundamental organizational feature of professional baseball to the present day.

The saving of the American League was no comfort for the fans of Baltimore. Earlier they had lost their best players to the Dodgers, then their best manager to the Giants; now they would be deprived of major league baseball entirely for a half-century. In conjunction with the peace between the two major leagues, the Baltimore franchise was sold to New Yorkers Frank Farrell and Bill Devery for $18,000, and they moved the ball club to Manhattan.

Johnson could not have been thrilled with his New York owners. The two were classic Tammany hacks. Both had been bartenders, and Farrell also owned a saloon along with a stable of racehorses and a gambling house. Devery had an even more colorful history. He was a police officer who rose through the ranks to become Chief of Police during Boss Croker's reign. M. R. Werner's history of Tammany Hall explains the true significance of the job:

> During the 1890's in New York City police bribery was so open and generally accepted that the particular motion of the hand behind the back and the palm turned up in the shape of a cup was used on the vaudeville stage then and later as the symbol denoting policeman.[5]

Gambling and prostitution required police protection to operate profitably, and Devery was willing to provide it. Tammany received a large and steady stream of income from its protection of vice.

Devery's moral standards on prostitution were curious. In one case revealed by the Lexow Committee, a state senate investigation into police corruption, Devery had received $500 when Henry Hoffman opened a bordello and perhaps $50 a month thereafter. One day, while walking by the house, Devery himself was solicited by one of the women. He called Hoffman into the police station the next day and railed, "Well, if them women cows of yours call me up again, I will take you by the neck and throw you out of the house."[6] For the offense, Devery's bagman collected an additional $10 a month from Hoffman. When pressed on these and related matters by legislative investigations, Devery's stock reply was, "Touchin' on and appertainin' to that matter, I disremember."[7] The code of silence was so dear to Devery that he commended a police officer suspected of drunkenness who declined to breathe in Devery's face.

By 1902, Croker was virtually retired in England, and Tammany's cohesion was gone for the moment. Devery split from Tammany, and in 1903 ran for mayor. He would not be held back by consistency. His campaign rallies featured free beer while he offered passionate speeches against vice. He even attracted the support of Carrie Nation, who gave an address in which to her audience's amazement she called Devery "a Prohibitionist."[8] Defeat relieved him of a potential distraction from the ball club.

The immediate problem for the American League entry in New York was that the team had no place to play. The New York Giants had acquiesced to the American League intrusion into New York because they were convinced that no land remained in Manhattan on which a stadium could be constructed.

The Giants were wrong. Farrell and Devery claimed a rugged, imposing spot not far from the Polo Grounds to build a facility for their ball club. In a matter of six weeks, rock was cleared, depressions were filled, and a ballpark constructed. Hilltop Park was a single-deck, wooden ballpark that seated 16,000 people on the highest point in Manhattan on Broadway between 165th and 168th Streets. The old Orioles were the new Highlanders, named for the ballpark in which games had to be compelling to keep the fans from being distracted by the spectacular view of the Hudson River and the New Jersey Palisades.

The Farrell–Devery years had their moments. In 1904, their second season, the Highlanders finished second in the American League just a game and a half behind the Boston Red Sox. Jack Chesbro won forty-one games that year, still the modern major league record for most wins in a season. The club drew 438,919 to Hilltop Park, well back of the Giants' attendance but far ahead of Hanlon's Dodgers. The 1906 season ended in another second-place finish, three back of the Chicago White Sox, and in 1909 over a half million went to Hilltop.

Despite these runs, the New Yorkers were not going to develop their potential in the hands of Farrell and Devery. The owners were so comfortable in an ethical swamp that in 1910 they signed Hal Chase to manage the Yankees. In fifteen major league seasons between 1905 and 1919, Chase acquired perhaps the most nefarious reputation of any player in the history of the game. He was a very able ballplayer, but, from New York to California, Chase was known for gambling and fixes wherever he landed.

The last years in Hilltop Park included a few memorable games. Washington's Walter Johnson pitched three shutouts in four days in 1908, a feat that says as much about the Highlanders as it does about the Senators' immortal. In 1912, Ty Cobb charged into the stands after a heckling fan and pummelled the fellow. When it was discovered that the victim was handicapped, Cobb was suspended and his teammates threatened a strike. In a rare diplomatic turn, Cobb took a fine and suspension, and talked his mates out of the show of solidarity.

The Highlanders' ineptitude may have helped thaw their relations with the Giants. In 1910, a City Series was inaugurated between the Manhattan neighbors. The following April, a fire destroyed part of the Polo Grounds, leaving the Giants without a home field. Brush accepted Farrell's offer to play at Hilltop until repairs were finished in June.

After the 1912 season, the Highlanders finished their tenth season at Hilltop, and their lease was expiring. The Giants were the preeminent franchise in baseball, and they invited the team that was becoming better known as the Yankees to join them in the Polo Grounds. The tenant would provide a little revenue to the Giants when the ballpark would be otherwise empty, and there was, at the time, no risk of serious competition for fans or press attention.

The Farrell and Devery adventure in ball club ownership ended in January 1915. The first Yankee owners sold their $18,000 investment for $460,000 to Jacob Ruppert and Tillinghast L'Hommedieu Huston. The high life was apparently more than Farrell and Devery could handle. Devery died in 1919 nearly destitute, and in 1926 Farrell's estate left a little over a thousand dollars to his heirs.

The new owners were better equipped to handle success. Ruppert was a native New Yorker, born to money in 1867. In a variation of the usual parental pressure, Jake's father talked him out of studying engineering at Columbia University so that he could learn the beer business from the bottom up. Few aspects of the enterprise escaped him, from washing barrels to the executive tasks.

While learning the family business, Ruppert also was a classic dilettante of the Gilded Age. He made the party circuit and dabbled in the arts. A lifelong bachelor, Ruppert also was a member of the Seventh Regiment, "the silk-stockinged, kid-gloved, socially dominant outfit of the New York National Guard."[9] He was given the honorary rank of colonel by Governor Hill in 1889 at the tender age of twenty-two.

In Frank Graham's description, "He had a town house on Fifth Avenue and an estate at Garrison on the Hudson. He collected jades, porcelains, Indian relics, first editions, race horses, yachts, dogs, and monkeys."[10] He was a member of prestigious social organizations including the Jockey Club and the New York Athletic Club. Despite this privileged background, when he turned to politics, he allied with Tammany Hall. Defeated in a local race, he was elected to Congress from a district on the Upper East Side, then reelected three times. He gradually lost interest in yachting and the horse and dog shows, but about the time of the first World War, his passion for baseball was building.

Tillinghast L'Hommedieu Huston was an altogether different sort. Born in Ohio in 1869, he pursued the engineering Ruppert had rejected. Huston grew up in modest circumstances, but he used his trade during the Spanish-American War by organizing the Second Volunteer Engineers and taking them to Cuba, where he rose to the rank of captain.

After the war, Huston remained in Cuba, making important connections with local officials and earning his fortune in public works projects. During this time, he made the acquaintance of John McGraw, who visited the island on vacations or training trips with the Giants. McGraw introduced Huston to Ruppert, and the two millionaires decided to buy a ball club together.

Although John Brush died in November 1912, McGraw steered Huston and Ruppert away from the Giants. He may have been protecting his own interest in having a stake in the team, but he offered to help them acquire the Yankees from Farrell and Devery in the knowledge that those two, as usual, needed cash.

Some years later, Colonel Ruppert described what he and Huston received for their money, "We got an orphan ball club, without a home of its own, without players of outstanding ability, without prestige."[11] Ruppert and Huston were strikingly different personalities who clashed throughout their years together, but they did fashion a strategy to sign players, organize an outstanding front office, and ultimately build a ballpark for the Yankees.

The new regime hired Bill Donovan to manage the club and Harry Sparrow, a friend of John McGraw's, as business manager. The one significant player added for the 1915 season was Wally Pipp, picked up from Detroit, but the Yankees remained a mediocre ball club. They finished in fifth place with a record of 69–83, an improvement of one place in the standings while winning one game fewer than in 1914. Attendance dropped by a hundred thousand from the previous year, down to 256,035.

Donovan lured Frank "Home Run" Baker out of a one-year retirement, and he was expected to improve the Yankee offense and draw fans to the Polo Grounds. Baker instead was injured chasing a foul ball and played only 100 games that season. Despite those limited appearances, Baker hit ten home runs, second in the league to Pipp's twelve.

The Yankees improved in this 1916 season to a fourth-place finish and a record of 80–74, their first winning record since 1910. Attendance jumped to 469,211, which was a hundred thousand short of the Giants but a little more than the pennant-winning Dodgers over in Brooklyn.

The Yankees were headed in the right direction, but Ruppert and Huston were discovering that money and determination were not enough to develop a contending ball club. The Yankees were a more promising franchise than they had been under Devery and Farrell, but they were stuck behind the elite clubs like the Giants. Like many struggling firms, they needed a break, and on November 1, 1916, they got one. On that day, Harry Frazee bought the Boston Red Sox.

Frazee was an impresario who had produced plays while building theaters in Boston, Chicago, and New York. He had promoted championship fights, and his acquisition of the Red Sox seemed to position him to play a dominant role in baseball. The Sox had just dispatched the Dodgers, four games to one, to capture their fourth World Series championship. Their star pitcher, twenty-one-year-old Babe Ruth, had won twenty-three games and was showing remarkable ability with the bat as well.

Frazee seems to have been just successful enough in the theater to launch plays that required a lot of money to be sustained. He left the Red Sox to operate under local management while he worked out of offices in Times Square where his 42nd Street neighbors included Ruppert and Huston.

The Yankees slipped back in 1917, with a losing record, a sixth-place finish, and a drop in attendance. Frustrated with his ball club, Ruppert took some decisive action. Til Huston had gone to Europe that spring with the American army when the United States entered World War I, and, while he was there, Ruppert changed managers. From a distance, Huston vainly lobbied for his friend Wilbert Robinson, who had brought the Dodgers their first pennant in the modern game in 1916, but Ruppert's interview of Robinson went badly. Over Huston's objections, Ruppert hired Miller Huggins, the manager of the St. Louis Cardinals, to pilot the Yankees. Huggins had a lackluster record with the Cardinals, but he had impressed Ban Johnson, who recommended him to Ruppert. Huggins's status became a source of serious contention between the Yankee owners.

The 1918 season belongs, in many respects, to the set of forgettable campaigns. The American entry into World War I threatened the entire season. The owners made the argument to President Wilson that baseball was an essential industry that should be permitted a normal operation while the carnage in Europe wound to its conclusion. They were partly successful, but the loss of key players and a critical cohort of fans seriously weakened the season. The Yankees managed to play 123 games, of which they won 60. The season is notable for the fifth World Series title for the Boston Red Sox, the last they would win in the twentieth century.[12]

While few outside of Boston remember the 1918 season, the following year remains infamous. The year 1919 is synonymous with the Black Sox, the Chicago team that threw the World Series that year, but that season included other elements that also shaped the future course of the game and of the Yankees in particular. Most important, chaos and corruption followed the slow collapse of baseball's National Commission, an awkward arrangement that ostensibly governed the game.

Long before the plot to fix the World Series was first conceived, a critical part of baseball's commercial foundation was under attack. The peace of 1903 not only ended the battle between the American and National Leagues, but also established the way in which the majors would recruit and develop their players. The 1903 arrangement established a subordinate relationship for the rest of professional baseball. Players could be claimed by major league teams from those other professional rosters virtually at will.

The other leagues organized the National Association of Professional Baseball Leagues, the body that continues to govern the minor league game. The "major league" status that the Americans and Nationals conferred on themselves was accepted by these other circuits who themselves created their own hierarchy. Class A, B, C, and D divided the minor leagues into tiers of quality and market size. The competitor–partner roles that the American and National leagues had resolved were also extended to the minor leagues. The connections among the various classes and between the minor and major leagues were governed by a pact known as the National Agreement.

The 1903 organization of professional baseball papered over a tension that exists to this day. The minor leagues serve two, sometimes conflicting, purposes: They supply smaller markets with professional baseball, and they develop players for higher quality leagues. The higher leagues can control, to some extent, the rosters of the lower leagues through options and drafts. When a team's roster is disrupted to serve the interests of a controlling franchise, the club's ability to provide the best possible game for its own fans is inevitably compromised.

From time to time, minor leagues bucked against the system that kept them in short pants, and 1919 was one of those times. The impact of World War I was especially difficult for the minors, as only twenty leagues could begin the 1917 season and only twelve would complete it. The following year was worse. Nine leagues began the 1918 campaign, and the International League was the only minor league able to finish.

In January 1919, the minors insisted on substantial changes to the National Agreement, ones that would have significantly reduced the ability of the majors to determine the commercial future of the minor league organizations. The major leagues rejected the demands, and, for the first time since 1903, formal ties between the major and minor leagues were severed, with minor league teams operating independently and securing the best prices for their players that they could.

The minor league clubs with terrific prospects could hold on to them until they received a fair price as determined in a free market. The lack of a National Agreement opened different possibilities for player development. The Yankees were one of the major league teams that eventually would revive syndicalism to directly own the minor league teams they required for fresh players.

As the 1903 agreement wobbled, Ruppert and Huston collided with Ban Johnson, still the preeminent executive in baseball. Unwittingly, the Yankee colonels undermined the authority of the American League president at the very time that effective leadership was essential to deal with the Black Sox scandal. The battle between the Yankees and Johnson began with one of the most common front-office pursuits: The Yankees wanted more pitching. Carl Mays won twenty-one games for the champion Red Sox in 1918, following twenty-two wins the previous year. For all his ability, Mays's mercurial personality led to problems with teammates and the front office. Mays walked out on the Red Sox in the middle of the 1919 season, and most of the focus centered on the proper reaction to his ill temper. Frazee, however, saw the matter in a different light.

The Red Sox owner appreciated that several clubs needed a pitcher of Mays's quality. He ignored Johnson's calls for a proper punishment and began to arrange a bidding war. The Yankees were joined by the White Sox, Indians, and other clubs in making offers of money and players. Alarmed that Mays might have intended all along to force a trade through an act of defiance, Johnson declared an end to trade talks until Boston applied some punishment to Mays. Rebellious in their own right, Ruppert and Huston challenged Johnson by acquiring Mays for $40,000 and a couple of pitchers.

Johnson reacted as forcefully as he had to Andrew Freedman's efforts to strangle the American League in its cradle. This time the threat was to Johnson's authority over the League, and, for the first time, the threat arose within the American League itself. Ban Johnson's power within the American League came, in substantial measure, from his direct participation in securing the financial base of many franchises. He had even spent his own money on occasion to put needed financial packages in place, but the Yankee owners were independently wealthy, with no commercial allegiance to the league president.

Johnson forced a meeting with Ruppert and Huston, then another with all the American League owners. The Yankees pressed the issue by going to court. They received a temporary restraining order against Johnson that allowed Mays to pitch for New York, and the troubled young man responded with a 7–3 record for the Yankees.

In the hearing that led to the final determination in the case, the Tammany connection appeared again: The judge turned out to be Robert Wagner, late of the New York State Senate. Wagner in fact had represented the Yorkville section of Manhattan on the Upper East Side, where one of his constituents had been Jake Ruppert. Despite that potential conflict, Wagner heard the case and ruled in favor of the Yankees.

The decision was a serious blow to Ban Johnson's place in the game's leadership. As president of the American League, Johnson had been one of three members of baseball's National Commission, its highest governing body. The Commission was often described as a court, a body that resolved disputes. Now that ersatz court had been challenged by Ruppert and Huston in a real tribunal that exposed the Commission as ultimately feckless. The timing of the Mays case compounded its impact. While Judge Wagner was preparing his decision, the Chicago White Sox were throwing the World Series to the Cincinnati Reds. The Black Sox scandal is the most notorious case of corruption on the playing field, but it was not the only instance of players throwing games for gamblers' bribes.[13]

The majority of baseball's rulers were determined that the game be marketed something along the lines of the Olympics, noble competition among athletes of splendid character. Baseball had organized on that principle after the Civil War, but, as its popularity grew, corrupting effects of alcohol, gambling, and winning at all costs became perpetual challenges. Ban Johnson had founded the American League, in part, on the notion that a game played to the higher standards would prove to be a more successful business.

Staying on that high road was not easy. Players who were annoyed at their managers or teammates were always a target for gamblers who would salve a bruised ego with some easy money. In terms of public confidence, rumors of a fix could be as damaging as the event itself, and some of the game's great players were tarnished by allegations that rarely could be completely disproved.

Before 1919, corruption could be treated as a marginal problem confined to the occasional player like Hal Chase or a couple of malcontents. No compelling evidence had been offered that the outcome of a pennant race or World Series had been anything but on the level. Now the World Series itself had been played with less integrity than a weekend game between a couple of local taverns. When rumors of the scandal were confirmed during the 1920 season, Ban Johnson, the baseball executive with the strongest credentials for integrity, was a marginal figure in saving the game.

These implications of the Mays case were lost as Ruppert and Huston worked another front. Miller Huggins had guided the Yankees to a winning record in another truncated season in 1919. The Yankees finished third with a record of 80–59. Attendance rebounded to 619,164, more than double the previous year's total; then, on December 26, 1919, the Yankees and Red Sox completed the most momentous deal in the history of the game. In a straight cash transaction announced publicly on January 3, 1920, Frazee received $100,000 for Ruth and another $300,000 in a loan. The security for the loan was a mortgage on Fenway Park. (This peculiar arrangement whereby one team owns another's ballpark is an obvious potential conflict of interest, one that was not allowed to stand when the Yankees tried a similar deal in the 1950s.)

The record is clear that Frazee sold Ruth to get money to finance theatrical ventures, but the explanation that Frazee offered at the time was not without some truth. He insisted that he needed the money simply to hold on to the ball club—whether fans would have preferred to have a player or a new owner was unexamined. Frazee contended that the Red

Sox were in jeopardy of becoming a "one-man team" by virtue of Ruth's contract demands. He noted that teams with only one great player are invariably losers. He also charged that Ruth was more trouble than he was worth. He branded him a selfish player, who was a distraction to other players who resented the special rules that the Babe felt should apply to him. Frazee concluded that the Yankees had taken a considerable gamble.

Ruppert and Huston knew that Frazee was not just covering himself. They dispatched Huggins to California to meet with Ruth to clarify what was expected of him in New York. The Yankee manager and the team's new star reached a tentative understanding that would be tested throughout Ruth's tenure with the club.

In a certain sense, the acquisition of Ruth is a classic example of baseball's alleged imbalance of wealth, the issue that preoccupies the game's leaders today. At first glance, New York simply rolled Boston because the larger market that the Polo Grounds could accommodate generated more revenue than could be secured in Fenway Park. As long as the Yankees were owned by the inept Devery and Farrell, teams like the Red Sox could be competitive, but, in the hands of wealthy and ambitious owners like Ruppert and Huston, the Yankees would inevitably dominate. Frazee, as so many owners before and since have done, cried poverty and asked what else he could possibly have done.

A closer look at the case reveals a lesson very applicable to today's game. Whatever the economic advantages the Yankees enjoyed over the Red Sox, the critical difference in the franchises was the seriousness of the owners about baseball. Over the years, people have purchased ball clubs for a variety of reasons. Frazee saw the Red Sox as a logical expansion of a theatrical base. When the base was threatened by setbacks, Frazee sacrificed the ball club. By contrast, Ruppert's principal business was under the direct threat of Prohibition. Instead of scavenging the Yankees to bolster the brewery, Ruppert continued to focus on improving the team, even while battling Prohibition as best he could. Both Ruppert and Huston were wealthy men, wealthier than Frazee, but the more important distinction was that baseball was a serious business to the Yankee owners while it was an amusing diversion to Frazee.

The acquisition of Ruth was the most memorable deal between the Red Sox and Yankees, but it was not the last, nor perhaps even the most important for the development of the Yankee dynasty. On May 7, 1920, during Ruth's inaugural season in New York, Harry Sparrow died. The loss of the Yankees' business manager left a critical vacuum in the front office because Ruppert and Huston had never fully repaired the breach over the hiring of Miller Huggins.

Once again, Harry Frazee came to the rescue. At season's end, Ed Barrow resigned as manager of the Red Sox and assumed the position of general manager with the Yankees. Having served as the Babe's manager in his final years in Boston, Barrow could fully appreciate the challenge that Huggins faced in controlling nature's child. He also knew what talent was left from a once dominant Red Sox club, and he knew that Harry Frazee would be willing to part with those players for the right price.

Barrow conferred with Huggins and mapped his strategy. He swung a deal that sent Muddy Ruel, Herb Thormahlen, Derril Pratt, and Sam Vick to Boston in exchange for Waite Hoyt, Wally Schang, Harry Harper, and Mike McNally. Frazee justified the trade by claiming that the Red Sox picked up four Yankee regulars for Wally Schang and three prospects. Frank Graham later offered a more accurate assessment: "Ruel became a great catcher in a Red Sox uniform, but Pratt was passed on to Detroit, Vick ate his way out of the league, and Thormahlen simply wasn't a true major-league pitcher. In New York, Schang averaged more than a hundred games a year for five years, Hoyt was a first-rate pitcher for eight years, Harper was a very useful one, and McNally was a handy fellow around the infield for a long time."[14]

The 1920 season was historic for baseball. Babe Ruth had found a stage suitable for his act, and the popularity that he inspired for baseball proved to be stronger than the revulsion that the Black Sox revelations triggered during September. Ruth was simply a phenomemon. While the worst fears about the World Series were being confirmed in Chicago, home runs were flying out of American League parks when the Yankees played. In his last year in Boston, Ruth set the major league home run record at twenty-nine. In his first year with the Yankees, he hit fifty-four.

One of the fifteen other major league *teams* hit more, the Phillies with sixty-four, but they finished last in the National League. Ruth was proving Frazee wrong. He not only was a greater player than anyone had anticipated, but he also had an uplifting effect on his team.

The Yankee colonels continued to battle Ban Johnson, fellow owners, and one another, but the ball club seemed unaffected. They won ninety-five games, more than any other Yankee team to date. Their third-place finish matched that of the previous year, but the impact of Ruth was clearly seen in the team's attendance. Drawing 1,289,422 fans represented the first time that any franchise went over a million at the gate, a point not lost on the Giants, who had been eclipsed by their tenants. John Brush's offer to Devery and Farrell to share the Polo Grounds suddenly needed to be reevaluated.

The Giants reacted quickly to Ruth's impact. A month after the season opened, on May 14, 1920, Stoneham and McGraw suddenly announced that the Yankees would not be allowed to play in the Polo Grounds in 1921. Ruppert professed shock, contending that he had an oral understanding with the Giants that the two clubs would work out a long-term lease. He acknowledged that, if the Giants wanted the Yankees to move, he and Huston would have to build a new park, and the two colonels bravely declared that one could be ready for the 1921 season.

A week after this announcement, the Giants reversed themselves. After meetings with Ban Johnson, Stoneham declared that the Yankees were welcome for the next couple of years and that discussions would begin for a long-term lease. Few took the gesture seriously. Ruppert likely had anticipated the benefits of his own facility, and the capricious move by the Giants would have been a final incentive to find a secure plant for the Yankees.

Johnson's role here is puzzling. Ruppert and Huston had become serious threats to Johnson's position within the game. Going to court over Carl Mays had been a virtual declaration of war on the American League president. But Johnson would have wanted to retain a strong American League franchise in New York, and that motivation, rather than any regard for the Yankee colonels, probably led to his intervention with the

Giants. Of course, Johnson also had a difficult association with John McGraw, so Johnson may have been going through some motions with little hope that they would bear fruit.

Harold Seymour notes in his history of the game that Ruppert and Huston had been urged to get the Yankees their own stadium from the time they acquired the club in January 1915. Seymour adds that some intriguing evidence suggests that Johnson spoke with the Giants' owner about acquiring the Yankees lease on the Polo Grounds, which would have given him the leverage to drive Ruppert and Huston from baseball.[15] By this point, whatever scheming Johnson had in mind was utterly futile. His own skills at organizational infighting were fading badly and Ruppert was growing more powerful all the time.

In September 1920, the Yankees were close to securing the Hebrew Orphan Asylum property at 135th Street and Amsterdam Avenue on the Upper West Side of Manhattan. About a mile south of the Polo Grounds, the site was accessible through mass transit. One month later, Ruppert and Huston went to Chicago for an owners' meeting; after negotiations with Charles Stoneham and John McGraw, they signed a lease on the Polo Grounds through the 1922 season. The Chicago meetings further shook baseball's organizational structure. Talks included consideration of a new twelve-team format that would be composed of the National League and the American League's rebellious franchises, including the Yankees, who were chafing under Johnson's anachronistic reign.

By the end of January 1921, the design of the new stadium was set, although the location was not yet confirmed. The Osborne Engineering Co. of Cleveland, Ohio, proposed a facility that would have been approximately twice the size of Braves Field in Boston, then the largest baseball park in the country. Osborne had extensive experience with baseball stadiums, including the Polo Grounds. The choice suggests that, for all of Ruppert's Tammany connections, he was serious enough about the design of the new ballpark that he went with the best in the business rather than a local company that might have had political connections.

A few weeks later, the Yankees announced that they had acquired property in the Bronx from the estate of William Waldorf Astor. The location was somewhat of a surprise, since reports had focused on the West Side property of the orphanage and several sites in Queens. The spot in the Bronx was within walking distance of the Polo Grounds over the Macombs Dam Bridge. It also enjoyed superior rapid transit facilities to the other sites where the Yankees had options. Ruppert and Huston had looked at the Astor property shortly after buying the Yankees in 1915. They ruled the site out then because it lacked adequate transportation. The development of the subway solved that problem, and the Bronx location became even more accessible than many neighborhoods in Manhattan. Ruppert and Huston sought a train station at the stadium site from the New York Central Railroad, something the Yankees are still petitioning for today.

The 1921 season was a milestone. The Yankees won their first pennant, finishing four and a half games ahead of the Indians. Ruth outdid himself with fifty-nine homers. Carl Mays recovered from the Ray Chapman tragedy and tied for the league lead in victories with twenty-seven. Bob Meusel, in his second year with the team, finished tied for second in the League for home runs with twenty-four. Attendance fell off, about 60,000, suggesting that the limits of popularity had been reached in the Polo Grounds.

The Giants enjoyed some consolation by beating the Yankees in the World Series, but even that victory was evidence of Ruth's stature in New York. The Yankees won the first two games of the Series by 3–0 scores. The Giants pitched around the Babe, but, when he drew a walk in the second game, he promptly stole second and third to delight the crowd and frustrate the Giants. The last stolen base was costly. Ruth scraped his elbow in the slide, and his arm became infected. He played the next day when the Giants rallied to win their first game, but made only a token appearance in the rest of the Series. The Giants prevailed five games to three under the old nine-game format, but Ruth's absence was an uncomfortably obvious factor.

The 1922 season was a bit bizarre. The Yankees, playing their final season in the Polo Grounds, began with Ruth suspended by Commissioner Landis for defying a ban on barnstorming or playing exhibition games after the 1921 season. This suspension covered the first six weeks of the new season, and Bob Meusel was included for his participation in Ruth's postseason travels. The Yankees caught a break because their only serious competition for the pennant was, of all teams, the St. Louis Browns. Ruth returned, and wound up with thirty-five home runs, losing his title to Ken Williams of the Browns. The Yankees held off the Browns for the flag, winning the pennant by a single game.

Again, they met the Giants in the Series, but this time the rout was on. The best the Yankees could do was a tie in the second game, a 3–3 ten-inning affair that was called because of darkness. The Giants shut down Ruth and the Yankee offense in taking four other games in a quasi-sweep of the resumed best of seven Series.

In the winter before the Stadium opened, the Yankees were a puzzle. Their owners had succeeded in clipping the wings of Ban Johnson, and they had established a decent working relationship with Commissioner Landis. They had built a first-rate front office with their hire of Ed Barrow from the Red Sox. The only complication was that Ruppert and Huston could not stand each other.

The focus of their problems was manager Miller Huggins, whom Ruppert continued to support while Huston pressed for a replacement. Huggins himself was a complication. He had shown great ability in guiding the Yankees to their first pennants, but his control of the ball club was in question. Ruth repeatedly tried to bully Huggins, and Barrow, the Babe's former manager in Boston, occasionally had to intervene to keep Ruth in line. Huston maintained that the team was in turmoil, but Ruppert and Barrow were satisfied with Huggins's work.

The Bad Boy himself had his fans concerned. His first two years in New York had been merely colorful, but 1922 had been troubling. The wild, unreasonable defiance that Ruth had displayed was an example of the worst features that Harry Frazee had predicted. At twenty-seven years old, Ruth should have been entering his prime, but his perpetual indulgence would begin to take a toll. The Yankees were much more than a one-man team, but Ruth was one man who was close to indispensable. The Babe would have to grow up or the Yankees would have to find a way for the organization to protect him from his own worst impulses.

Neither tensions between the colonels nor Ruth's behavior delayed the Stadium. The Osborne Engineering Company's surveyors and engineers first set foot on the stadium site on February 6, 1921. They studied the property to determine the grading and drainage that would be needed for construction. Postwar inflation had kept building costs high, but expectations were that the Stadium would begin to rise in May 1921. Right month, wrong year. The delays that frustrate developers and contractors are not entirely a modern innovation. The actual building began on May 6, 1922. The work was complicated, and bids were sought from various construction companies. The White Construction Co. of New York was the prime contractor, but they were not selected until April 18, 1922. That was shortly after Mayor Hylan finally approved the closing of Cromwell Avenue and 158th Street, two roads that ran right through the Stadium site.

These delays indicate that the building of a baseball stadium was a tremendous undertaking even eighty years ago. Hylan and Ruppert shared the critical Tammany connection, Til Huston was an engineer with the ability (occasionally expressed) to take over the engineering work himself if the bids were too high, and the Astor family owned the adjacent property to the Stadium, so no local opposition to the street closings arose—yet, with all these advantages, serious obstacles to beginning construction on the stadium had to be overcome.

Once under way, the Stadium was built in 284 working days. Its initial design included three decks on all sides of the structure. The familiar cut from foul line to foul line in the original Stadium was a decision based on cost savings and the need to let sunlight reach the grass. Perhaps the game was spared Astroturf for forty years by this fortunate choice.

By Ruppert's standard, the Yankees were no longer an orphan ball club void of star players without a home of their own. For all the problems between the two colonels, they had weathered the end of the Federal League's challenge to become a third major league, improved the ball club even during the trauma of World War I, and became important executives in baseball's inner circle while the Old Guard faded in influence. They picked up *the* star in the game along with Ed Barrow who would rival Branch Rickey in his ability to sustain top performances in the organization.

Through patience, persistence, local knowledge, and a bit of fortune, they also built the grandest structure in the game. Yankee Stadium was immediately recognized as not only the preeminent location in baseball but also as an important symbol of the American entertainment industry. Before 1923, a half a million had been a decent year's attendance for many franchises in the game. The Yankees now had a facility in which that number would be reached by the 4th of July.

At some point, at least a few of the other owners must have done the math and realized in horror that, with seating for 58,000, capacity crowds through a vital home stand in a torrid pennant race had the potential to draw 500,000 in a couple of weeks. Even if their own fans were equally eager to pay for a seat at the game, there simply were far fewer seats in Boston, Chicago, Detroit, or anywhere else in the league. A great team that packed the house in New York meant a revenue stream that could be put to use sustaining more great teams in a cycle that no other ball club was likely to be able to match.

The Yankees were set. They had the players, the front office, and now the stage for championships far into the future. The only remaining question was beyond the power of the Yankee colonels to answer with certainty: Would the fans continue to fill the Stadium?

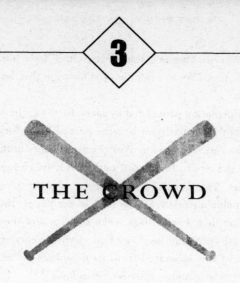

3

THE CROWD

When Bob Shawkey struck out Norm McMillan to end Opening Day, kids in the stands raced onto the field to catch up to Babe Ruth while the hero raced for the clubhouse. The *Bronx Home News* claimed that at least a thousand boys from the Bronx were after him. They had poured out of the right field bleachers, driving Ruth toward another youthful contingent that had burst the left field stands.

They caught and surrounded him, and the "Babe" walked to the door of the runway, flanked by shouting hundreds, who flung their caps in the air and cheered themselves hoarse. "Babe" had smashed out a home run and once more he reigns in the kingdom of boyish Bronx minds.[1]

"The kingdom of boyish Bronx minds" was an extraordinary realm of hope and imagination in which the most common dream was no doubt each boy's determination to someday replace the Babe himself. This childhood fantasy was hardly more improbable than the changes the

Bronx itself was realizing as it transformed itself from a bucolic region north of New York City to a middle-class borough that defined modern urban living.

This transformation proceeded in parts. In 1874, the section of the Bronx west of the Bronx River became part of New York City, while the area to the east remained in Westchester County until 1895, when it too joined the city to form what collectively was known as the Annexed District. The area had little common identity. Lloyd Ultan, the borough's notable historian, writes that, in the 1890s, Bronx residents would mention their local village when asked where they lived. As he described these communities, "The typical village encompassed only a few blocks and was separated from its neighbors by empty lots and fields of plowed farmland, orchards or meadows."[2]

This pastoral setting would more than triple its population between 1900 and 1920. Revolutions in mass transportation, housing, and public works were critical factors in this explosion. Just as important, the political culture of New York was developing, and it encouraged poor families to dream beyond their circumstances. Owning a decent home, educating children, working in a good job—these goals increasingly became part of serious planning rather than wishful thinking, and, as part of that plan, the Bronx became a tangible focus of middle-class aspirations.

The celebration of Opening Day culminated a tough road of more than two decades for a ball club, their hero, and also their fans. In 1899, the Yankees were a handful of players on a bankrupt Baltimore roster, and the four-year-old George Ruth was proving impossible to his parents. At the same time, the families of many of those who would fill the Stadium on April 18, 1923, were climbing out of poverty as brutal as any the nation has known. The Babe beat long odds to develop into their hero, but the kids who chased him and the working stiffs who paid to cheer him beat longer odds just to have their seats in the bleachers.

The Catholic Xaverian Brothers of St. Mary's Industrial School for Boys gave young George his way out. The fans who worshiped him found their own opportunities from parents who were more serious than Ruth's, from clergy, cops, teachers, and other adults who offered encouragement and discipline. To a great extent, those fans' emergence as a middle-class entertainment market depended as well on America's political culture finding a way through ideological zealotry to pragmatic policies that enabled cities like New York to make crucial adjustments to the demands of the new century.

When the full effects of industry began to appear in America after the Civil War, the country's challenge was elegantly presented by James Bryce, a member of the British House of Lords who toured America, as Alexis De Tocqueville had, writing about the country's government and institutions. In considering the scale of industrial power, Bryce concluded a chapter on the railroads with the observation that "the principle of monarchy, banished from the field of government, creeps back and asserts itself in the scarcely less momentous contests of industry and finance."[3] In other words, the American Constitution had successfully kept the power of the state from coalescing into a tyranny, but the new power of corporations and monopolies could be just as oppressive as any Roman despot. Bryce implied that Americans faced the challenge of solving the riddle of private power while retaining the advantages of the constitutional system. Failure to solve that riddle would risk a society of extreme wealth and poverty.

New York City in the late nineteenth century was a community at a dead end. The poor were stuck in squalid tenements in Lower Manhattan, packed tighter with every ship arriving from Europe. The horror was captured in picture and text by Jacob Riis in his classic work *How the Other Half Lives*.[4] Riis, himself a Danish immigrant, documented the lives of people who had come to America seeking freedom and opportunity and who often found poverty and despair.

Housing was a powerful symbol of the city's bankruptcy. Landlords who owned lots in lower Manhattan came to realize that even small backyards behind existing tenements represented a valuable asset in light of the press of immigration. Building to the property lines, the landlords created hovels of squalor that restricted air and sunlight to shocking levels with dangerous effects. These conditions created a nightmare of predator and prey. Drugs were commonly used to turn children and other helpless souls into thieves and prostitutes. Physical torture and emotional torment were other subjects not covered in the Emma Lazarus poem inscribed on the Statue of Liberty.

Arriving at Ellis Island, exhausted and bewildered, the immigrants understandably gravitated to whatever was familiar. Within a short walk from the foot of Manhattan, they could find a neighborhood where their native tongue was spoken. Italians, Germans, Greeks, Chinese, Russians—the newcomers pressed into a few blocks that seemed something like home.

While the masses of immigrants endured every natural and economic hardship, the rich decided their own housing was inadequate and began to play a game of dueling mansions. The Vanderbilts, Astors, Belmonts, and other dynasties transformed Fifth Avenue from empty lots to Millionaires' Row. William Henry Vanderbilt began the competition in 1879 when he moved into one of three new homes he had built between 52nd and 53rd Streets. Families with the means rushed to stake their own claims, and mansions soon defined the avenue for a two-mile stretch to the north.

These urban palaces became the settings for other games of wealth and status. Caroline Astor's capitulation to the social arrival of the Vanderbilts in 1883 was, for the city's elite, an event of historic dimensions. Museums and an opera house were built as chips in a contest of cultural poker, palaces of art in which social rivals could be welcomed or ostracized. The lighting of cigars with $100 bills and feasts in the dining room on horseback were only the most obvious derangements of wealth.

The poor had no money and many of the rich seemed to have no serious ambition. Marxists even began to take heart that America might be at the end of its rope. Friedrich Engels wrote an essay in 1887 that a true Labor Party could develop in the United States, a country that had denied even the existence of class distinctions through most of its history.[5]

Revolution, Marxist or otherwise, was not out of the question. Middle-aged New Yorkers in 1890 would have well remembered the Civil War draft riots between July 13 and 16, 1863—just weeks after Gettysburg. Faced with induction notices to replenish the Union army, many of the white working class became a mob that terrorized the city. They attacked anyone associated with the military draft that weighed most heavily on the Irish and others without the means to pay the $300 exemption.

The fury of impoverished immigrants focused on two targets: the wealthy Republicans, who were held responsible for the war, and the African Americans, who were seen as the beneficiaries of the workers' sacrifices. More Americans died at Gettysburg than in New York that month, but this class and racial insurrection was, in some respects, even more ominous. No one with the knowledge of that terrifying week could have been secure that "it can't happen here." The formula was the same then as now. Simmering resentments, idle young men, the stifling heat of midsummer—all awaiting the spark of an accident, argument, or arrest.

Insurrection did not require the particular pressure of the Civil War. Of special significance for baseball, entertainment had been an occasion of class strife in New York City. A bloody ruckus outside the Astor Place Opera House in May 1848 killed over twenty people in what was ostensibly a battle over the merits of two Shakespearean actors.[6] The dispute did not concern technical points of artistic performance but more basic considerations such as what sort of people were preferred at which theaters, what kinds of behaviors were expected from an audience, and similar symbolic issues. The Astor Place Riot was shocking because, as the *Philadelphia Public Ledger* wrote, "It leaves behind a feeling to which this community had hitherto been a stranger . . . a feeling that there is now in our country, in New York City, what every good patriot had hitherto considered it his duty to deny—a high and a low class."[7]

New York was not threatened by a lower class that preferred a rowdier version of Hamlet than that favored by the swells. What passed for entertainment among the desperately poor could be savage, bloody, and cruel battles that could jolt some adrenaline into people numbed by the tedium of poverty.

One account of Richard Croker's early days as a rising star of Tammany, written by one of his foes, described the kind of "sport" that the working poor were offered. Croker entered his dog in a fight with a dog belonging to Jim Cusick, the owner of a dog and rat pit on the West Side of Manhattan. Croker's and Cusick's dogs fought until Cusick's animal began to prevail. At that point, Croker himself joined the fight followed by Cusick. The battle raged for over forty-five minutes, and, at its end, we are informed that "when the smoke of the scuffle cleared away, the bloody pit was seen to be strewn with parts of human ears and pieces of human fingers."[8]

If the city's entertainment were limited to barbaric fights and sublime arts, perhaps the tensions would have overwhelmed any sense of community in New York. If watching animals tear one another to pieces was good fun, why not do as much to the rich who had all the advantages except numbers? Spontaneous rebellion or organized insurrection was possible when the masses of poor were driven to blood sports.

To the city's great fortune, other forms of recreation developed that helped to alleviate the strains. Cultural critic Neal Gabler refers to a study of New York in 1880 that found five types of places for diversion: (1) twenty-five theaters limited to the rich by a dollar admission; (2) theaters marketing plays to the Protestant middle class; (3) vaudeville and minstrel shows charging a quarter for the working class; (4) saloons and taverns; (5) "the vice districts"—where the commerce of sadism and rape could draw from all quarters of society.[9]

Baseball's development in the nineteenth century ran on a parallel track. The first organized games after the Civil War were among wealthy young men in prominent social clubs. The desire to win led to the use of a few "ringers" who would not have passed cultural muster. As the game's popularity reached the masses, social and commercial chaos followed. Gambling, drinking, vicious play, raiding other teams' rosters—all threatened to turn baseball into a slightly more elegant version of a dock fight. The challenge for baseball was to find a niche between high tea and Jim Cusick's dog and rat pit. In many respects, the commercial struggles before the accord of 1903 represented attempts to balance competition and cooperation among the game's franchises, but the owners also had to determine baseball's market, and thereby what kind of game would be offered.

In 1893, only six years after his hopeful essay, Engels wrote of the frustration of his dream.[10] He blamed the impediments of the Constitutional system, the ethnic diversity of the working class, and prosperity traced to high tariffs for removing the pressure on the workers to challenge the bosses. All that, and Babe Ruth had not even been born. Engels identified some of the reasons that New York did not explode, but he failed to see that America was beginning to reinvent itself and break out of the paralysis that had inspired revolutionaries. The political culture was rejecting both the Marxists' call for the radical destruction of private property and the Social Darwinists' assurances that a free market would winnow out the weak, leaving America stronger than before.

Progressive reformers made important contributions to the rise of a middle class by proposing the adjustments in government, politics, and public policy that have created the modern state. The regulation of business, the abandonment of complete faith in free markets, had begun at the national level with the Interstate Commerce Act in 1887, a law that purported to control the awesome power of the railroads. An omnibus antitrust law, the Sherman Act, was passed in 1890 to try to rein in the power of the great monopolies in steel, petroleum, finance, and the other essential industries. This attempt to control business through government was a novel exercise in the American experience. Regulation continued with the passage of the Pure Food and Drug Act in 1904. At the state level, laws to control child labor and impose minimum wages and limits on hours and other working conditions passed several legislatures. Often these reforms were stricken by courts on judicial review, but the popular sentiment that government could be trusted to control the new corporations and monopolies was being established.

In some cases, the rich themselves supported these reforms. Their motivation could have been a sense of justice or a realization that a hopeful working class was essential to social stability. For others, the incentive could have been more immediate. With effort, the horror of exploitation and accident among the poor could be ignored, but disease was a more democratic force. Building to the boundary of one's property turned every inch of land into a source of revenue, but it also prevented sunlight from reaching many of the living quarters and severely restricted the flow of air.

In this setting, an entire neighborhood could become a petri dish for disease. Riis described the logic of epidemics, "a child recovering from small-pox, and in the most contagious stage of the disease, has been found crawling among heaps of half finished clothing that the next day would be offered for sale on the counter of a Broadway store; or that a typhus fever patient has been discovered in a room whence perhaps a hundred coats had been sent home that week, each one with the wearer's death-warrant, unseen and unsuspected, basted in the lining."[11]

The realization that the effects of poverty did not respect social class helped drive the passage of legislation that improved conditions for the most desperate. Zoning laws required setbacks from property lines and other reforms improved the health and safety of tenants. Perhaps they improved as well the safety of New York's elite who escaped the fate of Parisian aristocracy a century before.

Engels's anticipation of revolution was not completely wrong, but it was misfocused. Sudden, radical upheaval was coming, but not so much in the realms of politics and government. Revolutions in technology were changing daily life and creating opportunities for many who had reached a dead end. Electricity and petroleum were the new sources of energy that combined with structural steel to force changes so dramatic that the country's economy was altered fundamentally.

Wall Street remained the financial center for the new industrial economy, and manufacturing provided jobs with better pay than many of the crowd had known before. Farming continued in New York City, even in Manhattan, well into the twentieth century, but conversations in the counting houses, the docks, the restaurants, theaters, and bars would focus on getting ahead rather than the need to overthrow the ruling class.

As dramatic as these changes were—and they rocked New York's culture, its economy, and its government—they were too subtle for some to notice. A comment attributed to John McGraw when the Giants considered evicting the Yankees from the Polo Grounds in 1920 reflected a common misperception: "If we kick them out, they won't be able to find another location on Manhattan Island. They'll have to move to the Bronx or Long Island. The fans will forget about them, and they'll be through."[12]

As a demographer, McGraw was stuck at the turn of the century. When New York consolidated in 1898, its population was concentrated in two boroughs. Manhattan had close to two million residents. Brooklyn was over a million, and the Bronx, Queens, and Staten Island combined for fewer than a half million.[13] As the Yankees were opening Hilltop Park, a large entertainment business could hope to prosper in Manhattan or Brooklyn, but anywhere else in the city was "the back of beyond."

If the Giants were counting on that old population pattern when they decided to bounce the Yankees, they missed a historic transformation. By 1920, Manhattan had passed the two million mark in population. Brooklyn nearly doubled in size, and went over two million itself. The Bronx had added a half million to grow to over 700,000. Queens was close to a half million, and Staten Island was over 100,000.[14]

The obvious question is: Where did all these people come from? Part of the answer is just as obvious: immigration. In 1900, the population of the new consolidated city was almost 3,500,000. In the next twenty years, it grew by slightly more than two million, the same number of New Yorkers who were first-generation Americans. But the numbers alone only hint at the revival of New York between the 1890s and Opening Day.

With the expansion of the city's legal boundaries in 1898, vast areas of land became more available to the masses who had been packed into lower Manhattan. Bringing these areas within the borders of New York City meant that the city government could target and coordinate projects—transportation services, for instance—that could join previously isolated communities into more prosperous commercial networks. Soon, people could live in the Bronx and work in lower Manhattan.

Where the Bronx's new residents lived was another of the great changes of the day. Apartments that were built just after 1900 were often called "new-law" tenements in reference to a 1901 housing act that targeted the tenements of Riis's book. Clifton Hood has noted that, in contrast to the squalor of the old tenements, "For $16.00 to $20.00 dollars a month residents could rent a brand-new apartment that included two bedrooms, a combined dining-living room, a kitchen with hot water and a gas range, and an interior toilet and bathtub. These new-law tenements had good heating and lighting, carpeted hallways, and tastefully decorated foyers and facades."[15]

This kind of housing at those prices was the very opportunity that the working class of lower Manhattan needed. The poorest among them might still be blocked, but those with any edge at all could take advantage of the new housing to begin the life that had brought them to America in the first place. Soon, the tenants were aspiring to become homeowners. People were trading tenements for apartments that generally sought to retain the advantages of communal living through some kind of common garden or courtyard. The decade of the 1920s produced the greatest volume of new housing in the city's history. Over 400,000 new apartment units were constructed along with more than 106,000 single family homes and 111,000 two-family dwellings.[16]

Apartment construction was facilitated in the 1920s by an interplay between technology and the law. Advances in self-service elevators allowed their installation and operation in middle-class residences. No longer were they limited to luxury high-rises. At the same time, the building code required any structure above six stories to be completely fireproof. In other words, five- and six-story apartments with elevators proved cheaper to build than taller buildings, and the convenience of the elevator allowed marketing to middle-class occupants. The Bronx relied little on single family homes for its development. Architects experimented with distinctly different designs as they balanced market forces with artistic innovation and compliance with building and zoning codes.

Housing needs during World War I forced direct government construction, but, once the war was over, the political culture of the time caused those programs to be abandoned. Government remained in the housing market through policies that were targeted to stimulate private construction. Ten-year real estate tax exemptions were one such device intended to encourage new building during the early 1920s.

Jacob Riis had estimated that one of the worst of the neighborhoods he studied, a place crudely known as "Jewtown," packed 330,000 people into a single square mile.[17] Many of these families escaped to the Bronx, bringing a strong cultural sensibility with them. From the time the Stadium opened through the end of the 1920s, the number of Jews on the Lower East Side fell from over 700,000 to just under 300,000.[18] Most of them went to the Bronx, where the number of Jewish residents grew to 585,000 in 1930, nearly half of the borough's entire population.[19]

Worker cooperatives thrived in a cultural climate that blocked government projects. The Amalgamated Clothing Workers of America was the most important union in the garment business, and it developed several cooperative housing projects throughout New York, including the Bronx. Economic advantages of these co-ops included housing costs that were estimated to be 25 percent below market rates. Groceries and other staples could be purchased at co-op stores at a reduced price. Day care allowed both parents to secure jobs, and a bus service provided transportation to subway stations.

Social aspects of the co-ops were at least as pronounced. As Richard Plunz puts it:

The cooperatives were in a sense also a microcosm of the whole of the Jewish Bronx. The life within the elite private buildings of the Grand Concourse was less intense and less directed, of course, but all the same, these buildings shared a common "culture of housing" which imbued similar urbanistic ideals and cultural heritage, regardless of specific differences of social class or politics.[20]

The co-ops had their own newspapers, libraries, and meeting halls. The urban sensibilities that nearly suffocated in the tenements of the Lower East Side developed in the Bronx in the co-ops. And, as baseball rose in importance in American culture, Bronx neighborhoods had the wherewithal to discuss the games, share opinion, and draw converts to the American pastime. Babe Ruth and the Shalom Aleichim Cooperative are not an obvious pair on the face of things, but the great Jewish co-op was as equipped to integrate the Babe into their community life as any neighborhood in New York.

The most common way to commute from the developing neighborhoods in the Bronx to the jobs of Manhattan was the subway. In *722 Miles*, Clifton Hood's excellent history of the subway system, he writes, "Today farms, villages, and country estates; tomorrow, a city. From 1904 to World War I this process of rapid, comprehensive urban development was repeated throughout the Bronx in neighborhood after neighborhood along the IRT's [Interborough Rapid Transit] Broadway and Lenox Avenue branches."[21] This development of the subways was an essential part of changing the Bronx from something like the Northwest Territory for Manhattan into a functioning part of New York City. The new technology allowed the linking of neighborhoods, thus the expansion of the city.

The politics and economics of this development are familiar. As Hood puts it, land speculators "gained advance knowledge of the subway's route from Interborough executives and municipal politicians, bought vast tracts of unimproved land along the line, and then sold their property to building contractors at tremendous profit."[22] Although honest graft retained its appeal, direct government participation in the subways remained controversial.

Hoods reviews the different proposals for funding, constructing, and operating the subways. In the 1890s, various models of regulatory commissions, public authorities, and other private enterprise were openly considered. Much as cities do today with sports stadiums, New York was trying to find a partnership between business and government that would combine efficiency with fairness.

New Yorkers were concerned about spending tax money for businesses that would be owned by a few wealthy magnates. They were also troubled by the prospect of Richard Croker's Tammany Hall exploiting the subways for their own questionable ends. Federal financing of railroad construction was offered as an example of the legitimacy of public investment, but critics countered with the *Credit Mobilier* scandal as evidence of the mischief that could attend that kind of venture.

Back and forth, the argument developed between those concerned about the combination of wealth and power to exploit the many for the benefit of the few and those concerned that a serious expansion of government control of business would kill enterprise and initiative. No doubt much of the debate was hot air, but important ideas were refined to develop pragmatic ways to help the city. Ideological purity proved less important than finding answers that solved problems and created opportunity. A healthy preference for private enterprise remained, but, having had bitter experience with tenements, child labor, and other abuses, New Yorkers willingly considered new responsibilities for government.

In the case of the subways, the initial compromise included public ownership with private companies operating the lines. The system became a favorite target for Mayor John Hylan, who himself had been fired from a job with the Brooklyn Rapid Transit Company (BRT) in 1897.[23] Hylan was further enraged by a tragic accident on November 1, 1918, when a BRT train, operated by an inadequately trained strikebreaker who was also ill and exhausted, derailed with horrifying results. Over ninety people were killed as the subway cars broke and twisted into lethal weapons of wood and steel.[24]

Hylan's attacks on the subway system focused on his championing of the nickel fare, a sum that made little financial sense even in 1920, but was politically unassailable for decades after. Hylan fashioned the arguments for a transportation system that would enjoy tremendous popular support, and that also carried him to a great reelection victory in the 1921 mayoral race. New Yorkers had understood that the combination of new housing and rapid transit were essential components of the modern urban life they were enjoying.

The Bronx was designed to be more than the terminus of subway lines. The borough's most elegant street was a tribute to the automobile as the preeminent mode of American transportation. In the 1890s, while subways were largely in the realm of ideas, a bold plan for the construction of a boulevard in the Bronx began to take shape.

The Grand Concourse first took shape in the mind of Louis Risse, a French immigrant who enjoyed the Bronx as a hunting preserve in the late 1860s. Years later, Risse was an engineer in the Bronx who convinced his boss, Louis Heintz, of the wisdom of a magnificent boulevard modeled on the Champs-Élysées. As Risse described it, "A boulevard is a promenade, a drive, an avenue of pleasure, everything in fact except a commercial thoroughfare."[25]

Because the Grand Concourse was designed well before Henry Ford built cars for the masses, one of the first purposes of the project was to provide a place for New York society to race their horses. Cars, at this time, were so slow that they were shunted to paved roads that ran parallel to the central paths that horses and buggies traversed. Wide sidewalks complemented the vehicular roads, so that pedestrians would be an important part of life on the Concourse. The roadway also connected New Yorkers with parks that had been acquired in the northern part of the Bronx. Van Cortlandt Park and Bronx Park, the home of the Bronx Zoo and the New York Botanical Garden, were accessible through this new road.

Construction began in 1902, and was expected to take about three years. It took about twice as long, due primarily to the geological challenges that greatly complicated the project. Underpasses ingeniously prevented interference with the north–south flow of traffic on the main road, and also solved some of the engineering problems.

The future of the concourse was secured with the opening of the IRT subway line just two blocks away in 1917. Rapid transit facilitated living in the elegant, new section of the Bronx while commuting rather easily to Manhattan. Yankee Stadium's opening in 1923 added to the appeal of the neighborhood, and the Concourse Plaza, an exclusive hotel, opened the following year.

Just north of the Stadium, a posh home was built in 1924 by the former baron of New York baseball, Andrew Freedman.[26] The magnate's idea of charitable works is reflected in his will, which stipulated that the house would become a residence for the elderly who had once been rich but who had fallen on hard times. Restored to their former glory, these fortunate few could enjoy "a seventy-five foot drawing room, an oak-paneled library stocked with classics in several languages, a billiard room, and marble fireplace."[27] In the 1980s, residency requirements were changed so that the applicants need only be poor without going to the trouble of first being rich.

The Grand Concourse became a litmus test for the Bronx. Compared variously with Park and Fifth Avenues, it was for a time the place to live for many New Yorkers. Art Deco apartments rose in the 1930s, and they remain one of the great collections of that period. The boulevard itself became what Risse intended, a place to be seen, admired, and envied.

When hard times hit the Bronx, the Grand Concourse was an easy, bitter symbol of dreams that had shattered. After World War II, renovation plans invariably pronounced a strategy for making the Concourse grand again. Turning back the clock has proven impossible, but finding a new purpose for this remarkable road remains a reasonable goal.

In addition to antitrust, zoning, and other regulatory reforms, the Progressive Era also included a modernizing of government finance. The income tax was established by constitutional amendment in 1913. The following year Congress created the Federal Reserve to provide something like a central bank for the United States. In 1921, a major reform of the budgetary process was fashioned with the creation of the Bureau of the Budget, which brought principles of corporate budgeting to the state.

Popular control of government was also extended to make America's political system more democratic. The Seventeenth Amendment to the Constitution, the second of two passed in 1913, established the popular election of U.S. senators, replacing the original practice of having them chosen by state legislatures. The Nineteenth Amendment was passed seven years later to secure women's suffrage throughout the land.

This modern state appeared to have some of the organizational advantages of corporations at the same time that it was subject to more popular control. Private enterprise was favored for housing (and, initially, for the subways), but responsibility for some other products and services fell to the public sector.

Parks and recreation became important responsibilities for government, and they formed the foundation of Robert Moses's power in New

York. Beaches and pastoral preserves were increasingly regarded as public amenities to which all were entitled. Other public enterprises included docks, bridges, roads, tunnels, canals, and the water supply. In each case, private ownership and management were displaced, and those losing their businesses understandably howled in protest.

In his annual report in 1923, the Commissioner of Public Markets proposed a new venture, the construction of public terminal markets. These facilities were defined as markets at the end of transportation lines where food would be received from producers and sold to wholesalers who in turn would distribute the food to retailers who would sell directly to the public. The Commissioner of Public Markets in the year of Yankee Stadium's inaugural was Edwin J. O'Malley, who wrote that more than ten billion pounds of food arrived in New York every year from each state in the union. More than half of that food, he estimated, rotted at the railway terminals, which, of course, theoretically doubled the price of the remaining produce. The economic pressures on families were especially terrible during World War I when so many men were in the army. Rumors of food profiteering abounded, stories that food was being dumped in New Jersey to drive up the price in New York.

O'Malley categorically rejected the utilitarian dogma of the free market. "The greatest good for the greatest number becomes but an illusion when entrusted to the mercies of those far removed from the people and having contact with them only to extract from them."[28]

O'Malley made the case for terminal markets by noting their capacity to handle the volume of food arriving in the city and efficiently move it to retail outlets before it began to rot. Storage facilities protected the food from sudden and severe changes in the weather. He also alluded to the terror of many of the Irish families of New York. Arguing that the city had a food reserve of two weeks, he invoked the awful word "famine." He went on:

A strike on our local transportation lines or on the waterfront, a great blizzard, ice floes in the harbor, the interruption of the free movement of trains into the city, are difficulties which might spell disaster to our food supply reserve and reap a heavy toll of suffering, misery and possibly death.[29]

He stressed the particular dependence of the four hundred babies born in the city each day, the sick, and the elderly on an ample, healthful food supply.

As it happened, the splendid example of what O'Malley was proposing for every borough was rising in the Bronx. In fact, it was rising in the shadows of Yankee Stadium. The city was spending $7.5 million to build the Bronx Terminal Market on fifty-two acres by the Macombs Dam Bridge.

On a theoretical level, O'Malley's case was that the free market was deficient in getting food to hungry New Yorkers. One of the familiar abuses of monopoly, the witholding of the product, drove prices artificially high. Whims of weather could destroy additional produce that lay exposed on the subways of New York. And no private interest could afford to hold an adequate food supply in reserve in case of emergency. In this instance, regulation was not the answer, public enterprise was. The spectre of Bolshevism complicated any argument for public ownership, but the necessity of a reliable food source was more dear to New Yorkers than free market ideology.

The prospect of multimillion dollar terminal markets throughout the boroughs was a textbook opportunity for "honest graft." The opening of the Bronx Terminal Market guaranteed that the area across the Harlem River from the Polo Grounds would be a focus of economic activity. Much of the work at the market would necessarily begin at or before dawn. Food would be on its way to retail centers well before noon. Many of the workers would finish their shifts in the early afternoon— just in time for a baseball game.

The Terminal Market was an example of the innovative middle path that Americans were discovering between unregulated markets and the radical destruction of private property. This middle path was essential to the development of the middle class that was the foundation of baseball's economy. Confined to the privileged few, baseball could not have grown beyond the gentlemen's clubs of Manhattan. Targeted only to the denizens of Jim Cusick's dives, baseball would have been reduced to a war of sharp cleats and beanballs.

As it was, one reason baseball enjoyed its phenomenal growth was that millions of people grew into New York's middle class. They were able to do so because of their own ambition, because of the expansion of private business that gave them jobs, and because of various government policies that helped the city break out of the stagnation that had threatened it in the late nineteenth century. In our own time, we sometimes condense our understanding of public affairs to ideological preconceptions of the left or right, perfect for a television screen but otherwise not very helpful. The rise of New York's middle class demonstrates that these narrow debates miss important factors, and they mistakenly restrict the credit for progress to an incomplete list of contributors.

While its functioning boundaries, infrastructure, and public policies changed between 1899 and 1923, New York City's culture made its own adjustments. In public schools, factories, and churches; in opera houses, the Armory show, and other points of high culture; in gambling houses, burlesque shows, and the track; in police precincts, Tammany headquarters, and reformers' living rooms—in word and deed, New Yorkers were defining who they were.

The Great War had provoked strains between those who supported England's brave fight against German aggression and those, like many German immigrants, who were understandably inclined to the other side. Many Irish Americans reacted fiercely to the British decision to divert war resources at Easter in 1916 to suppress the rising in Dublin. Few immigrant groups in New York could escape pulls of loyalty that the war engendered.

On a more ethereal level, the arrival of modern art shocked many patrons and critics who were perplexed at the radical presentation of the new age. For people desperate for order in the turbulent times, painters and composers were holding up the mirror that confirmed that traditional order had collapsed. The upside was that creativity had more room than before, but, if one looked to the arts for comfort and reassurance against the strains of the day, these were trying times.

The Russian Revolution in 1917, overthrowing the Czar in March and establishing the communist Soviet Union in November, was a defining event for America through the century. Americans who grew up in the Cold War often saw the rivalry as the central organizing principle of public affairs. From time to time, attitudes about the Soviet state intruded into American politics with all but the most vocal and persistent critics of all things in the "workers' paradise" suspected of disloyalty.

Such suspicions roiled New York after World War I as supporters of labor unions became the object of fierce accusations that they wanted to replicate the Russian experience here. Frederick Lewis Allen in his classic work *Only Yesterday* offers a review of the turmoil:

> Those were the days when column after column of the front pages of the newspapers shouted the news of strikes and anti-Bolshevik riots; when radicals shot down Armistice Day paraders in Centralia, Washington, and in revenge the patriotic citizenry took out of the jail a member of the I.W.W [the Industrial Workers of the World or "Wobblies" were one of the more radical unions of the time]——a white American be it noted——and lynched him by tying a rope around his neck and throwing him off a bridge; when properly elected members of the Assembly of New York State were expelled (and their constituents thereby disenfranchised) simply because they had been elected as members of the venerable Socialist Party; when a jury in Indiana took two minutes to acquit a man for shooting and killing an alien because he had shouted "To hell with the United States"; and when the Vice President of the nation cited as a dangerous manifestation of radicalism in the women's colleges the fact that the girl debaters of Radcliffe had upheld the affirmative in an intercollegiate debate on the subject: "Resolved that the recognition of labor unions by employers is essential to successful collective bargaining."

These were some of the threats to the steady, stable progress that New York and America were pursuing in the early part of this century.

Race riots, short hair, and comfortable clothes for women, the stunning attempt to outlaw drinking through the Eighteenth Amendment—these added to the sense that some people had of a world gone mad. In the face of so much turmoil, we might expect a resurgence of Anglophilia, especially since we entered the Great War on the same side as England. A return to English roots was the hallmark of the Nativist reaction to the Irish immigrants who arrived during the 1840s, but, in the early 1920s, native New Yorkers seemed to be as leery of the English as any other nationality.

An example of this concern is seen in an investigation conducted between 1921 and 1923 into the history textbooks used in New York City public schools. Mayor John Hylan had called for the inquiry, assigning Commissioner of Accounts David Hirshfield to the task. Part of Hylan's charge warned Hirshfield that "the school children of this city must not be inoculated with the poisonous virus of foreign propaganda which seeks to belittle illustrious American patriots."[30]

Hirshfield took the mayor's point, and provided a list of offensive themes that he discovered in his research. Among the objectionable charges:

That the American Revolution was merely a "civil war" between the English people on both sides of the sea and their "German" king;

That the United States Constitution and most of our free institutions were borrowed from England;

That the Mexican War was a grab of territory;

That our country's history has been "hitherto distorted through unthinking adherence to national prejudice";

That it is now being "set right" through "newer tendencies in historical writing" and "methods of modern historical scholarship."[31]

These propositions are now fairly standard in American histories, but, at the time, they were controversial because they pointed education in a different direction.

Hirshfield, in bold print, stressed that he did not defend the accuracy of everything in the old texts, but "those American histories were written from the American point of view, intended to awaken love for America and for everything American, to instill patriotism in the breasts of the young and excite their admiration for the heroic men and splendid women who laid the foundation of our independence and made this Nation a fact."[32]

The romantic tone of Hirshfield's report distinguishes it from modern public policy analysis, but the substance is not so far removed. The report is a classic example of a values debate. The new texts were asserting a more scientific approach to history in which objectivity and neutrality are central features. Hirshfield asked, in his spirited way, about the traditional function of molding citizens. How can children grow to respect our community if they are not told emphatically about its heroic past?

The school investigation is confirmation that New York City in the 1920s had become a vanguard for the country. Hirschfield's tone seems to be reactionary, but the report triumphantly asserts that America is its own place. The country is decidedly not English, so the importance and value of immigration are implicitly but fundamentally recognized. The report also reveals that, to the consternation of the mayor and his allies, a sophisticated understanding of American history was being offered to New York's children throughout the city's public schools.

Looking back at that time, we may wonder why an honest look at George Washington was possible in the public schools, but an unvarnished account of Babe Ruth beyond the ballpark was inconceivable in the city's sports sections. Perhaps the answer is as simple as Ruth's importance to the treasury of the Yankees, their competitors, the newspapers that covered his play, and the products he endorsed. Washington was safely preserved on the mantel, but Ruth was alive to sell tickets, the evening edition, and automobiles.

What could hold such a dynamic community together? In the 1920s, commercialism and celebrity were powerful forces, and they have remained so ever since. They join an array of myths about America and New York that inspire and frustrate those who bet their lives that their best prospects to realize their ambitions lie in this country and this city. The Yankees offered an entire roster of reasons to believe that you can make it here. Fame and fortune are possible, perhaps not in the great Stadium in the Bronx, but surely in factories, docks, banks, theaters, or any of the commercial avenues that the city now required.

You could now also be your own Jake Ruppert in a Bronx co-op, a Queens single-family wood frame, an upscale apartment in Manhattan, a cottage on Staten Island, or a dwelling above your storefront in Brooklyn. You could live as no one in your family had likely lived before, and you could get to work or play miles from home without having to make the investment in a car. But you could even do that too, if you wanted.

The Yankees were prepared for a marvelous time, and New York was too. The city had found its way through the social, political, and economic forces that had destroyed much of the rest of the world. Surveying the wreckage of Europe's war and the perils of the American past, New Yorkers would take to the swagger of Babe Ruth as an entirely reasonable expression of how great it was to be alive and in New York in the Roaring Twenties.

THE RUPPERT ERA

Jacob Ruppert remained the Yankees' owner until his death in 1939. Under his leadership, the team became an important part of New York life, something more than an engaging amusement, tracking the atmosphere of the city through the frivolity of the 1920s and the hard times of the 1930s. The Yankees were developing a mystique, part of which centered on an interplay of baseball, politics, and entertainment that assumed new importance in the 1920s.

President Warren Harding attended a game at the Stadium about a week after Opening Day, and Babe Ruth obliged with another home run. The two met before the game as Harding, like the Tammany Democrats, basked in the reflected glory of the home run king. By public reputation, Harding was the Babe's kind of president, a man with similar appetites as Ruth's and the same willingness to indulge them. The appearance of a president at any event confers significance and suggests that something important is under way. Harding, in a small way, helped the Stadium become a place to be and be seen.

Those unable to get to Yankee Stadium were finding new ways to be linked to the festivities. Newspaper editors understood the Stadium as a celebrity magnet, so Yankee games were certain to receive thorough coverage. More important, electronic curiosities that had been concocted in places like Thomas Edison's workshop were maturing into industries that needed products to sell to viewers and listeners. Recorded music could be played back on phonographs, bringing the artistry of individual performers to audiences of unprecedented numbers. Movies were quickly becoming an art form with "talkies" arriving by the end of the decade. This combination of moving images with sound was not just an amusement. Newsreels gave the public the incredible chance to see the physical manner of public figures and hear their actual voices.

In that regard, newsreels were particularly good to Babe Ruth. Baseball historians have valid reason to believe that the Babe was a better player even than Honus Wagner, Ty Cobb, and Joe Jackson, but those three are remote figures because we generally see them only in still photographs from their playing days. Ruth, who scarcely needs any help, nonetheless gets it as the first star of the newsreel era. He is far more accessible because, albeit in grainy black and white images, we see how he moved, along with his gestures and facial expressions. We also know how he sounded, a wry and cocky voice that fit so well his larger than life figure.

Ruth helped to set the new mold for national prominence. Whether a politician, inventor, artist, or millionaire—if you could bring a presence to newsreels or the radio airwaves, you could be a celebrity in the cinema age, a status unrivaled in American popular culture. With Babe Ruth at center stage in the nation's largest market, the Yankees were positioned to exploit these new commercial opportunities to maximum advantage.

While the public eye was on his right fielder, Jake Ruppert was building an enterprise far more enduring than one great player. On May 21, 1923, a month after Yankee Stadium opened, Ruppert bought out Til Huston to become the Yankees' sole owner. The tension between the two colonels had never completely healed after Ruppert hired Miller Huggins while Huston served the American army in France. Babe Ruth's continual challenges to Huggins's authority kept the issue alive despite the team's improved play.

Huston's engineering background had been a great help in the Yankees' securing the right kind of home, but he and Ruppert had too many battles with too much bitterness to sustain the kind of focus that the franchise needed. Ruppert paid about one and a quarter million dollars for Huston's interest in the Yankees, about a million dollars more than Huston had paid for his part of the club back in 1915.

The buyout stabilized the front office. Ruppert was the ultimate authority. Ed Barrow ran the business operations; Miller Huggins, whether Ruth liked it or not, was the manager. In the new climate, the 1923 season was a grand success as the Yankees won the pennant by fifteen games over Ty Cobb's Detroit Tigers. They capped the year by winning their first World Series. They beat the Giants in six games over six days in the two great ballyards that were only walking distance apart.

This first championship was also the last for many of the Yankee starters. They finished two games back of the Washington Senators in 1924, and had a disastrous collapse in 1925. The Ruppert organization then retooled the club, and put a different and far better team on the field in 1926.

When we first look at the Yankees in the 1920s, we see Babe Ruth and a supporting cast dominating baseball through the decade. More accurately, Ruth played on several teams with the Yankees. The first relied greatly on the players maneuvered from Harry Frazee, but the Red Sox owner got out of the game in July 1923. The Frazee offerings were replaced by prospects that the Yankees had scouted, signed, and developed themselves. Ruth is entitled to every accolade he ever received, but the Yankee team was also becoming a product of a first-rate organization.

Among the changes between the 1923 and 1926 editions: Lou Gehrig famously had replaced Wally Pipp at first base; Tony Lazzeri took over for Aaron Ward at second; Mark Koenig was the new shortstop after Everett Scott's streak ended; and Earle Combs succeeded Whitey Witt in center field. The Yankees needed only the 1925 season to reload and resume their dominance.

This pattern would repeat long after Jake Ruppert passed from the scene. Other franchises could occasionally develop a powerhouse team that contended for championships over a few years. The unique aspect of the Yankees was that they could produce just that kind of team decade after decade.

After the 1925 season, in which the team finished seventh with attendance at 697,267, the Yankees would not have another year that disappointing until 1966. Over the thirty-nine seasons from 1926 through 1964, the Yankees finished first an incredible twenty-six times. Six times they finished in second place, and they had another six third-place finishes. A single drop to fourth place completes the longest reign in American professional sports. The Yankees compiled nineteen World Series titles during that span.

In the late 1920s, the Yankees returned to the World Series through three consecutive Octobers. They fell to the St. Louis Cardinals in 1926, when Grover Cleveland Alexander capped a brilliant career by coming out of the bullpen in the seventh inning to strike out Tony Lazzeri and save the seventh game.

The 1927 Yankees are often cited as the greatest team in baseball history. They won 110 games during the regular season, winning the pennant by nineteen games over Connie Mack's Athletics. They dispatched the Pittsburgh Pirates in four games, with Ruth hitting .400 with two home runs.

A kind of footnote to the 1927 season sheds some different light on the ownership issue. In January of that year, Rogers Hornsby was traded by the St. Louis Cardinals to the New York Giants. Hornsby had been given a small share of ownership in the Cardinals, and he intended to keep it even while playing for the Giants. The obvious conflict was resolved by Commissioner Landis who ordered the stock sold.

Hornsby as owner was an extraordinary departure from the class distinction that had separated players and owners. From time to time, owners have talked about teams really belonging to the fans, but they have jealously guarded their own control over the essential business aspects of their franchises. Employee ownership has never been a serious model in baseball despite some of the potentially stabilizing advantages it could bring to the modern business.

With order restored, the 1928 season in the American League was a closer race to the same conclusion. The Yankees won 101 games to edge the Athletics by two and a half games, then they took revenge for their 1926 loss to the Cardinals by sweeping St. Louis four straight in the World Series. The potential of Yankee Stadium to affect a game was evident on September 9 when the Yankees played a doubleheader against the Athletics. Philadelphia was a half game ahead of New York at breakfast, but trailed the Yankees at dinner. A record crowd of 85,265 cheered the Yankees to a 5–0 and 7–3 sweep of the Athletics. In addition to the tremendous crowd, an estimated 100,000 were turned away.[1]

The danger of accommodating these large crowds was tragically demonstrated the following spring when two people were trampled to death leaving a game. An estimated 9,000 fans were in the right field bleachers on May 19, 1929, when a soft rain began to fall. A few went to the exit where they continued to watch the game. To leave the Stadium, these fans had to walk down fourteen steps, and this led to disaster when the skies opened up. Thousands of people raced for the exit and pressed against those on the stairs. Inevitably, people fell, and the tiny area at the foot of the stairs became "a screaming, struggling mass of people."[2] In addition to the fatalities, sixty-two people were injured, many of them children who had watched the game in "Ruthville."

This kind of risk to public safety was another link between the Yankees and public officials. The Fire Department, building inspectors, police, and transportation officials have become essential actors in the safe operation of the Stadium. Disasters like the one in May 1929 are terrible reminders that the places where we gather for entertainment can quickly become sites of tragedies.

The 1929 season ended sadly as well. On September 25, the ball club suffered the sudden death of manager Miller Huggins. Like Casey Stengel and Joe Torre later, Huggins had compiled a mediocre record as manager before being signed by the Yankees. As with his successors, once in New York, Huggins set an incomparable standard. The Yankees slipped to second place in the American League, and the front office scrambled to find a manager who could lead the club through another time of transition.

While Yankee fans enjoyed seeing the team as a triumphant symbol of New York City in the Roaring Twenties, politics and governing in New York and America initiated their own changes that later would prove critical to the stadium game. These portentous changes began on April 25, 1924, with the death of Charles Murphy. His passing left Tammany Hall without effective leadership, and Tammany began a decline that it has never reversed.

Al Smith and Robert Wagner had become important state and national figures by the time of Murphy's death, but neither was in a position to exercise the peculiar skills that were needed to control Tammany. If there is any merit to Plunkitt's distinction between honest and dishonest graft, only the most brilliant political management could limit Tammany to the more noble form of corruption. Without Murphy, the machine deteriorated into a morass of hack politicians grabbing what they could.

The symbol of the times was the mayoralty of Jimmy Walker, who was first elected in 1925 to succeed John Hylan. Walker had been a New York state senator whom Tammany preferred to the more independent and Brooklyn-based Hylan. By disposition, preparation, and talent, Jimmy Walker was a songwriter rather than a public servant. "Will You Love Me in December as You Do in May?" remains perhaps his most familiar composition. Family pressures drove him from Tin Pan Alley into politics, but he simply saw public office as another stage for easy entertainment. By most accounts, Walker was a thoroughly engaging fellow who possessed the charm that can seduce an electorate for the season of a campaign. During the 1920s, the need for conscientious governing was not apparent to many people—certainly not to Walker—so his casual approach to his responsibilities was tolerated and even celebrated.

Governor Smith supported Walker's run for mayor after receiving worthless assurances that Beau James would stop his drinking and philandering. In a sense, Walker was a trim, better dressed version of Babe Ruth without the equivalent of home runs on the job. The potential alliance between Smith and Walker for the betterment of New York was illusory because Walker had no capacity for serious governing.

In 1927, while the Babe was hitting his sixty home runs, Walker began an affair with Betty Compton, a twenty-three-year-old actress. Forsaking discretion as well as his wife, the mayor moved into a suite at the Ritz. He had made it so easy for the press to fill blank pages with his nightly cavorting that they overlooked his arrangement with Compton while continuing to focus on his wardrobe, parties, and quips.

With this breezy treatment of his responsibilities, Walker was able to keep his foes at bay through a remarkable reelection campaign in 1929. Walker's opponent could not have offered a sharper choice to the voters. Fiorello LaGuardia was a Republican congressman from Harlem who had championed every unfashionable cause during the 1920s. As ambitious as anyone in public life at the time, LaGuardia savagely attacked the rich, the utilities, banks, national Republican administrations, and Tammany Hall. He demanded vast public works programs, aid to the poor, public housing, education, regulation, and other staples of the Progressive agenda. In increasingly emotional and erratic tones, LaGuardia campaigned by pointing out the shallowness and cost of the party over which Walker so cheerfully presided. Beau James ignored the taunts as well as some economic indicators that the party was about over.

The most dramatic sign of hard times ahead was the collapse of the stock market in October 1929 just weeks before the mayoral election. We associate the event with the beginning of the Great Depression, but a number of months passed before the city and the nation were gripped by the fearful poverty that would last until World War II. In the weeks following the crash, optimistic predictions abounded, and the New York City electorate voted in expectation of continued prosperity. Walker won a tremendous victory over LaGuardia, but his reelection simply meant that he would preside over his own demise.

One immediate cause of Walker's undoing could be traced a year before his reelection to a notorious murder in Manhattan. The *New York*

Times obituary announced, "Rothstein—Arnold, beloved husband of Caroline and devoted son of Abraham and Esther. Reposing at Riverside Memorial Chapel, 76th St. and Amsterdam Ave. Interment private."[3] The gambler had been shot at a meeting called to collect some recent losses that he had incurred.

The *Times*'s story on Rothstein's shooting described the game in which he had lost over $300,000 as beginning shortly before midnight on September 29 and lasting well into the next day. Rothstein lingered for a day after the shooting, occasionally conscious, but he may not have identified his assailant. In any event, the case was never closed.

To baseball fans, Rothstein is known as the man who fixed the 1919 World Series.[4] The reformers' game of "connect the dots" linked Walker to Rothstein through a robbery a month after the 1929 election. On December 7, a political fund-raiser in the Bronx was interrupted at 1:30 in the morning by masked gunmen while the guest of honor, Judge Albert Vitale, was making his speech.[5] Vitale was the boss of the Tepecano Democratic Club, a local Tammany unit. A detective was present, and he and two court attendants surrendered revolvers to the robbers. Several thousand dollars in cash and jewelry were also taken.

The bold robbery had a bizarre aftermath. No one called the police to report the crime, and, a few hours later, Vitale himself summoned the police detective who was his fellow victim to the Tepecano headquarters. When he arrived, the detective was presented by Vitale with his gun, the other two revolvers, and all the pilfered cash and jewelry. Even in Jimmy Walker's New York, that was news.

The robbery was likely the work of another Tammany group with ties to organized crime. The political effect was stunning. The public summoned a reaction that had been in abeyance for years: They were shocked. Vitale's behavior suggested that the judge himself was personally tied to the crime bosses, and the city bar association demanded his removal from the bench. An old LaGuardia charge began to resonate— that Vitale had been in debt to Arnold Rothstein for $19,600.

The electorate that had laughed with Jimmy Walker a month before now demanded that the corruption be investigated. The new governor,

Franklin Roosevelt, was forced to appoint a commission that would risk exposing Tammany Hall's connections to organized crime. The Wigwam had survived the Lexow investigation of the 1890s, so recovery was possible, but FDR, ambivalent at best about Tammany, appointed a man to head the commission who had the capacity to bury Tammany and the personal desire to do so.

Judge Samuel Seabury was a paragon among the good government reformers of New York City. His ancestry traced to the *Mayflower*, and his ambition had focused on the very seats that Tammany pols had taken in his place. He had wanted the governorship as a stepping-stone to the presidency, but Al Smith, with Charles Murphy's considerable help, had beaten the patrician to it.

Seabury was sincerely offended by Tammany's practices in the Hall's best days, and he loathed the return to crude bribery and shakedowns that had characterized its recent years. Beginning in 1930, with patience and persistence through several years of public hearings, Seabury exposed the waste and theft of Jimmy Walker's reign. The mayor himself took the stand, and his charm no longer deflected tough questions. The Great Depression had taken hold, and the city was suffering. Too many New Yorkers had become too familiar with hunger, cold, and fear. A sharp wardrobe and a snappy tune had become preposterous in the circumstances.

Other New York politicians saw an opportunity in the changed climate and competed fiercely for the top prizes in state and national politics. Al Smith, badly hurt by Murphy's passing, continued his pursuit of the Democratic presidential nomination. Franklin Roosevelt, with presidential ambitions of his own, had reluctantly agreed to Smith's urging that he run for governor of New York in 1928. FDR, still struggling to resume a public life after his polio attack in 1921, had preferred a longer timetable: the governorship in 1932 and a presidential run four years later.

The political choreography was scrambled by Smith's defeat for the presidency in 1928 while FDR won the governorship. Roosevelt suddenly had the inside track, and he pressed the advantage ruthlessly. His association with Smith deteriorated, and many New York Democrats faced a painful choice when Smith suddenly jumped back into the presidential picture in 1932. FDR blocked Smith's late challenge, then dealt with Jimmy Walker.

Roosevelt needed the support of New York City Democrats in the fall campaign, but he could not be seen to be complacent about Tammany corruption. Having lost all support, Walker resigned his office. In the tradition of William Marcy Tweed and Richard Croker, he moved to Europe while the storm over Tammany raged.

In 1933, after a year with John O'Brien filling out Walker's term, Fiorello LaGuardia was elected the mayor of New York. LaGuardia won his own bruising battle to secure the fusion nomination of Republicans and reformers. His firebrand politics and perhaps his bloodline were offensive to the old guard like Seabury, but he simply was the only alternative to having Tammany in Gracie Mansion. In his own way, LaGuardia was every bit as flamboyant as Jimmy Walker had been. The obvious difference was that LaGuardia was serious about governing the city and capable of doing so.

The election results of 1932 represented another historical milestone for American government. In the face of the Great Depression, Herbert Hoover, a thoroughly decent man, extended the government as far as his limited conception of the state permitted. He had won international fame directing relief efforts after World War I, giving him a reputation as a humanitarian that was unsurpassed perhaps in the world. His tragedy was that, in the crisis that his own country suffered, he could have served far more effectively as a private citizen. As president, Hoover could not bring himself to direct public assistance to the suffering millions. A man of deep conviction, he was inflexible when experimentation was essential. The Democrats made sure he became a caricature of aloofness and indifference. A bright man, Hoover lacked the political skills to sustain his country's confidence.

The Republicans were on the verge of a national collapse, and Tammany Hall had been discredited thoroughly by the Seabury investigation. Into this vacuum, Roosevelt and LaGuardia brought the latest manifestation of the Progressive tradition. The New Deal resumed the liberal experiment after it had been put aside by the Republican restoration of the 1920s. We can easily chart how the state expanded: the size of the budget, the number of agencies, the expansion of regulatory power, the introduction of Social Security, the legislative protection of workers' rights to organize and bargain collectively. Beyond those aspects, the importance of the New Deal for our purposes is that it established that government participation in capital projects was an essential part of the modern economy.[6] The New Deal expanded the kinds of public spending that the electorate would accept as legitimate. One type is the category of public works or enterprise that no individual interest can justify. The Erie Canal was an example of public works that helped New York City become the dominant city in the country in the nineteenth century by linking midwestern commerce through the Great Lakes and the Hudson River, then to the ports of Manhattan and Brooklyn. The Erie Canal was a tremendous boon to thousands of businesses, but no single business or small group of firms could have afforded the project. A collective effort coordinated through government accomplished the task and strengthened the regional and national economies.

The New Deal relied on that experiment and others like it to propose new types of government enterprise. The logic of this type of spending was clear: If development that would benefit the community cannot be supported by voluntary investments of the private market, government should intervene and spend taxpayers' money because it will be returned many times over.

The expanded concept of public works needed new forms of government organization to be successful. The original Madisonian system, dating to 1787, had worked brilliantly at keeping power from coalescing to the detriment of personal liberty. The trick in the twentieth century, as the liberals saw it, was to preserve the protections against the abuse of power by the state while creating new techniques for correcting the abuses and inadequacies of corporate power.

In his study of government corporations, Jerry Mitchell points out that Franklin Roosevelt had extensive experience with public works and their agencies. The Panama Railroad Company, chartered by New York, had been acquired by the federal government in 1903 during the administration of his cousin Theodore Roosevelt, and it was the key administrative component in the construction of the Panama Canal. The Port of New York Authority had become a model of the new type of enterprise in the 1920s. As Assistant Secretary of the Navy under Woodrow Wilson, FDR was one of the administrators who developed fresh perspectives on economic development during World War I. Mitchell notes of FDR that, "before he was New York's governor, he worked for a time in a law firm that was involved with the use of bonds to build public projects. He was also a Progressive reformer and therefore a champion of organizations that could prevail over the dishonesty of political machines and the economic self-interest of large business corporations."[7] The growth of public works in the New Deal was predicated on the Progressive assumption that the public weal could grow through new types of enterprise. As Roosevelt believed, America was not limited to a choice between a public works corruptly administered through an organization like Tammany or an economic market in which individual gain was the sole criterion for investment.

The Progressives had become convinced that bold, centralized strategies were needed for the American economy to realize its potential. Jordan Schwarz describes the premise of the New Deal:

> The New Dealers believed that national economic growth was stifled by the monopolization of capital and manufacturing in the northeast quadrant of the country—making the South and the West undeveloped countries. They concluded that relief and recovery were stopgap solutions to the problems of unemployment and stagnation; poverty required development through hitherto unimagined quantities of public investment that could inspire labor mobility and private investment.[8]

The map of major league baseball reflected these limits in America. Until the 1950s, St. Louis and Chicago were part of what was known informally as the "western division" of the American and National

Leagues. Washington, D.C., Cincinnati, and St. Louis were strung along the southern boundary of the majors. Los Angeles, with a strong entry in the Pacific Coast League, beckoned as a potential major league market, but its isolation and the complexities of travel were too daunting. Three-quarters of America had to follow major league baseball through newspapers, radio, and newsreels until their cities grew enough to support teams of their own, and that growth would not have been possible without the commitment of resources by the federal government.

The Tennessee Valley Authority (TVA) became the prototype of what many of the New Dealers were trying to accomplish. The TVA was a government project, but, as a public authority, one that was modeled on corporate organization. In its classic design, modern bureaucracy—whatever the sector: business, government, or nonprofit—needed a concentration of power in a kind of pyramid form so that those at the top could direct the resources of the organization in a coordinated effort to a common purpose. This efficiency is antithetical to the paralysis fashioned in the Constitution for the original branches of American government. Separation of powers, checks and balances, and distinct constituencies for each office give public officials the means and incentives to block one another's aspirations in a kind of traffic jam in which no single interest group can prevail.

The TVA brought a substantial part of the South into the industrial age. Rivers were tamed to permit barge traffic that expanded commerce. Dams introduced electric power to the region, changing life in the home, schools, and the workplace. Flood control prevented the loss of topsoil, turning desolate valleys into productive cropland. Many of these effects are challenged nowadays by people who doubt the ultimate success or wisdom of trying to tame nature to this extent, but the impact in the 1930s was truly stunning.[9] The TVA was thought to combine the efficiency of business with the public purpose of government, and it offered the hope that its success could be replicated throughout the country.

Massive power projects helped develop the desert of the American Southwest and the isolated forests and streams of the Pacific Northwest. This public infrastructure permitted the growth of the modern American cities of the Sunbelt. If nature were an impediment to economic development, then nature would be changed, and it would be changed largely through public policies that relied on the application of modern organizational principles.

While the New Deal transformed America through these projects, New York City was applying the formula on the municipal level. LaGuardia cooperated with FDR from the beginning. As his biographer Thomas Kessner described LaGuardia's strategy, "Teaming the best public planner in the nation with one of the brightest experts on public finance, he dispatched Robert Moses and Adolf Berle to Washington to deliver the message that New York was prepared to compete for federal projects and prove that it could manage them with integrity and efficiency."[10]

Political rivalries swirled as they always do among the ambitious, but LaGuardia and Roosevelt had common interests in advancing a liberal agenda that challenged both the vagaries of an unfettered market as well as the corruption associated with Tammany's care for the disadvantaged. In a brutal economic time, New Yorkers saw bridges rise, parkland developed, and roads laid to link families, markets, and communities. Public efforts joined private developments like Rockefeller Center and the Empire State Building in brazenly defying the gloom that was among the serious effects of the Depression. Whether the bounty was the first electric light in a home in Alabama, irrigated farmland in Arizona, flood prevention in Oregon, or a more efficient link between Queens and Manhattan—public enterprise could generate wider economic growth and lift the spirits of a community.

Through the Ruppert years, the Yankees continued to offer winning teams to New York. Bob Shawkey, the Opening Day pitcher in 1923, was named Yankee manager in 1930. Following Huggins's death, Babe Ruth had hoped to be named the Yankee manager, but the Babe's day in the New York sun was drawing to a close. Ruth still led the American League with forty-nine home runs, but Hack Wilson of the Chicago Cubs took some of the familiar spotlight with his incredible year, hitting fifty-six homers and driving in 190 runs. The Yankees finished third, sixteen games back of the Athletics, and the front office seized an opportunity when Wilson's manager, Joe McCarthy, was fired at the end of the season. Shawkey had expected to remain as manager, but McCarthy was highly admired by the Yankee brass, who wasted little time in signing him.

The new manager had no more use for Ruth's antics than had Huggins, and McCarthy was a more effective disciplinarian. He required a dress code and demanded professional conduct from his players. Gehrig, Bill Dickey, and the other new stars responded well, and even the Babe picked up his game for his final few seasons. The Yankees finished well back of the Athletics again in 1931, but they were ready to reassert themselves the following season.

The Yankees' 1932 edition rang up 107 wins and beat the Cubs in the World Series in four games. Since their 3–2 loss to the St. Louis Cardinals in the seventh game of the 1926 World Series, the Yankees had been back to the fall classic three times: in 1927, 1928, and 1932; and they had yet to lose another game. In the third game of the 1932 Series, Babe Ruth pointed toward the centerfield stands in Wrigley Field before hitting a home run precisely there. The famous "called shot" was his last World Series home run. The Babe had two more seasons with the Yankees, both of them second-place finishes. Even in the twilight of his career, his unique place in the game was evident. In both 1930 and 1933, the Babe pitched a complete game victory, showing some of the form that had first established him among the game's greats.

The Yankees had their third straight second-place finish in 1935. Gehrig, Tony Lazzeri, and Bill Dickey were the stars of the team and they were joined in 1936 by rookie Joe DiMaggio. For the next four seasons, the Yankees won the American League pennant and the World Series. The National League champions won only three games against the Yankees in those four years. All challengers had been routed: the Athletics, Cardinals, Giants. The Yankees were again the best team in baseball.

Where Ruth's swagger was emblematic of the Roaring Twenties, the quiet dignity of Gehrig and DiMaggio fit the Depression years. These men were the children of immigrants who personified the importance of hard work and a low profile. Gehrig's consecutive game streak was a kind of homage to people who went to work every day whether they felt like it or not. During the Depression, it might even have suggested a fear that, if you missed a day of work, you might be replaced. You could ask Wally Pipp.

The Yankees during the late 1930s developed the lordly image that would characterize the franchise, but this was not a team of the well-to-do. The immigrants and working class who were battling through the Depression found players who were like them. The Babe was a great hero while the party was on, but different icons were needed for the hard times.

Attendance at Yankee Stadium dipped a bit during the 1930s. The club drew 1,169,230 in 1930, but would not crack the million mark again until 1946 when over two million celebrated the return of peace after World War II. The Detroit Tigers, by contrast, drew over a million three times during those years. No benefits were needed for Ruppert, however. The Yankees were consistently over 900,000 during the Depression.

On September 9, 1931, the Yankees and Giants played a benefit game of their own for an unemployment fund. A crowd of 60,549 raised $59,642.50 to help the jobless.[11] The game was the first meeting between the neighbors since the 1923 World Series. No great surprise—a 7–3 Yankee win and a homer by the Babe.

Yankee Stadium was also the site of the heavyweight championship fight between Joe Louis and Germany's Max Schmeling on June 22, 1938. Louis had been defeated by Schmeling two years earlier, the same year in which Jesse Owens had dominated the Berlin Olympics. With the dexterity that accompanies American racism, Louis was a beloved champion when he entered the ring against Schmeling even though there were many restaurants in the country where he would not have been served a meal. Louis knew that many of his countrymen held him in the same disdain that the Nazis did, but that did not distract him from the work at hand. He destroyed Schmeling in the first round, thereby proving, to some fans, the superiority of the American way. Louis would just have to be careful where and how he celebrated.

About a month after the Louis–Schmeling fight, the Yankees were in Chicago for a series with the White Sox. Before a game on July 29, Jake Powell, a backup outfielder for New York, was being interviewed on radio. In a question unasked since free agency, the interviewer inquired about what Powell did for a living in the off-season. Powell replied that he was a police officer in Dayton, Ohio. Pleasantries were exchanged until Powell cheerfully offered that one of the benefits of the job was "cracking niggers over the head."[12] Ten years later, in Powell's obituary, the New York Times delicately referred to "a radio broadcast in which the player made a remark that was interpreted widely as offensive to Chicago's Negro population."[13] The reaction at the time was closer to pandemonium. The station, WGN, was owned by the *Chicago Tribune*, and it immediately stopped the interview. It then tried to cover itself with the announcement that it was not responsible for the remarks of the ballplayers. Commissioner Landis, who might not have been particularly troubled if the slur had been made privately, met with Powell, then suspended him for ten days.

Powell himself began the backpedaling that would become all too familiar whenever the nation's ugliest trait would break through the media. He offered the ever lame, "I don't remember saying anything like that at all, and I certainly would never mean to say anything offensive to the Negroes of Dayton, Chicago or anywhere else. I have some very good friends among the Negroes in Dayton."[14]

His manager found another familiar target—the messenger. McCarthy fumed:

The ball players do not want to engage in these broadcasts. In fact, most of them are afraid of them and want no part of them. But they are pestered and pestered until finally one of them gives in. Then in an unguarded moment something is said, maybe only in a joke, but it's taken the wrong way and then there is trouble.

I don't know what Powell said, but whatever it was, I'm pretty sure he meant no harm. Probably just meant to get off a wise crack. So the radio people ran out cold with apologies and I'm out a ball player for ten days in the thick of a pennant race.[15]

McCarthy issued another edict. No more interviews unless with a prepared script.

In his own troubled way, Powell apparently tried to atone for his remarks. Red Smith wrote a column when Powell died, and he included the story that, after the Yankees returned from their road trip, Powell went to the north end of Harlem one night and visited bars in a pilgrimage of amends that reached its conclusion at the south end of the community. "In each he introduced himself. He said he was Jake Powell and he said that he had made a foolish mistake and that he was sorry. Then he ordered drinks for the crowd and moved on to the next joint."[16]

Life was crowding the Yankees in another way. During the stretch drive of 1938, fans would tire of Powell and focus on the pennant race as the Yankees locked up their third straight title. The only complication was that Gehrig's play had deteriorated. A bad slump was the common opinion, but a few fans and reporters thought that the consecutive game streak was finally taking its toll. The truth was too horrible to imagine. When his fatal illness was finally known and faced, Yankee Stadium offered one of the most poignant moments ever recorded, on Lou Gehrig Appreciation Day on the following 4th of July.

Less dramatic, but just as significant for the Yankees, Jake Ruppert died on January 13, 1939, at the age of seventy-one. Ruppert had built such a solid organization that his passing had no discernible effects on the field. The Yankees continued to win championships in the house that Ruppert had built. Joe McCarthy, a quiet professional like Huggins, directed his roster of stars. The minor league operations under George Weiss found and developed replacements as the stars aged. Babe Ruth's old Boston manager, Ed Barrow, remained in charge of front-office operations, and he showed the heart of the baseball business when he cut Gehrig's salary by three thousand dollars after the 1938 season.[17]

The Ruppert era was an extraordinary period. Yankee Stadium was its most enduring monument, justifying every expectation the Colonel had entertained. Against their will, the fans at the stadium occasionally had to grapple with racism and an athlete dying young, but mostly they were able to enjoy some of the best baseball ever played by some of the greatest players the game has produced. Through tragedy, folly, and championships, the Yankees' hold on the fans deepened.

On a parallel track, American government was assuming new economic and social responsibilities, and experimenting with new ways of meeting obligations. The fall of Tammany did not end graft, honest and otherwise, but it did discredit the machine model of public service. Professionalism, albeit suffused with politics, became a standard of government administration, and public works an effective way to stimulate local economies while creating an infrastructure that was fundamental to sustaining private commerce. Baseball was not on the agenda of public works during the Ruppert era, but the strategies and administrative instruments for putting it there were developing rapidly.

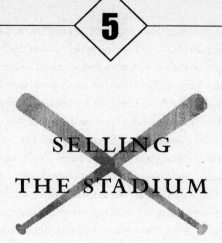

SELLING
THE STADIUM

Del Webb and Dan Topping entered the Yankee picture on January 25, 1945, when they joined Larry MacPhail in purchasing the franchise from Jake Ruppert's estate. The trio paid $2.8 million for the ball club, Yankee Stadium, and the farm system. Since the Stadium alone had cost $2.5 million when it was built twenty-three years before, the investment was promising.

MacPhail was the only one of the partners with experience in major league baseball. Equal parts genius and drunk, MacPhail had originated night baseball with the Cincinnati Reds in 1939, rebuilt the Brooklyn Dodgers from bankruptcy in the early 1940s, and, with the substantial backing of Topping and Webb, now owned the prize franchise in the game.[1] In the mold of Frank Farrell and Bill Devery, he proved unable to handle success.

Dan Topping was familiar in New York circles. He was an heir to the Anaconda Copper fortune, so his personal stakes in the Yankees of roughly a million dollars was more than tip money, but not unreasonable for a man of his circumstances. His co-owner Webb freely professed that Topping was the first among equals, telling a reporter from

Sports Illustrated in 1960, "He's a sincere, straight man. I have a 50% interest in the Yankees, but . . . Topping is the boss of the ball club."[2]

In some respects, the new owners had acquired a national team. Like Notre Dame, the Yankees found fans in every town and at least as many people who loved to see them lose. They were also, of course, the glamour franchise in the game and a "promising investment." Otherwise, Webb's involvement would have been unlikely. He was thoroughly a westerner, a native Californian who had made a fortune in Arizona as a building contractor, and he would shortly embark on several ventures in the Southwest that would dwarf the returns from owning the Yankees.

The new era began with some of the problems that Jake Ruppert had encountered early in his ownership. In particular, contention had returned to the front office. Ed Barrow had continued running the Yankees after Ruppert's death, and, at the time of the purchase, the new owners announced that he would continue to do so, but within a few weeks, MacPhail assumed control of baseball operations by taking the jobs of president and general manager. Barrow became Chairman of the Board, exercising little influence in the MacPhail regime.

Joe McCarthy had enjoyed one of the most distinguished careers as the Yankees manager, but the job was becoming increasingly taxing. He guided the Yankees to a fourth-place finish in 1945, then retired early the next season. Bill Dickey succeeded him as a player–manager, but he quit with a few weeks to go, turning the reins over to Johnny Neun as the Yanks came in third in the American League.

The 1947 season was tumultuous and historic. As Jackie Robinson prepared to break baseball's color barrier in Brooklyn, the Dodgers' manager, Leo Durocher, was trying to weather a storm of controversy relating to his friends, his wife, and his habits. Durocher's sins included a familiarity with racetracks, antagonizing the Catholic archdiocese by marrying actress Laraine Day after she received a divorce in Mexico, and, in his absence and apparently without his knowledge, having his apartment used by actor George Raft for a crap game in which a businessman claimed he had been cheated out of $18,500. Durocher was attacked regularly in print by columnist Westbrook Pegler for associating with Raft, who was a friend of some questionable characters. Durocher was a vicious bench jockey and a ruthless competitor, but his private behavior was no different from that of some of his accusers.

MacPhail was one of the people urging Commissioner Happy Chandler to punish Durocher. So, more important, was the archbishop of Brooklyn—complete with threats of a Catholic boycott of Ebbets Field. In the face of this pressure, Chandler summoned the necessary moral outrage to suspend Durocher for a year. His bill of particulars referred to "a series of publicity-producing affairs."[3] Durocher was gone, Burt Shotton was brought in to manage Jackie Robinson's debut, and the Yankees sought to reclaim their rightful place under the guiding hand of Bucky Harris. The Yankees responded, winning the American League by twelve games, then edging the Dodgers in seven to win their first World Series since 1943. But victory was too much for MacPhail. At the party at the Biltmore, MacPhail apparently had some kind of breakdown, punching and harassing members of the press and the Yankee organization. Topping dragged him into the kitchen literally to beat some sense into him. MacPhail was chastened briefly, then fired farm director George Weiss in a drunken rage.

MacPhail's hangover included losing the Yankees. Topping and Webb got rid of their headache with a $2 million buyout. MacPhail had doubled his investment, but, like Farrell and Devery, the money would not last. His was one of the tragic lives that spot the game's history—brilliance lost in alcohol, drugs, or mental illness.

Topping and Webb settled the front office, retaining Weiss and promoting him to general manager. Topping assumed the role of president, but Weiss was the key figure in the operation of the ball club. Bucky Harris, tainted as MacPhail's hire, could not survive a third-place finish in 1948, even though the Yankees were only three games behind the pennant-winning Cleveland Indians.

Weiss installed Casey Stengel, who had been managing the Oakland Oaks of the Pacific Coast League. Stengel came with some baggage.[4] He had a reputation from his days with the Dodgers as a clown who had none of the majesty associated with Yankee managers like McCarthy and

Miller Huggins. Stengel also had had two stints as a major league manager, first with Brooklyn in the 1930s, then the Boston Braves through 1943, and he had only one season with a better than .500 finish while piloting those two lamentable ball clubs.

Weiss knew that Stengel had played for both Wilbert Robinson and John McGraw, and that he had learned volumes from each. He had kept up with Stengel over the years and hired him with complete confidence. All Stengel did was take the Yankees to World Series titles in each of his first five years, a standard unlikely to be approached again. The final one of those championships in 1953 put the Yankees in a position of such value that Webb and Topping were able literally to capitalize with the sale of the stadium just a couple of months after the Yankees took the Dodgers in six.

While Topping ran the Yankees, and enjoyed the Hamptons, Del Webb was busy with construction projects that required baseball to hold its nose and close at least one eye. Baseball was willing to do both.

Webb enjoyed one of those careers that seem to reflect the mythology of the self-made man.[5] He was born in Fresno, California, in 1899. After dropping out of high school, Webb became a carpenter, earning fifty cents an hour. He also picked up a little money playing semi-pro baseball. During a game at San Quentin prison in 1926, he was exposed to typhoid from the drinking cup of an inmate, and the disease had a devastating effect. He lost half of his 200 pounds, and had to move to Phoenix to take advantage of the climate.

His baseball career was at an end, and Webb encountered another tough break when the contractor for whom he was working paid him with a bad check before skipping town. Webb took over the contractor's business, obtaining capital assets of ten wheelbarrows, twenty shovels, and ten picks. Within five years, the firm was worth three million dollars. Webb was one of the developers who prospered through public works projects during World War II. His included the construction of military bases, hospitals, and internment camps. The camps, according to *Sports Illustrated,* were intended "to accommodate 10,000 Japanese internees."[6] The inmates, of course, were not Japanese but Americans of Japanese ancestry.

Webb's firm developed a reputation for efficient and effective operations that led to doing $100 million worth of work for the government during the war. The tension between these public contracts and the Western culture of rugged individualism was exploited at an awards dinner in Phoenix in 1949. Robert Goldwater, brother of the future senator and presidential candidate, cheerfully introduced Webb as "an ignorant sonuvabitch who built a million dollars with a hammer and a nail and a case of whisky thoughtfully distributed in Washington."[7]

At the same time that he was buying his interest in the Yankees, Webb was pursuing another venture. In one of his versions, he claimed that he took over the construction of the Flamingo Hotel in Las Vegas after friends at the bank that was financing the project asked him to come to the rescue.[8] Only after he began work, Webb later claimed, was the Flamingo sold to Benjamin "Bugsy" Siegel. Webb said that he tried to escape the deal, but that Siegel had a binding contract as well as a bulge under his jacket pocket.[9] In this account, Webb mentioned that he never had a problem with Siegel, who paid more quickly than most customers. In a 1969 interview, he said of Siegel, "Bankers, lawyers, and industrialists—I never knew anyone whose word was better."[10]

In a different spin on his introduction to Las Vegas, Webb suggested that he went in with his eyes open. "I consulted with Hoover [J. Edgar] for a long time before we went into Vegas, because we were worried about the gangster element. Hoover encouraged us to go in."[11]

When Siegel was shot dead in Los Angeles on June 20, 1947, he owed Webb money for the recently completed casino. Perhaps with some reluctance, Webb took a part ownership in the Flamingo in lieu of direct payment. His partners in the venture included the notorious Meyer Lansky and Gus Greenbaum, a Phoenix mobster who subsequently had his throat slit. Webb's connections with organized crime figures received a cursory review at the time by baseball commissioner Happy Chandler, but, in the 1970s a group of journalists, the Investigative Reporters and Editors (IRE), conducted a systematic review of government documents and concluded that in addition to active ownership with mobsters in Las Vegas hotels and casinos, Webb purchased a 3,000 acre ranch near Phoenix in 1959 at an exorbitant price from owners that included a Detroit mob boss, Joseph Zerilli.[12] Land buys at peculiar prices were a common technique of settling other commercial transactions that needed to be kept off the books.

The Yankee owner survived in Las Vegas from the pioneering days after World War II through the competition of various organized crime families to the emergence of Howard Hughes, a Webb intimate, as a major player in the Las Vegas casino game in the late 1960s and 1970s. He built the Sahara and Mint hotels in the early 1960s, and again he was compensated with "points" or part ownership. The points were camouflaged because Webb's fellow baseball owners took the official position that these were construction projects for which the builder received direct payment.

The fig leaf that covered Webb's commercial association with organized crime shows that baseball had treated its powerful insiders differently from its scoundrels in uniform. The very people who suspended Durocher tolerated Webb's associations. The double standard did not end with baseball officials. The Federal Bureau of Investigation (FBI) kept a file on Mickey Mantle during the 1950s because of his carousing, but the Bureau reports no record on Webb despite his extensive dealings with organized crime.[13]

At a later point in his career, Webb offered yet another variation of his involvement with the mob. In discussing his construction of the Sahara hotel and casino, Webb offered this disingenuous explanation: "We took five years making up our minds. We consulted our Wall Street investment bankers [Lehman Brothers]. We were afraid we'd have a hell of a time with the mobster element, but we figured we could run hotels and casinos on a business-like basis and not have a goddamn thing to do with the gangsters."[14]

This spin shows an evolution of the cover that baseball accepted for Webb's business. At first the story was that Webb was not really involved with gangsters because he accepted lump-sum payments rather than a continuing interest in the project. Later, when the long-term Las Vegas partnerships were undeniable, Webb and the baseball establishment excused them with the distinction that Webb's interest was confined to the hotel and that he had no stake in the casino.

Webb addressed the potential conflict of interest in his activities in 1961, but he construed the threat to baseball to an unreasonably narrow degree, "I played baseball for nine years, and I've been associated with the Yankees for sixteen years and no one has seen me bet even a nickel on a baseball game."[15]

With a moment's reflection, we can see that gambling is only one of the ways that organized crime could have corrupted baseball. Arnold Rothstein's gambling ring that fixed the 1919 World Series is the most dramatic example of criminal influence, but, with its enormous financial resources and its emerging control of drug traffic and prostitution, mob figures had the capacity to put straying baseball owners, executives, and players into impossible dilemmas. The threat of blackmail could have just as easily influenced baseball as much as bribery affected the pitching, fielding, and hitting of eight White Sox players in 1919. Imagine a mob figure buying a cheap, undeveloped plot of land in a city without major league baseball, then forcing an owner through the threat of personal or financial ruin to relocate his club to that site. No evidence suggests that such coercion ever occurred, let alone that Webb had any role attempting it. But the 1950s were a decade of franchise upheaval and stadium deals, the collapse of the minor leagues, and the eve of major league expansion. The appearance of potential mob influence should have triggered a far more diligent reaction from the game's executives than the acquiescence that served as a policy.

Jake Ruppert built Yankee Stadium as a showcase for an emerging dynasty, but his successors had a different use for the Stadium. On December 17, 1953, Dan Topping and Del Webb sold Yankee Stadium, the ground on which it stands, adjacent parking lots, and a minor league park in Kansas City—all the assets were transferred to Arnold Johnson, a Chicago financier, for the amount of $6.5 million. The agreement reflected what one reporter at the time called "a world where groups of men often work out mutually profitable deals involving millions of dollars without any individual having to shell out much of his own cash [by] an enterprising grasp of what can be done by the ingenious use of things like leasebacks, second mortgages, large cash loans and special stock issues."[16]

In some respects, the deal resembled Babe Ruth's sale by the Red Sox to the Yankees. In part of that deal, Ruppert had acquired an interest in Fenway Park as collateral on his loan to Harry Frazee. Now it was the Yankee owners selling their team's ballpark for financial gain. One important distinction is that Frazee was desperate for money to underwrite his theatrical ventures, but Topping and Webb were not in such straits. What Topping and Webb had in common with Frazee was that baseball was not their primary commercial concern but a diversion from more serious interests.

The sale of the Stadium was part of a pattern of transactions in baseball beginning in the 1950s in which ballparks, the most expensive capital investment clubs made, were cut loose by the franchises and turned over to local governments. The owners' willingness to divest their ballparks—made possible by their communities' willingness to assume the cost of replacements—made baseball franchises entirely portable and franchise relocation both a feasible option and a credible threat. In its physical details, moving a franchise became only slightly more complicated than going on a road trip.

Arnold Johnson was a financier from Chicago who had ties to the Yankee partners. Johnson and Topping were fellow directors of the Automatic Canteen Company, a firm in which Johnson owned 2.5 percent of all shares, Topping 1.3 percent, and Webb another 1.3 percent.[17] Webb was also a partner of Johnson's in a construction project for apartments in Phoenix.

After buying the stadium property, Johnson immediately sold the land at the Stadium site and the adjacent parking lots to the Knights of Columbus for $2.5 million, then leased the property back for a twenty-eight-year period at a rent that would ultimately pay the Knights $4,850,000.[18] Johnson covered himself against swings in the real estate market by including options to buy back the land in the fifteenth and twentieth years and also three successive fifteen-year renewal options that could have extended the duration of the lease to a total of seventy-three years.

Johnson then leased the Stadium itself and sublet the property that he had rented from the Knights to the Yankees. Topping and Webb agreed to their own twenty-eight-year deal that would pay Johnson a total of $11.5 million. In another part of the deal with Topping and Webb, Johnson gave the Yankee owners a twenty-year second mortgage on the stadium and the lease rights to the land in exchange for $2.9 million.

A ten-year first mortgage on the Stadium had been granted to the Atwell Corporation, described at the time as "a trading instrument for private funds and estates." This agreement was reassigned two months later to a copartnership called Salkeld & Co., raising $500,000 for Johnson. Another $100,000 was secured through a mortgage of the Kansas City property.

The mortgages, along with the sale of the Stadium grounds and parking lots to the Knights of Columbus, gave Johnson $6 million, just half a million short of the amount he paid Topping and Webb for the Yankee property in New York and Kansas City.

The net financial effect of these deals was that Johnson raised the money to buy Yankee Stadium and related properties through an elaborate series of paper transactions that risked none of his own money. If the transactions had been simply a series of complex financial maneuvers, head spinning to most of us, that left a few rich men richer than before, then their significance would be limited. But they were more than that.

In 1954, Arnold Johnson acquired the Philadelphia Athletics from the family of Connie Mack. The heirs had been squabbling hopelessly about the franchise, and Johnson was prepared to solve the Macks' financial problems and improve the Athletics' impoverished state by moving the club to Kansas City. The prospect of getting a major league franchise was the inducement Kansas City needed to pass a bond issue to acquire the local minor league park and improve it. The owner of the park, of course, was Arnold Johnson, and the contractor who would make the improvements was, not surprisingly, Del Webb.

By the fall of 1954, Johnson had his plan in place. He secured some additional financing from business contacts in Chicago, and planned to sell Connie Mack Stadium (known also as Shibe Park) to the Philadelphia Phillies to raise further revenue. Johnson was set to become a major league magnate, but one of the game's Old Guard challenged the entire venture.

Clark Griffith was a contemporary of Connie Mack's, and the two had been friends and rivals dating back to their playing days in the 1890s. Griffith was the longtime owner of the Washington Senators, and, perhaps of some importance, had been the first manager of the Yankees after their resettlement in New York. He guided the Highlanders from 1903 through 1908. At an American League meeting on November 8, 1954, Griffith raised an objection to Johnson's joining the ranks. "Rule 20" required that "No club or stockholder or official of a club shall, directly or indirectly, own stock or have any financial interest in any other club in its league."

Johnson had two problems in the face of Rule 20. First, he was the Yankees' landlord through his ownership of the Stadium. Second, he was a creditor to Del Webb and Dan Topping through the second mortgage on the Stadium, the one that gave Johnson nearly $3 million.

The American League owners declined a local offer from Philadelphians to acquire the Athletics. They approved the Johnson offer, but imposed the condition that he square the purchase with Rule 20. The Athletics cost Johnson $3.5 million. He picked up $1.65 million from the Phillies for Connie Mack Stadium. Another $650,000 came from the sale of Blues Stadium to the taxpayers of Kansas City. Assorted debts that the Athletics had accumulated were obligated to a concessions company, the Jacobs Brothers, who were repaid through a contract at the renovated Kansas City park. Even Roy Mack put a substantial amount of his gains back into the franchise as a minority stockholder. Once again, Arnold Johnson had secured a lucrative asset without risking his own money.

To comply with Rule 20, Commissioner Ford Frick ordered Johnson to divest himself of Yankee Stadium. Johnson complied by selling the Stadium to an old business associate, John Cox, an attorney and businessman from Texas. Although Frick had demanded assurance that Johnson would have no association with the Yankees that would violate Rule 20, the sale of the Stadium between Johnson and Cox was completed without a written contract. This casual arrangement was considered during Congress's investigation into baseball's antitrust exemption in 1957, and the treatment of Johnson by the committee is instructive for its kid-glove treatment of the Athletics' owner:

> MR. SINGMAN. In the absence of a written contract of sale, what assurance did the commissioner's office or the American League have that you retained no interest whatsoever in the Yankee Stadium Corp., since they have no way of knowing what the terms are?
> MR. JOHNSON. I believe the principal thing that they would have is my integrity as a businessman over the last 30 years.[19]

Julian H. Singman then asked if that assurance was the only evidence that Johnson did not retain an option to repurchase the property at a later date. Johnson replied that his word should be sufficient because as an independently wealthy man he would have no need to cut such a deal. Rather than press the matter with any number of examples of the leisure class behaving like scoundrels, the committee beat a retreat. Singman capitulated, "We appreciate that. And we do not mean to infer anything."[20]

Whatever was left of the integrity of the hearing became the target of Edward Vollers, one of Johnson's attorneys and the man who had drafted the transfer of the Stadium from Johnson to Cox. Vollers interjected his own guarantee that the agreement contained no provision that might allow the Stadium to revert to Johnson. Singman replied that he understood and had asked the question simply because the prospect had been raised by others.

Vollers cut him off with the statement, "Mr. Johnson is not that character of man."[21] Singman rejoined, "We appreciate that. Thank you."[22]

Then Singman asked why Vollers himself did not want a written contract of sale, and Vollers replied, "Because that is the way Messrs. Cox and Johnson do business."[23] Johnson then sealed the matter by adding, "And that is really true."[24] Singman, routed, said, "All right. Thank you."[25]

Yankee Stadium was a multimillion dollar asset that Arnold Johnson had transferred to a twenty-year business associate without a written bill of sale. The sale had been required by the commissioner of baseball to make sure that the business relationship between Johnson and the Yankee owners was severed now that they held rival franchises. Frick himself ignored the substantive failure to comply with his edict, and the congressional investigation of the arrangement was embarrassingly timid. Whenever a question became interesting, a hint of indignation from Johnson or his attorney backed the committee down.

Rather than move into the truly intriguing area of whether the ties between Johnson and the Yankees were connected in any way to Del Webb's ties to organized crime, the committee asked Johnson to review his dealings with the Yankees. In his opening remarks, he asserted that he had purchased the Athletics not to make money but because he loved baseball and wished to develop a winning ball club. He then addressed what he called "gossip" about his relationship with the Yankees:

> I want to say that we are not anybody's "farm" club. We are not any-
> one's "country cousin." I might just as well be blunt and put it plainly.
> The only interest I have in the New York Yankees or any other major
> league club is beating their brains out every time we play them, and I
> mean that.[26]

The gossip that Johnson wanted to rebut concerned the extraordinary number of trades between the Yankees and Athletics and the tendency of the Yankees to get the better of the deals. Between the time Johnson bought the club in November 1954 and the summer of 1957, fifty-seven players in the two organizations had traded places. While the Yankees won pennants in the eight-team American League from 1955 to

1958, the Athletics finished sixth, eighth, seventh, and seventh during those seasons.

At that time, the commissioner of baseball had generic authority to protect "the best interests of baseball." The issues that Congress was ineptly investigating should have been the focus of a vigorous inquiry by Ford Frick. Whether the ties between the Yankees and Athletics were in the best interests of baseball is an arguable point, but its significance is limited primarily to the world of major league baseball. Webb's ties to organized crime were a more disturbing public issue. Whether criminals might have influenced business decisions within baseball was worthy of a serious investigation by Congress and the FBI.

The congressional hearings of 1957 were little more than a charade. Serious public issues like race, suburban growth, and declining inner cities were effectively ignored. Congress instead focused on questions that Ford Frick should have been pressing while ignoring the larger issues of possible fraud that could properly have been investigated in a governmental arena with subpoena powers and other tools. Congressmen found that their own best interests, insofar as baseball was concerned, were to have occasional hearings with comic touches—like Casey Stengel's legendary display of the peculiar syntax of "Stengelese"—fulminate a bit about the public trust that the game enjoyed, then, most important, do nothing.

In the 1950s, Estes Kefauver of Tennessee and John McClelland of Arkansas were two senators who attained national prominence with tough investigations into organized crime. Kefauver even secured the vice presidential nomination of the Democratic Party in 1956, so an examination of Webb's associations with mob figures should have enjoyed some popular political support. Career interests, if not a commitment to the public interest, could have motivated a serious review of some of baseball's business connections, but Congress chose theatrics instead.

If anyone had cared, the question of why the Athletics should have left Philadelphia is intriguing. The team's record had certainly become dismal. Last-place finishes were especially depressing when the Phillies had revived with the Whiz Kids pennant in 1950. Attendance in their final season in Philadelphia was just over 300,000, and it jumped over a million during the inaugural campaign in Kansas City. But that says much more about a poor organization and the transitory fortunes of any ball club than about the ability of Philadelphia to support two franchises. At the time of the move, Philadelphia was the third largest city in the country with a population of just over two million. Kansas City was less than a fourth that size, so after Johnson overhauled the organization, would it not have been better off in the larger market?

The abandonment of multiteam cities was a common adjustment to postwar trends because, with more people leaving cities for suburbs, the attendance base was shrinking. Boston, St. Louis, and New York were also left with one team at the end of the 1950s. But attendance for the remaining club actually declined in Boston and New York in the first year that they had their towns to themselves. Johnson took the Athletics to Kansas City as part of a complex arrangement that took advantage of the Yankees' historic minor league ties to that city. A good deal for him. Why the other owners accepted the move is more puzzling.

In fairness to the memory of Del Webb, Arnold Johnson, and their baseball partners, no evidence in these pages suggests any criminal or nefarious motive to their commercial ventures. Yet the willingness of league officials not to examine them is at least ironic: Joe Jackson and the Black Sox banned for life and erased from official memory; Leo Durocher suspended for a year for knowing people who knew people; and Del Webb enjoying his championship team and his Vegas connections.

Whatever the propriety of Del Webb and company's machinations behind the scenes, the team's on-field success during those years only added luster to the Yankee aura. Many of those who are now deciding the future of Yankee Stadium, voters included, came to know the team in this era. Mayor Rudolph Giuliani formed his notable attachment to the Yankees as a boy watching the Yankees of Casey Stengel. These are the teams that Billy Crystal and Bob Costas have evoked to millions of viewers watching *City Slickers* or the Game of the Week. Roger Kahn is probably correct that more emotion attaches to the Brooklyn Dodgers for their single triumph in October 1955 than any Yankee championship, but Yankee fans have been more richly rewarded for their devotion than those of any other franchise.

Stengel's inaugural season of 1949 was historic for the Yankees. They not only beat the Red Sox by a single game, but, in establishing himself, Stengel beat Joe McCarthy, now managing Boston. The Yankees that year had only one twenty-game winner, Vic Raschi, but Joe Paige reflected Stengel's great talent for handling his roster by appearing in sixty games as a relief pitcher and saving twenty-seven, both marks leading the league. Most important, Stengel had to handle the difficult problem of a hobbling Joe DiMaggio. Two more different personalities are hard to imagine, and Stengel faced the task of making decisions about the Yankee lineup with the legendary player entering the twilight of his career.

The 1949 Series was brief, but the first two games at the stadium were 1–0 affairs, each side winning one. Tommy Henrich's ninth inning home run off Don Newcombe in the opener is the most memorable moment. The third game was a 1–1 tie in the ninth inning at Ebbets Field. The Yankees scored three in the top of the inning, and held off a Dodger rally to win 4–3. The fourth game was another tight affair that the Yankees won 6–4, and they captured the Series the next day with a 10–6 win in Brooklyn.

DiMaggio bounced back in 1950 to hit .301 with thirty-two home runs and 122 runs batted in. The Yankees won the pennant by three games over the Detroit Tigers, and they faced the Philadelphia Phillies in the World Series. The Whiz Kids won the pennant on the last day of the season to take their first National League title since 1915. The magic ended in a hurry for Philadelphia. Again, the first two games were 1–0, but the Yankees won them both. They edged the Phillies in the third game 3–2, rallying for a run in the eighth and ninth innings, then rookie Whitey Ford won 5–2 for the first of his record ten World Series games to complete the sweep.

The National League had its most famous pennant race the following year, and again the Yankees were unimpressed. After the great stretch run that forced a tie with Brooklyn, the New York Giants won the deciding third game of the playoff with a ninth inning home run that you might have heard about. This was the first meeting between the Yankees and Giants since 1937, and the Giants took command with a 5–1 victory in the opener at the stadium. The Yankees bounced back in the second game, but the Giants again took a lead with a 6–2 win across the Harlem River in the Polo Grounds. After observing an honorary travel day, the Yankees won the fourth game also by a 6–2 score, then pounded the Giants 13–1, and closed out the Series with a 4–3 win back at their home field.

The 1951 season was DiMaggio's last. He was slowed by injuries and pressed by Mickey Mantle. Certainly, there was room in the outfield for the two of them, but one star was rising while the other was in decline. DiMaggio was all about timing, and he knew that his career was over.

After three championships in a row, the Yankees were challenged in the American League by a new contender. Al Lopez was developing a terrific team in Cleveland. The Indians had finished second the year before and they gave the Yankees another run in 1952. Cleveland came up short by two games, and Stengel's team prepared to face Brooklyn again in another seven game Series with plenty of moments for Dodger fans to chew on through the winter. Brooklyn won three of the first five games, but they could not close the deal, even though the last two games were at Ebbets Field.

The 1953 season was more of the same. The Yankees put more distance between themselves and the Indians, winning with a seven game margin. Dodger fans will argue that this might have been the best edition of that club ever. The Bums won 105 games, Carl Furillo won the batting title hitting .344, and Roy Campanella, league MVP, led the National League with 142 runs batted in. Add Duke Snider, Gil Hodges, Pee Wee Reese, Billy Cox, and Jackie Robinson, and the Dodgers had a marvelous blend of hitting, power, speed, and fielding. Carl Erskine anchored a solid pitching staff to give the Dodgers reason to hope in October.

Brooklyn lasted one fewer game than they had the year before. Again, the what-ifs prevail. The Dodgers tied Game Six, with Carl Furillo's two-run homer in the top of the ninth, but Billy Martin singled home the winning run in the bottom of the inning.

The Brooklyn team was undeniably one of the greatest ever, but the Yankees were undeniably that much better. The pitching staff in those days still relied on Vic Raschi, Allie Reynolds, Ed Lopat, and Whitey Ford, with Johnny Sain coming out of the bullpen. The transition from DiMaggio to Mantle was smooth. Phil Rizzuto was still a marvelous shortstop—the key, in Ted Williams's opinion, to the Yankees' ultimate successes. Yogi Berra was a gifted defensive catcher and one of the most dangerous bats in the game.

Backing the stars was an array of role players who would arrive for a season or two, often at the end of their careers. Stengel's particular genius was using these flickering gifts at precisely the right moment. Platooning was the term, and it was sometimes taken to be a rather mindless strategy of right-handed batters against left-handed pitchers. Stengel understood it as an elaborate balancing act among competitive athletes who longed for the spotlight. He maintained that the key to managing was keeping the ten guys who hated you away from the ten who were undecided.

At this point, the Yankees had compiled a record as the greatest team in the history of the game. Not only had they won five consecutive championships, one better than McCarthy's four from 1936–39, they did it against demonstrably better competition. The integration of the game in 1947 dramatically improved the Dodgers and Giants, as eventually it would the other franchises. The Yankees were among the last teams to take advantage of the new pool of talent, but, despite hampering themselves in this way, they beat the best that the new game had to offer.

Oddly, in 1954, Stengel led the Yankees to their best record in his tenure, yet their string was broken. Winning 103 games secured second place that season when the Cleveland Indians won 111. New Yorkers were still able to celebrate baseball as Willie Mays and the New York Giants took the National League pennant, then upset the Indians in a stunning four-game sweep.

The Yankees resumed their dominance of the American League in 1955, but that critical margin in the World Series began to sputter. The Dodgers were a veteran club in 1955, and they ran away from the National League. Winning their first ten games, they were never challenged, and the pennant was secure in early September. The Yankees had a tougher time with Cleveland, but they resumed their rivalry with the Dodgers. The edge that the Yankees had enjoyed in so many crucial games was now with the Dodgers, who won their only championship in Brooklyn, rallying in seven games after dropping the first two.

In 1956, the Dodgers were still a veteran club. In fact, they were beginning to show their age. They fought back tough challenges from the Milwaukee Braves and the Cincinnati Reds, rising clubs in the National League. Another seven-game series, but the Yankees recovered their touch. This time they were the team to rally from a two-game deficit. The Dodgers managed just one run after the fourth game (the first shutout being Don Larsen's perfect game), and it was enough to tie the Series at three games apiece. A 9–0 blowout in the seventh game concluded the extraordinary Yankee–Brooklyn rivalry. The next time the two teams would meet in October, they needed jet airliners instead of subways to get to one another's stadium.

The Yankees won their third straight pennant comfortably in 1957. Al Lopez had moved to the Chicago White Sox, and they were now the closest competition the Yankees faced. The Milwaukee Braves had youth; the Dodgers had gray hair; and the Braves had their first pennant in their temporary Wisconsin home. A hot pitcher, Lew Burdette, won three games in the Series for the Braves, Wes Covington killed rallies with a couple of spectacular catches, and Henry Aaron hit .393 in the Series with three home runs. After winning the World Series in each of his first five seasons, Stengel now had one in his last four.

Both teams won their leagues comfortably in 1958, setting up a rematch in the Series. The Braves got off to a strong start, winning the first two games at home. The Yankees won the first game back at the stadium, but Warren Spahn shut out Whitey Ford in the fourth game, giving the Braves a three-games-to-one lead in the Series.

Bob Turley emerged as the Yankee hero. New York took three games in a row and Turley won two of them. Game Six required extra innings, and two runs in the top of the tenth to counter the single run that the Braves got in the bottom of the inning. More what-ifs, but the Yankees had recaptured the World Series title. It would prove to be their last with Casey Stengel.

Webb and Topping believed that Stengel, in his late sixties, was getting too old to manage the team. The last time the Yankees finished as low as third, it cost manager Bucky Harris his job. Stengel's record and his close tie to George Weiss spared him another season after the Yankees finished 79–75 in 1959.

The 1960 season was a terrific rebound for New York. They won ninety-seven games, took the pennant by eight games, and faced a new challenge from the Pittsburgh Pirates in October. The Yankees did everything but win. They scored an incredible fifty-five runs, had a team batting average of .338, a team slugging average of .528, stroked ninety-one hits, and 142 total bases—all of them records for a seven-game series.

As often happens in sports, when you are stuck in a position you should have been able to avoid, something bad will happen. In this case, the Yankees should never have been taken to a seventh game. When they were, a bad hop grounder helped the Pirates rally for five runs in the eighth inning, then Bill Mazeroski hit his famous home run over the left field fence to win the Series for Pittsburgh.

Maz's home run not only won the World Series for Pittsburgh, it also sealed Casey Stengel's fate. Taking the arbitrary position that Stengel's seventieth birthday was the time to make a change, Webb and Topping clumsily fired Stengel while trying to dress it as a resignation. They waited a couple of weeks, then fired George Weiss.

Stengel returned to his role as a beloved clown when he came back in 1962 to manage the New York Mets until the middle of 1965. The Mets were comically inept in those years, and Stengel helped keep the bumbling entertaining. By the time the Mets restored National League baseball to New York, the stadium game had changed fundamentally. The

Dodgers and Giants had left for California, largely due to the inability of New York public officials to accommodate Walter O'Malley's interest in building a new stadium for the Dodgers with his own money. What had become far easier was to put up the public purse to provide a new facility, as the city was doing with the Mets and Shea Stadium.

Webb and Topping sold the franchise to the Columbia Broadcasting System (CBS) in 1964. Webb tried to return to baseball in the early 1970s when the Chicago White Sox franchise was for sale. Commissioner Bowie Kuhn told him that he would have to divest his casino holdings if he wanted back in the game.[27] Webb did the math, and passed up the opportunity. He died on the 4th of July 1974.

The Webb and Topping era covered a time when the World War I generation of stadiums were largely abandoned as obsolete. In their case, obsolescence meant that they were too small, architecturally inadequate, located in the wrong part of town, and otherwise unsuited for putting people in the seats and giving the team a revenue stream that would allow it to remain competitive.

For the most part, the replacements for these ballparks were public, multipurpose stadiums that promised economic development and status for their communities. The Webb–Topping sale of Yankee Stadium was a textbook on how to make the stadium game work for the ball club. Exquisite financial intricacies replaced the old model of bringing people to the ballpark, charging them admission, and selling them some food. The Stadium sale and accompanying arrangements showed the major league owners that their stadiums could trigger unrealized income. Since that time, obsolescence did not have to mean cracks in the foundation. A stadium deal that did not maximize the owner's income needed to be restructured, or the franchise needed to consider a more sympathetic community. The stakes in the stadium game had risen considerably.

The sawmill that stood on the site of Yankee Stadium.

The site before construction.

Governor Al Smith throws out the first ball
on Opening Day, 1923.

John Philip Sousa, in dark uniform, leading the Seventh Regiment
band on Opening Day.

Jacob Ruppert, Kenesaw Landis, and Tillinghast Huston (*l. to r.*) on Opening Day, 1923.

Babe Ruth signs for the historic 1927 season in the company of Ed Barrow and Jacob Ruppert (seated).

Claire Ruth unveiling the monument to the Babe.

Del Webb, Dan Topping, and George Weiss (*left to right*) congratulate Bill Dickey for joining the Yankees coaching staff in 1948.

John Lindsay presents home plate to Claire Ruth and first base to Eleanor Gehrig.

The design for the renovated stadium.

Joe DiMaggio amid the Stadium's reconstruction.

The view from the upper deck right field before renovation.

The same view after renovation.

Two fans: Mayor Rudolph Giuliani and George Steinbrenner,
Grand Marshall of the New York City Steuben Day Parade in 2000.

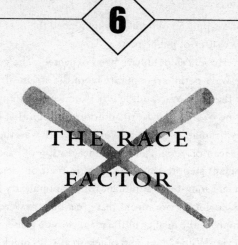

THE RACE
FACTOR

After a generation of poverty and war, America in 1946 was ready to celebrate. One indication that the hard times were over was attendance at baseball games, which rose dramatically as GIs returned home. The Yankees, who had not drawn a million since 1930, packed two million into the Stadium every year between 1946 and 1950. The Giants drew their first one-million gate at the Polo Grounds in 1945. The Dodgers got back to a million in 1945, then added another 700,000 the following year. Even the St. Louis Browns poked back over a half-million in 1946, a total achieved only six times in the dismal history of that forgettable franchise.

The growing popularity of baseball was accompanied by some fundamental changes in the business of the sport, and these changes in turn were to have a powerful influence on the stadium game that would begin to be played in the next ten years. Specifically, the popularity of baseball was rising in new markets that demanded major league franchises of their own. Restless owners and eager entrepreneurs triggered franchise relocation and expansion, and, in almost every case, the urgency of attracting a new team or keeping an old one quickly turned the issue of the team's stadium into a matter of public policy.

Baseball's resurgence could have been expected. The game seems to be one of the ways people recuperate from the strain of war. Baseball took off after the Civil War, and, led by Babe Ruth, boomed during the 1920s following World War I. An additional reason that baseball's appeal grew so dramatically after World War II was the infusion of African-American players. The racial integration of baseball was not only an important step in America's fitful pursuit of social justice, but also an important long-term stimulant for the popularity of the sport.[1] Eliminating the color barrier meant that great players were immediately available to improve the quality of the major league game. Jackie Robinson, Monte Irvin, Willie Mays, and other great stars quickly made baseball a better game than it had been when the elite players were drawn from an artificially restricted labor pool. In addition, these new players gave black baseball fans more reason than ever to follow the game and go to major league ballparks.

In baseball's great racial epic, Jackie Robinson's place as an American hero appears to be secure. The commemoration of the fiftieth anniversary of his rookie season with the Brooklyn Dodgers was celebrated throughout baseball in 1997, and his number 42 has been retired on every roster. He may be as well known as any baseball player including Babe Ruth.

Beyond Robinson the icon, the history of baseball's integration is less familiar.[2] Occasional stories in 1997 noted that a few months after Robinson's arrival in Brooklyn, on the 4th of July Larry Doby became the first African American to play for an American League franchise. His immediate impact was minimal. While Robinson hit .297, led the National League with twenty-nine stolen bases, and won the first Rookie of the Year Award, Doby appeared in only twenty-nine games, mostly as a pinch hitter. His distinguished record began the following year when he hit over .300 for the first time. In 1952, he led the American League in home runs and runs scored, and, two years later, led in homers again and in runs batted in.

The St. Louis Browns brought up two African-American players about a week after Doby appeared.[3] Hank Thompson, a second baseman, played briefly that season, was out of the majors in 1948, but returned to begin a solid career with the New York Giants in 1949. Willard Brown was a centerfielder for the Browns who was the first black player to have the common experience of a single, brief appearance in the majors. He returned to the Negro leagues and later played a few seasons of minor league ball.

The Dodgers introduced Dan Bankhead, the majors' first black pitcher, on August 26, 1947, then added Roy Campanella and Don Newcombe over the next couple of seasons in an obvious strategy of using black players to strengthen the ball club. The Indians brought the legendary Satchel Paige to Cleveland in 1948 and added Minnie Minoso in 1949. Hank Thompson integrated his second team in 1949 when he joined the New York Giants along with Monte Irvin.

While the American League seemed content with the strategy of waiting for someone to be Babe Ruth and deliver three runs with one swing of the bat, Jackie Robinson helped to distinguish National League baseball as a game of speed and aggressive play. Robinson did not invent this game—Ty Cobb and the St. Louis Cardinals' Gashouse Gang were earlier practitioners—but, as a former collegiate star in football and track, Robinson injected a remarkable athleticism into baseball. His style of play introduced a dramatic tension that baseball sometimes lacked, and fans and baseball's more thoughtful executives were eager for more.

The public reaction to baseball's integration punctured the last excuse for the color barrier. We might think at first that major league owners were unaware of the great black players who were available earlier in the century. But their own players had barnstormed against the stars of the Negro leagues in the off-season, so ignorance did not explain the ban on African Americans. Perhaps a potential negative reaction from white players concerned the owners. But the players had negative reactions about a lot of things, and the owners were utterly indifferent to those complaints. Maybe the owners were willing, but blocked by

Commissioner Kenesaw Landis? He had frustrated Bill Veeck's attempts to buy and integrate the Philadelphia Phillies during World War II. But Landis was not controlling the owners. The commissioner also objected to farm systems, and the owners developed them in complete defiance. The final plausible explanation for ignoring black players could have been a concern that attendance would drop, that white fans would refuse to patronize games that included blacks.

As integration began, it turned out that fans cared about the quality of baseball. When teams improved with the addition of black players, the crowds increased.[4] When the club deteriorated, people stayed away. Integration itself represented no financial sacrifice for the owners, yet most clubs, including the Yankees, were very slow to take advantage of this new opportunity.

By 1954, the Yankees were one of eight teams yet to integrate, half of the major league roster at that time. The Pirates, Cardinals, and Reds joined the Yankees in playing their first black player in April of that year. The Yankees had insisted that they were eager to sign an African American as soon as they found one who met their standards. They were finally satisfied in 1954 when they made Elston Howard their first black player. Attendance at the Stadium dropped 60,000 for the year as the Yankees lost their first pennant since 1948.

The delay in signing an African American is sometimes attributed to the Yankees' sense that their market was the tony suburbs around the city, places that preferred watching games in all-white comfort.[5] Especially damning for the Yankees was manager Casey Stengel's reputed remark at the signing of Elston Howard, "Well, when they finally get me a nigger, I get the only one who can't run."[6] Robert Creamer, Stengel's biographer, characterizes the remark as "stupid" rather than "racist"—one could, of course, conclude that it was both. Creamer adds that Howard himself did not believe that his manager was a bigot.

This patience that Howard displayed in the face of such provocation seems to have been one of the qualities that appealed to the Yankee brass. Webb, Topping, and Weiss showed no interest in a player, like Jackie Robinson, who would defiantly challenge the bigotry about him.

Tony Kubek's memoir of the 1961 Yankee team points out that Vic Power was a prospect who showed considerable promise in the Yankee farm system.[7] Kubek then concludes, "But the Yankees weren't sold on his personality. The front office was afraid Power might fly off the handle when confronted with the pressure of being the first black Yankee. Eventually, he was traded because the Yankees wanted their first black player to be their kind of guy."[8]

Kubek quotes Dan Daniels from *The Sporting News* that Howard was picked "because of his quiet demeanor, his gentlemanly habits and instincts, and his lack of aggressive attitudes on race questions."[9] Howard was also a catcher on a team that had Yogi Berra. He was not going to attract a lot of attention either through his manner or his game. The Yankees had integrated, but had done so on their terms. They displayed no sense of urgency on the issue. They waited patiently, if not indifferently, for a player who would not change them by his personality or his play.

At first glance, Howard was the perfect player for the Yankee front office. He remained in the background while the team continued to win. He took the Yankees off the hook of integration. Because the team continued to pile up championships, no one could argue that the roster could be improved, and, by his presence on that roster, the Yankees had conformed to an emerging social requirement for professional sports teams. By contrast, for example, the Boston Red Sox were preposterous in arguing that they could not find the right player for their team while they finished one mediocre season after another, finally integrating in 1959, three years after Jackie Robinson retired.

When Yogi Berra reached the later stages of his career, Howard finally had his chance to catch regularly for the Yankees. Kubek, the Yankee shortstop, remembered Howard's arm. "His throws were bullets, but when you caught them at second base, they went into your glove like a feather."[10] Whitey Ford pointed out to Kubek that Howard caught closer to home plate than Berra had. He was able to catch sinkers before they hit the ground, and Ford concluded that he received more strike calls on low pitches because of Howard's proficiency. Other Yankee pitchers raved about his skill in guiding through the game, encouraging them when they tired and showing them that he would catch breaking balls in the dirt—all essential parts of the art of catching.

One of Elston Howard's last public appearances was as a coach in the Yankee dugout in a game at Fenway Park on June 18, 1977, keeping Reggie Jackson and Billy Martin from coming to blows on national television. His expression during the melee displayed both patience and weariness as the Yankee manager and their star player blustered and fulminated. He had played a unique role, both special and limited, as the Yankees' first black player. He had endured the separate accommodations for black players in spring training sites in the South during the 1950s and early 1960s. He had remained a coach, while managing spots in New York and elsewhere were recycled to the same familiar hands.

Elston Howard died at the age of fifty-one. He is certainly remembered, but he is not in the pantheon of early black stars like Jackie Robinson, Henry Aaron, and Willie Mays. That tells us a lot about the pantheon. We properly celebrate the players whose brilliance proves that the all-white game was an inferior version of what we have seen since 1947. We properly honor the men whose toughness was harder than the bigotry that was vented on them. Our inability to appreciate fully the other personalities who played essential roles in driving racism from the diamond reflects our own limitations, not theirs.

A quick scan of the front offices of major league franchises suggests that racism lingers, unconsciously perhaps, but as real as a Red Sox roster from the 1950s. Men and women with the qualities of Elston Howard could fill some of those front-office positions, but progress in that area will remain slow until the owners finally grasp that they are forgoing talent that could enrich their franchises.

The Yankees were demonstrably slow in the 1950s to sign black players, but concluding that their personnel moves reflected calculated bigotry requires a reach beyond the evidence. Unmistakably, however, the integration that was painfully slow in the ball club was moving far more quickly in the borough. The demographic makeup of the Bronx was changing dramatically in the postwar years while the Yankees remained essentially an all-white team. Census data compiled by Ira Rosenwaike in his book *Population History of New York City* shows the startling transformation of the borough.[11]

	Total	Whites	African Americans
1940	1,394,711	1,370,319	23,529
1950	1,451,277	1,351,662	97,752
1960	1,424,815	1,256,284	163,896
1970	1,471,701	1,080,859	357,681

In the first fifteen years after World War II, the white population of the Bronx remained fairly steady. During the same period, a great influx of African Americans transformed several neighborhoods in the borough. For a time, one could hope that the Bronx would serve the new arrivals as it had so many others in its brief history as an urban center.

The melting-pot metaphor of America suggested that the new migration to northern cities would ultimately mean an infusion of traditional values for the Bronx. Parents would work hard, perhaps at two jobs. Children would be encouraged to take advantage of education as a means to advance. Families would attend church, developing an appreciation for whatever opportunities they enjoyed and reinforcing moral standards. The behavior of work, thrift, temperance, loyalty, honesty, patience, and persistence that had been identified with the country's religious heritage would work its wonders again. White families would see that their new neighbors aspired to the same goals and practiced the same values to realize them. Suspicions would be overcome, and the community would be strengthened anew; but the myth, in this case, was unrealized.

As the numbers in the Rosenwaike book indicate, the black population of the borough more than doubled during the 1960s, and the white segment dropped by one-sixth. The total number of Bronx residents did not change much between 1940 and 1970, but the internal composition of the borough did. On its face, the Bronx looks like a classic case of white flight. The arrival of African Americans or Puerto Ricans into a neighborhood would be assumed to translate into lower property values or worse, so those who could relocate were generally advised by family and friends to do so, but the change in the Bronx was more complex than simply See black, run.

The loss of manufacturing jobs is often cited as a central factor in the borough's demise.[12] Skilled manual labor had been the key to prosperity for most impoverished families in twentieth-century America. Even some high school education was often unnecessary to function successfully in local factories. World War II had placed a premium on those jobs as much of the traditional workforce was transferred to the military as manufacturing plants worked around the clock to satisfy wartime demands.

With the end of the war, peace challenged prosperity. The workforce swelled with the return of millions of young men from the armed services looking for jobs. Employers who were eager to reduce their costs wanted to relocate in communities that were less sympathetic to the influence of labor unions. New York was exactly the kind of city that hemorrhaged entry-level blue-collar jobs to the Sunbelt. When large numbers of blacks and Puerto Ricans arrived in New York in the 1950s, the racial tensions were exacerbated by the declining opportunities for the working poor.

The formula in American mythology for social and economic advancement was no longer working in New York because one of its key ingredients, accessible jobs leading to well-paying stable careers, was no longer in place. In the face of that historic change, postwar public policies were literally paving the way for the able and ambitious to follow those jobs out of the cities. Interstate highways and other road construction sustained the place of the automobile as an essential tool in getting ahead. For those who stayed in New York, public housing fostered a segregation that left the city racially balkanized. Government mortgages, the GI Bill, and school construction encouraged more middle-class migration to the suburbs. New York risked returning to the frightening class divide of the Gilded Age, this time with the division exacerbated by the ferocious demon of race.

Rosenwaike's numbers reflect African Americans migrating to New York for the same reason so many Europeans had come to the city for a

hundred years: the prospect of a better life. They arrived at the moment
that the instruments of opportunity were changing radically. Their inability to adjust entirely and instantly to historic change lent evidence,
for those so disposed, to hoary and facile racial analysis. Well-inten-
tioned public policies then offered ways out of the Bronx for those with
some means who were unwilling to gamble that the progressive dynamic of New York would work its wonders again.

By the mid-1970s, substantial parts of the borough had gone to the
modern urban hell of drugs, gangs, arson, homelessness, abandoned
children, violent crime, and other tragedies. Movies, books, television,
and other popular entertainment warned anyone without direct experience that a trip to the Bronx risked one's life. Metaphors alluding to
Europe after World War II were exhausted in accounts of life in the
Bronx. Politicians made pilgrimages to Charlotte Street to bear witness
and promise a new day. The Grand Concourse held out longer than
some other neighborhoods, but it too collapsed in the 1970s. Compar-
isons with Park Avenue or the Champs-Élysées were now only a reference point for the glory that was gone. The boulevard became a major
thoroughfare in a slum, and right in the middle of the mess was Yankee
Stadium.

The fall of the Grand Concourse was particularly stunning. An article
by Isa Kapp in *Commentary* in 1949 had portrayed a thriving Jewish community in that setting.[13]

At the threshold of the Bronx, just past a miniature Negro slum and
the Cardinal Hayes High School, there immediately emerges a Jewish
community as dense, traditional and possessive as William Faulkner's
Yoknapatawpha County, and through it flows a great middle-class
river, the Grand Concourse. There is no mistaking even its inlets and
tributaries: the waters that seep over from the evergreened foun-
tained courtyard of the Roosevelt Apartments to the modest tan
brick of Morris Avenue carry an irrepressible *elan*, a flood of self-in-
dulgence and bountiful vitality, vulgar and promiscuous withal, luxu-
riant and pleasurable.[14]

Kapp described the neighborhood in broad, easy sweeps that tried to capture the rich dynamic of Jewish life. She was brutal when she saw shallow materialism, and she caricatured the preferences and aspirations of people who had found a home at the Grand Concourse:

> The dress-manufacturer's son naturally gets his MD, specializes, the daughter becomes a psychiatric social worker. To confirm their faith in themselves, and in America's promises, they become conspicuous consumers of silver foxes, simultaneously of learning, gift-shop monstrosities, liberal causes and Gargantuan pastries. A generous expansive life! At the same time, a life utterly without taste. The rugs are too heavy, the spirit of the Jewish holiday is kept alive by fur pieces, the frame is always more expensive than the picture.[15]

Yet Kapp allowed that what offended her was not a permanent condition, "the vulgar, predictable middle-class homogeneity is infinitely mobile, transformable, and energetic."[16] She wrote that the stifling conformity— symbolized by "the utter degradation" of hiring an interior decorator— would likely pass in the next generation as individuality returned.

This marvelous aspect of an argument within a Jewish community was no doubt repeated in its own way in other immigrant neighborhoods. What should be retained of the old traditions? What should be embraced in the new culture? How much leeway should individual members of the group be allowed before social pressures are applied? As in any family, these questions could be answered with great passion, but, in the case of the Grand Concourse, they were not always answered with an eye to the larger forces that were transforming the neighborhood.

The Grand Concourse had always been in part a street of imagination. It was as much a totem of aspirations as it was brick and mortar. By the 1960s, a staple of local news could be a story on how the neighborhood was changing. For a moment, the future of the community was in the balance. An article in the *New York Times* in 1966 addressed the racial migration that Rosenwaike's numbers indicate. The headline for the story—"Grand Concourse: Hub of Bronx Is Undergoing Ethnic

Changes"—is straightforward enough.[17] In the parlance of the day, the article described the movement of Jews to the suburbs as "Negroes" and Puerto Ricans moved in. The journalist, Steven V. Roberts, made a perceptive observation about the dynamic of this change, "The transition of the Concourse began, in fact, not with a rejection of non-whites but with a rejection by young white families of the world of their parents."[18]

After offering a couple of examples of young families who were leaving the area, Roberts continued, "For others, liberated by education and affluence from the narrow and exhausting lives of their parents, the relentlessly bourgeois character of the Bronx was just what they wanted to get away from."[19] Isa Kapp had predicted that the bourgeois conformity that she disdained would pass in the next generation. It did, but not perhaps in the way she had anticipated. The kids did not stay to change the Concourse. They headed for the suburbs to define their lives in a new setting.

Once again, a public policy intruded to aggravate a tough situation. Co-op City, a middle income development of 15,000 units, was preparing to open in the northeast part of the Bronx. Its managers were overwhelmed with applications from the Grand Concourse. While Co-op City served as a magnet to draw people from the Concourse, other factors were pushing people out. Some landlords, in a reprise of the old tenement days of the nineteenth century, rented apartments to several families—often black and Hispanic—then cut services. Profits swelled as rents increased and maintenance costs were reduced despite the effects on the neighborhood.

Again, public policy failed to respond as needed. Rather than enforce building codes rigorously, public services themselves were cut. Roberts's article claimed that "police protection, sanitation, recreation facilities have grown less reliable."[20] The inevitable decline in the community mixed inexorably with the racial change. Whites insisted to Roberts that they had no problem with black neighbors as long as they could pay their way and held to the same standards that had prevailed before. Anthony Hill, described as a young, black air force veteran, reflected the frustration of the very people that the whites said they welcomed. "If the whites won't move out when middle-income Negroes move in, property values won't go down. But if the whites do move, then the lower classes will start to move in, and then values will go down."[21]

To forestall that decline, Bronx Borough President Herman Badillo stressed the need for code enforcement, and he noted that efforts to that end had failed for lack of funds. Other public officials called for a concerted public effort to save the area. Congressman James H. Scheuer, who represented the area, insisted, "We need a massive infusion of talents, money and services to provide the same integrated community facilities that will be built at Co-op City."[22]

Scheuer's point is especially important. The challenges of big cities would be relatively easy to solve if all that were required was money. Billions of dollars have been spent to promote economic development, reduce crime, and extend economic opportunity, but the money must be spent on sensible programs, thoughtfully administered. Money is not the only resource that the problems require. Time, energy, imagination, and perseverance are at least as important.

In 1972, the *Times* again looked at the Grand Concourse, and posed the essential issue: "Like an aging couple no longer sure of their purpose in life after their children have moved away, the Grand Concourse in the Bronx faces an uncertain future: genteel aging or despairing poverty."[23] The reporter, Robert Tomasson, wrote, "But the mystique that made the Grand Concourse a status symbol for Jewish families for more than half a century is largely gone, and with it has gone the neighborhood's religious and social cohesion and its distinctive economic stability."[24]

The *Daily News* covered these same changes more bluntly in a feature for its Sunday magazine in April 1980.[25] The article focused in part on Rita Barish who, with her husband Phil, had owned a small candy store off the Grand Concourse. In 1951, their troubles were little kids blowing the paper wrappers on straws around the store, bigger kids trying to read "girlie" magazines while other youngsters tried to squirt seltzer bottles. "By the late '60s, that world had already started to crumble. The tailor next door was held up, then the grocery. Rita started getting to the store by 6:30 in the morning, so as not to leave Phil there alone.

When the crime started to get bad, the evening paper trade dropped off and the store started closing earlier. Who wanted to come out at night?"[26] Quite possibly Anthony Hill, the air force veteran, would have wanted to. The fear of crime drove decisions that accelerated the decline of the neighborhood: buy iron gates and steel shutters for the storefront; close earlier; eventually, get out altogether. The decisions that made sense for individuals left the streets of the community to night predators. The decent people who were unable to flee became the prey of a criminal element.

Fear of violent crime was not the only disturbing development. The author of the *Daily News* article went back to what had been the Barish candy store to ask for an egg cream, and received a blank stare in return. The feature describes "three jewels in the Concourse crown" as the Lewis Morris Apartments, a spectacularly elegant dwelling that had boasted Bobby Darin among its residents; the Concourse Plaza Hotel, built with the stadium in 1923 and the home of a number of Yankees; and the Loew's Paradise movie theater, where, "If she were lucky, a Concourse girl got her first serious kiss at Loew's at 188th St., under an azure ceiling in which clouds drifted among thousands of perpetually twinkling stars."[27] These treasures were all lost in the demise of the neighborhood. The *Daily News* reported the same dynamic that the *Times* had described, "The first minority families were fiercely upwardly mobile, but their arrival set the stage for others—unstable, on welfare, or close to it."[28] Anthony Hill's wish—that the whites hold their ground next to the newcomers on the line of middle-class values—remained unfulfilled.

Great Society programs in the 1960s transferred plenty of public money to the South Bronx, but not necessarily other essential resources. Aid to Families with Dependent Children, Medicaid, Food Stamps—all attempted to give poor people the means to sustain a decent standard of living. At the same time, building codes were ignored, policing strategies were ill-suited to the new problems, and some landlords were able to exploit their tenants with impunity. The dynamic of decline that the *Times* and *Daily News* effectively covered could sound at times like a force of nature. More accurately, the ruin of the Grand Concourse represented a failure of public and private forces.

Public decisions about the Yankees and their place in the Bronx were complicated by some popular assumptions about the Dodgers and the borough of Brooklyn. Those assumptions were largely mistaken, but they were a powerful force in shaping the expectations of the Yankees' owners and the options of New York's public officials.

In the 1950s, the Brooklyn Dodgers were one of the most prosperous franchises in the game.[29] Unlike the Braves, Browns, and Athletics, the teams that had moved cities before them, the Dodgers had no problem paying their bills. Walter O'Malley was troubled by the future rather than the present. He anticipated that the Braves, resettled in Milwaukee, would be able to sign the top prospects because of their stadium deal, a new ballpark owned by the county that freed the Braves from the burden of upkeep.

By contrast, Ebbets Field was showing its age. Fresh paint did not solve the problem of only seven hundred parking places, so O'Malley began looking for an alternative to the old ballpark so that the Dodgers could remain competitive with the Braves. O'Malley found the answer at the intersection of Atlantic and Flatbush Avenues. The site included a terminal of the Long Island Railroad, and it had plenty of room to park the cars of commuting fans.

Folklore about the Dodgers move has generally ignored this option. The tremendous wealth that O'Malley realized in Los Angeles combined with bitterness in Brooklyn at being abandoned by its beloved Bums. California gold was linked to the hard feelings in Brooklyn, and the Dodger move came to be explained as a maneuver by the greedy O'Malley who knew that he was going to make millions in the Golden West. In the retelling, the race card inevitably popped up, and O'Malley was also painted as recoiling from the sight of Brooklyn's growing African-American and Puerto Rican populations.

Buzzie Bavasi was the Dodgers' general manager at the time of the move and he recounted a conversation with Walter O'Malley after the 1956 season. As Bavasi relates, O'Malley had summoned him to his office, then pointed out the window and said, "Look down there. What do you see?

"Across from our office was the welfare office. I looked out the window and the problem was apparent.

" 'I see a long, long line of poor Puerto Rican people getting their welfare checks,' I said.

"The Puerto Rican part did not bother Walter. What did bother him was the word 'poor.' By looking out the window, he could see the future. And the future he saw involved too many people without enough money to adequately support the Dodgers."[30]

Bavasi's recollection raises a very subtle but important point: the relationship between race and class in America. On its face, the Bavasi story supports basic American mythology by presenting the white businessman as indifferent to the race of his customers as long as their money was green. Bigotry is irrational because it means that people willing to part with their money are rejected for a reason that is arbitrary and self-defeating. At the same time, color is often associated with class, so the arrival of black and Hispanic fans to see the Robinsons and Clementes might well have troubled white owners who feared that their revenue base was declining.

Walter O'Malley's purported personal indifference to the racial mix of his customers might not have been shared by some of the fans. Peter Golenbock's oral history, *Bums*, includes some evidence that Jackie Robinson's breakthrough brought some tension to Ebbets Field. One Dodger fan told Golenbock that by the mid-1950s, "You had a different crowd. It was more subdued, because you weren't as apt to jump up and scream across the aisle at someone because neither the white fans nor the black fans were comfortable with each other."[31] He was also told, "When the blacks started coming to the game, a lot of whites stopped coming. And the black allegiance was only to Robinson and the black ballplayers."[32]

The merits of these concerns may have been baseless, but the significance of Golenbock's oral history is that much of America's mystifying culture of race centers on perception. If, in the retelling, the Dodgers left Brooklyn because Walter O'Malley dreaded black fans or race riots, then the future of the Yankees in the Bronx was also compromised because the demographics of the borough were following a similar pattern. Rosenwaike's numbers show Brooklyn reflecting the same forces that were changing the Bronx:[33]

	Total	Whites	African Americans
1940	2,698,285	2,587,951	107,263
1950	2,738,175	2,525,118	208,478
1960	2,627,319	2,245,859	381,460
1970	2,602,012	1,905,788	696,224

In the boroughs that were home to the Yankees and Dodgers, the overall population had stabilized, significant numbers of African Americans were moving in, and whites were headed for the suburbs. No doubt many who decried O'Malley's treachery were doing so from Connecticut, Westchester, or New Jersey.

The white fans had left, in many instances, because their economic futures had left. William Julius Wilson, a distinguished sociologist, found the same economic forces at work that we had noted earlier, "Following World War II, fundamental technological and economic changes facilitated the increasing decentralization of American businesses. Improvements in transportation and communication have made the use of open and relatively inexpensive tracts of land outside central cities more feasible not only for manufacturing, wholesaling, and retailing but also for residential development."[34] This historic change seems to reflect an economic incentive of lowering costs: Land for new homes and factories is cheaper; building a new plant may well be cheaper than retrofitting an old one; the suburbs offer more room for a home than any affordable apartment in the city. The economics may have been compelling, but race was inextricably linked to the forces of money.

Wilson notes that as white industrial workers improved their standard of living through union organizing in the 1940s and 1950s, white employers often fought back by hiring black workers to break strikes or swell the labor market.[35] The great middle-class, urban labor market that had been part of the foundation of baseball's popularity in the first half of the twentieth century was changing radically. White businessmen could be sympathetic to the demands of blacks for economic opportunity because, even if they weren't concerned about social justice, they understood that the larger labor pool could reduce their costs. At the same time, blue-collar solidarity was split by race, and that was an especially ominous development for the business of baseball because the owners had to reconfigure their fan base. If your job and home were no longer a short hop from the ballpark, then how would you get to the game or who would take your place in the seat?

Why would the owner of one of the most prosperous franchises in the game want to move three thousand miles from the market that was making him rich? If he knew the future of Chavez Ravine and the first 3,000,000 gates in baseball, that would explain the move, but he could not have known that over 40,000 fans would pack Dodger Stadium night after night. At the time of the move, the Dodgers had not secured a place to play at all in Los Angeles. The first few seasons were passed in the Memorial Coliseum that a doomed public relations project attempted to portray as a kind of Fenway Park West. Dodger Stadium was a dream that had to endure a ballot referendum and court cases including one that went against O'Malley. Construction was delayed years beyond what had been anticipated, driving up costs significantly. Some sure thing.

The Atlantic–Flatbush option makes perfect sense not because Walter O'Malley was so devoted to Brooklyn but precisely because he was such a cunning businessman. He would not have easily left the city that he had known all his life, the political climate that he had learned while his father built the Bronx Terminal Market, or the fan base that the Dodgers had finally secured after decades of struggle. Staying put made sense. Going west was the gamble, even a rash one.

Two lessons from the Yankees' case can be applied to the Dodgers. First, O'Malley, the shrewd businessman, figured that you could make money with a baseball team in a borough that whites were leaving while blacks and Hispanics moved in. If you had the right stadium and efficient access, he was certain that fans would come. He was certain enough to bet his own money, which should get our attention. O'Malley's proposal to the city of New York was that he would buy the land that he needed, then finance the stadium with private capital. What he asked in return was that the city would assemble the various parcels at Atlantic and Flatbush into a single property that he could afford to purchase. Acquiring each item individually would drive the prices up to a prohibitive point, so he requested the city to use its powers under the Federal Housing Act of 1949 to condemn the property, then sell it to the Dodgers.

O'Malley had figured out what Yankee fans later would prove: People will visit where they might not live. The demographics of Brooklyn and the Bronx reflect white flight, but the attendance at Yankee Stadium suggests that fans will set aside any misgivings they might have to get to the games, especially if the team is a contender. Given the kind of corporate citizenship that Walter and Peter O'Malley demonstrated in Los Angeles, we can reasonably assume that Walter O'Malley would have used his influence to see that fans were comfortable coming to a Dodger Stadium in Brooklyn. Because he was such a humanitarian? No, because it would have been good business.

This first lesson has been largely lost in the overreaction to the second: Sentiment would not hold a franchise. When the Yankees began to press their own stadium demands in the late 1960s and early 1970s, it was against the backdrop of the loss of two historic National League teams. In short, could the Yankees really have left New York? The unmistakable answer was that, if the Dodgers could leave Brooklyn, any team could leave any city.

Because the folklore surrounding the Dodgers' move insisted that O'Malley had been demanding that the city give him a new stadium, the obvious conclusion was that, if you fail to give an owner what he demands, you will lose his team. The conclusion is ironic because O'Malley was demanding *less* than what New York was offering. The city was willing to build a public stadium—in fact Shea Stadium that the Mets moved into in 1964. O'Malley did not want, as he put it, to be a tenant in a political ballpark. He wanted Robert Moses, in his capacity as Chairman of the Mayor's Slum Clearance Committee, to use his authority to assemble the package of land at Atlantic and Flatbush for O'Malley's purchase. That would have been the extent of the city's involvement, a one-time exercise of eminent domain rather than a permanent role of landlord.

Moses declined to accommodate O'Malley, and O'Malley declined Moses's overtures about moving the Dodgers to a public stadium in Queens. During their impasse, the opportunity to build a stadium with private financing arose in an unlikely place. Public officials from Los Angeles approached O'Malley about moving the Dodgers to a public site near the civic center of the city. The success of the venture is well known, but it was unknowable at the time of the move. The Dodgers left Brooklyn because the public officials of New York could not fashion the right deal, not because O'Malley rejected their largesse.

CBS then bought the Yankees, integrated with some enthusiasm, and watched as both the Yankees and the Bronx became nightmares. The story of these years then takes an additional twist: The terrible team in the terrifying borough still drew crowds. The two-million gates had ended years before. Stengel's championship in his rookie year as manager drew 2,281,676, about a hundred thousand less than the third-place team that had cost Bucky Harris his job the year before. Stengel's second season attracted a little over two million, and his third championship in a row drew a little under that number. For the rest of Stengel's reign, the club drew in the neighborhood of a million and a half. This record was better than that of any other American League team, but few fans in other cities were paying to watch a championship ball club.

When the dynasty collapsed in the CBS years, attendance plunged, but not so far as we might have expected. With the exception of 1972, attendance remained above a million each year. The drop was about one-third of what the gate had been during the 1950s, but the team had become truly dreadful and the Bronx was a place that white people were fleeing at an extraordinary pace. Certainly, some African-American fans might have been going to games because they wanted to see black men in pinstripes or because they now lived nearby in the Bronx themselves. Just as likely, white people who would not prefer to live in the Bronx were willing to visit it to see the Yankees, even if the team seemed to be imposters lost in the Stadium of Mantle, Berra, and Ford.

The critical point about race for our purposes is that it has played an important background role in conversations about Yankee Stadium, and those conversations have missed some important facts. One is the persistent attendance at Yankee games of at least a million people a year, even during the years when the team was not worth walking across the street to see. When the Yankees rebounded to championship form in 1976, they nearly doubled their attendance to go back over 2,000,000, even though the neighborhood around the stadium was enduring some of its worst horrors. Racial folklore might predict that white people will not willingly go to a black neighborhood, especially one with a reputation for random violence, but the folklore is wrong. Yankee fans bottom at a million in the worst of times, and they can match all but fashionable expansion teams when they have a quality team.

The truth about race, the Yankees, and the Bronx is complicated, too complicated to be captured in the easy tales we sometimes pass along about race in our culture. The ball club was slow to integrate, but it won championships regardless. Those great teams of the 1950s captured the hearts of many boys who have become the men who will decide the Yankees' future in the Bronx, but the annual attendance for those teams had dropped about a half million from where it had been in the late 1940s. The Bronx integrated during this time, and went into a social and economic decline that had little to do with race directly. In the worst of that decline, the Yankees put a terrible team on the field and still drew over a million fans per year. In time, the team would resume its championship form, and the fans would return as never before.

7

CBS AND THE STADIUM DEAL

On August 24, 1970, Michael Burke, president of the New York Yankees, sent a letter to Mayor John Lindsay identifying four elements that were vital to the "physical circumstances of the Yankees."[1] Burke was running the Yankees for the Columbia Broadcasting System (CBS) that had purchased the franchise six years earlier, and the four factors that he insisted had to be considered as a single entity included the forty-seven-year-old Stadium; inadequate parking; traffic congestion; and the neighborhood.

Burke then offered a wish list in order of preference: (1) a new, domed multipurpose stadium; (2) a new, open-air multipurpose stadium; (3) a renovated Yankee Stadium reflecting major modernization. Burke wrote that the stadium's location was "very good," but that parking, traffic, and "the texture of the environment" needed to be addressed. Specifically, Burke contended that 10,000 to 12,000 parking spaces were needed either adjacent to the Stadium or within easy reach. He blamed the traffic configuration for causing thousands of fans to abandon the trip to the Stadium even though they had tickets in hand.

Thousands more, he claimed, arrived annoyed and frustrated from the ordeal of driving the final blocks to get to the game.

The point about "the texture of the environment" was a delicate way of introducing the race issue. Burke characterized going to a ball game as "a sense of occasion . . . approached with a certain gaiety and an expectation of enjoyment."[2] But the Stadium's neighborhood made fans apprehensive about attending a Yankee game, "fearful about what might come to them—especially at night."[3] Burke then offered a remarkable equivocation: "The basis of this fear is not specific in most cases, but the state of mind is nonetheless real."[4]

Burke's statement was disingenuous. By the summer of 1970, the basis of people's fears about the South Bronx was quite specific: They feared violent crime. Over a million fans, of all descriptions, watched the Yankees at the Stadium in the summer of 1970, but the South Bronx was not otherwise a tourist attraction. Having evaded race as a factor in "the physical circumstances of the Yankees," Burke declined to give Mayor Lindsay any specific recommendation about that problem.

If his wish list were realized, the Yankees would remain at their old location and play in a new, domed, multipurpose stadium with ten to twelve thousand parking spaces nearby plus a reconfigured escape route back to the more secure pockets of the tri-state area. Those elements were clear to Burke. The nervousness about race and class would remain, as they so often do in America, percolating on a back burner.

Other than this last point, the letter is a straightforward presentation of the challenges the Yankees faced concerning their building. The salutation is a cheerful "Dear John," and Burke signed off with a chummy "Mike." The letter's tone, appearance, and content are familiar and cordial to a point that we might miss the irony: Why was Burke telling the Yankees' problems to the mayor of New York? The answer, a surprising one, is that Burke was responding to Lindsay's initiative. As reported by Joe Durso of the *New York Times*, Burke recalled on April 5, 1971, "Last August the Mayor came to Yankee Stadium for the annual game against the Mets and said to me, 'Look, we've really got to do something for the Yankees. Will you come to a meeting next week at my office?'" Durso wrote that "Burke thought that over for something like one-fifth of a second and replied, 'Sure.' "[5] How did John Lindsay come to be so concerned about the Yankees?

CBS had acquired the Yankees on August 13, 1964, when Del Webb and Dan Topping sold 80 percent of their stock in the ball club to the network for about $14 million. The broadcasting giant was one of the most powerful corporations in the world, and it was trying to diversify its riches to keep pace with the growth of the entertainment field. CBS would own the Yankees for less than ten years, the shortest tenure of any owner, but its reign would be memorable in three respects: (1) for the first time in memory, the Yankees would become a simply awful ball club; (2) when CBS would sell the franchise in 1973 to a group headed by George Steinbrenner, they would take a loss on the deal—something not even Bill Devery and William Farrell were able to manage; and (3) the City of New York would begin to sink nearly $100 million in the acquisition and renovation of Yankee Stadium while the network enjoyed unrivaled prosperity and the city approached the verge of fiscal collapse.

Despite its stunning implications, the sale to CBS was approved almost immediately by the other American League owners. Only Arthur Allyn, owner of the Chicago White Sox, and Charlie Finley, owner of the Kansas City Athletics, opposed the deal. They complained first about the process that sprang the venture on the other owners at the end of a series of meetings, and they were also troubled by the potential implications of having CBS within the owners' tent.

Television had become a crucial part of the baseball business during the 1950s, with weekly national broadcasts that featured the Yankees more than any other team. These televised games brought major league baseball to new markets, and the effects on franchise moves and expansion were significant. Pay television, what we have come to know as cable and satellite systems, was fiercely resisted by the broadcast networks and now the premiere network owned baseball's premiere team.

Official explanations of the sale reflect the state of major league operations at the time. Commissioner Ford Frick claimed that he had learned about the deal ten days before it was announced, and that he had spent the time satisfying himself about three issues: whether the Yankees identity would be maintained; whether the sale would constitute a conflict of interest; and whether baseball's position in securing future television contracts would be compromised.

Frick announced himself satisfied on all counts, indicating that he had either an extraordinary capacity for gathering and analyzing information or, more likely, that his views on the matter were not central to the transaction.[6] The Commissioner declared that CBS would bid for the World Series and other broadcasts on the same basis as the other networks and it is possible that he actually believed this.

Del Webb had said that "firm negotiations" had been under way for only the week or two before the sale, so the public was asked to believe that this transfer was a relatively simple proposition that was wrapped up in a matter of days once the parties focused on specifics. More likely, the purchase reflected discussions over a long time between CBS chairman William Paley and his friend Dan Topping. The two men traveled in rarified circles in New York as part of an elite that normally did not need to concern itself with the public's reaction to its preferences.

The predictable antitrust fulminations began shortly after the sale was announced. Emanuel Celler, chairman of the House Judiciary Committee, declared that the sale "clearly indicates that baseball is a big business and always has been."[7] The Justice Department sent mixed messages, and New York's senators, Kenneth Keating and Jacob Javits, urged caution in assessing the sale. In other words, something significant had happened, but no obvious basis seemed to exist for the federal government to block the transaction.

American League owners had approved the acquisition, and the commissioner seemed oblivious to it. No other party was in a position to veto the sale. Arthur Daley, of the *New York Times*, reflected a prevalent concern that something ominous would result from a rich broadcasting company owning a baseball team, claiming that "this strange union brings on feelings of disquietude."[8] Daley was not terribly specific about his concerns, but he did maintain that television had destroyed both boxing and minor league baseball and that professional football had escaped the ruin of the small screen only by the policy of blacking out local games.

Daley's insight was similar to Representative Celler's, and neither's was especially penetrating. Both men seem to have been troubled by a distinction regarding baseball that some continue to invoke today: It used to be a game—now it's a business. Daley offered, "It's the possible ramifications of this deal that produce such feelings of anxiety. It's true that baseball has changed radically until only Tom Yawkey of the Red Sox, Phil Wrigley of the Cubs, and Mrs. Charles Shipman Payson of the Mets are more interested in the sport than the money. The carpetbaggers and the quick-buck men have taken over a game that once had true sportsmen at the controls."[9] Daley concluded, "Even Walter O'Malley, money-mad though he is, still loves the Dodgers to the bottom of his warm, Irish heart. If this deal is a portent of the future, it is an ominous one. The dollar sign is beginning to obscure the standings of the teams."[10]

The sale even made a ripple in international affairs as *Izvestia*, the official government newspaper of the Soviet Union, sympathized with the players: "In the best tradition of trade in human bodies, the New York Yankees were not even told about the deal."[11] Suggesting that Mickey Mantle was, in some way, comparable to Dred Scott was the kind of hysteria that was common during the Cold War. Closer to the mark, *Izvestia* reported, "The sensational sale of the New York Yankees is another proof that some sports are being turned into an appendix of commercial television. TV companies pay hundreds of thousands and millions of dollars for the right to televise baseball and other matches. However, they get still larger sums from companies whose goods they advertise during those matches."[12] The players were then described as struggling at the base of that pyramid, "sportsmen bought and sold by businessmen."

CBS's acquisition of the Yankees was not the radical step that Daley—let alone the Soviets—described; instead, it was a fresh jab at an old nerve: the connection between money and love in sports. Baseball, the Olympics, tennis, golf, and other sports have wrestled with a fundamental dilemma: To restrict the game to those who play only for the love of the sport and competition inevitably means that access is confined to the rich. In the case of baseball, the organized game had begun among gentlemen's clubs in Manhattan. The expansion of the sport to the masses required some financial compensation for men to take time to play the game.

At any number of points, baseball fans lamented that a line had been crossed, that the purity of the contest was compromised by financial considerations, that what had been a diversion was now a business. Almost a century before the sale of the Yankees to CBS, consternation attended the first professional baseball leagues. Teams raided opposing rosters and turned seasons into chaos. The reserve clause provoked player revolts decades before Marvin Miller was even born. We have earlier reviewed the mischief of syndicates, Andrew Freedman, and the Baltimore franchises at the turn of the twentieth century. Shortly after the pact of 1903, minor leagues rebelled against their control by the American and National Leagues. Babe Ruth's sale in 1920 was the second time he had been auctioned for financial reasons—Jack Dunn was forced to let Ruth go to the Red Sox in 1914 to save his Baltimore Orioles from the Federal League. Connie Mack disbanded one of the greatest teams ever in 1915 rather than pay them a market rate. These were some of the aggravations that baseball suffered before Yankee Stadium was built. The history of the game simply belies the easy distinction between business and sport that Daley, Celler, and many others made in 1964.

Instead of railing at the obvious—that business played an essential role in modern sports—we do better to ask what kind of influence CBS exerted on baseball and how the game and its interested parties fared because of that influence. Part of the answer comes from changing the perspective. Instead of asking what CBS meant to the Yankees, consider what the ball club meant to the network. The answer, in many respects, was "not much."

One account of the purchase noted that CBS could finance the entire venture with its profits from the musical *My Fair Lady,* the Broadway hit that the network had underwritten.[13] The network had assumed a preeminent position in the broadcast industry, with phenomenal growth in the fifteen years before the sale. During that span, CBS's net income had grown by 900 percent, earnings per share by 600 percent, and net worth by 550 percent. The *Times* concluded, "Few companies in any type of enterprise can match that record."[14]

CBS was a vast collection of entertainment businesses in 1964. The television network was one of seven divisions in the corporation. It was composed of 205 affiliated television stations, and the network itself owned five stations outright in New York, Chicago, Los Angeles, Philadelphia, and St. Louis. The CBS Radio Network also owned stations in those five cities as well as in Boston and San Francisco. Columbia Records gave CBS an entrant into the growing field of recorded music. CBS also had an international division, and CBS Films was the largest exporter of movies for television.

Staying apace with technological change, CBS Laboratories Division conducted research and development for business, government, and academic institutions. Some of this work was financed by government contracts, especially in cases of military use.

In some respects, the crown jewel of the corporation was CBS News. Its standard had been set by the courageous and historic work that Edward R. Murrow had done on radio from the rooftops of London during the Blitz in World War II. A corps of newsmen with the Murrow stamp of approval continued to dominate the network's news division in the 1960s. Most important was Walter Cronkite, who came to define the anchor position. The News division wrestled with conflicting pressures to continue to produce important work on serious issues and commercial demands for more revenue, which usually translated into lighter fare.

Sometimes the choices to go for more money cost the network its proud reputation. In his book on American media, *The Powers That Be*, David Halberstam excoriated CBS for offering, "to its undying disgrace," the show *Hogan's Heroes*, a comedy set in a German POW camp during World War II. Halberstam concluded, "The immorality of the decision to place this program on the nation's airwaves was staggering, yet the competition seemed to demand it."[15] The battle for ratings became an increasingly sophisticated contest, and marketing research suggested that high quality could be incompatible with high ratings.

The acquisition of the Yankees gave the network an immensely popular asset and one that also carried with it considerable prestige. Halberstam saw the purchase as a reflection of a profound personal change in the founder of CBS, William S. Paley. "Bill Paley had one dream, of having a million dollars in the bank. Now his company was churning out profits of $20 and $30 million a year, but it wasn't in the bank, that would be old-fashioned. Rather the money was going into the acquisition of other companies, the expansion of the empire."[16]

In a *New York Times* magazine piece, about CBS and the Yankees, Leonard Wallace Robinson also was impressed by the chairman's personality. The article noted that the television industry was maturing, which meant that virtually every market in the United States had a station and that programs were saturated with commercials. The growth of the industry had been phenomenal, but the future would have to pursue new directions for the expansion to continue. Taxes were another reason to diversify. CBS executives wanted to invest the corporation's profits so that they would yield direct benefits to the network instead of going to the public purse. But in addition to financial considerations, Paley and CBS president Frank Stanton may have been motivated by their reputations among friends. Robinson cited an anonymous industry source in the *Times* article who observed that both Paley and Stanton "have a hunger for a certain kind of top-level status you can't get in television broadcasting."[17] The source noted that the CBS executives socialized with the rich, powerful, and well educated, "You certainly can't expect to be the toast of such friends if you keep putting on 'nothing' stuff like *The Beverly Hillbillies*. On the other hand, if you own the Yankees or, say, a big reputable publishing company, you've arrived."[18]

Mike Burke, interviewed for the article, was evasive about how active CBS would be in the operations of the ball club. He pointed out that the network had not involved itself in *My Fair Lady* beyond the financing, but another Broadway play, *What Makes Sammy Run?*, received direct suggestions about casting. Burke avoided any commitment about which model would apply to baseball. Yankee Stadium was another matter. From the outset, CBS intended to improve the facility, but its initial objectives were quite modest:

> Vice presidents are already talking about moving certain aisles so that the view from some 5,000 seats now partially or wholly blocked by girders will be cleared. They may also try to make the box seats more comfortable, bring the antique public-address system up to date and improve parking facilities. They have even contemplated the possibility of putting a restaurant out where the left-field bleachers now stand, so that one could watch a game while eating or drinking— presumably beer of a certain brand.[19]

No suggestion appears in the article that the public would be on the hook for even these limited changes in the stadium.

Within days of the sale, the Department of Justice announced that it was investigating the transaction. Antitrust officials interviewed Charles Finley and Arthur Allyn, the two owners who vociferously opposed the takeover. The review continued for several months and was finally concluded at the start of November with a decision that no antitrust problems were created by the sale.

The CBS move into baseball was the first intrusion into the sport by a national broadcasting company. What was just as unsettling to some teams and fans was the very old concern that a single owner with pockets far deeper than his or her competitors could capture the best talent in the game and drive serious competition from the field before the first pitch on Opening Day. New York owners, in the biggest market, were always suspect in this regard going back at least to the days of Andrew Freedman. In that regard, CBS soon put every troubled soul to rest.

The Yankees were in third place in the American League on the day they were sold to the network. Yogi Berra was in his first season as the club's manager, and he was doing a decent job directing men who, a year before, had been his teammates. Legends were still in the lineup, and they had something left in the tank. Mickey Mantle finished third in the

American League in home runs with thirty-five and runs batted in with 111. Whitey Ford won seventeen games with a 2.13 earned run average, both also good for third among American League pitchers. Roger Maris had a solid year in right field. Tony Kubek anchored shortstop. The brilliant fielder, Clete Boyer, played third base, and Bobby Richardson, nearly the hero of the 1960 World Series, played second.

The youngsters on the team never quite materialized. Tom Tresh, the left fielder, was supposed to replace Mantle as Mantle had replaced DiMaggio. Joe Pepitone, the first baseman, played twelve seasons in the majors, but was unable to reach the impossibly high standards that had become commonplace in the Bronx. Mel Stottlemyre won nine games for the Yankees in his rookie season in 1964 and proved to be a fine major league pitcher on what became a terrible ball club.

The Yankees played well down the stretch after the sale. They won ninety-nine games, edging the Chicago White Sox for the pennant by a single game. They then dueled the St. Louis Cardinals in a classic seven-game World Series. In a terrible blow to New York, Whitey Ford, one of the greatest postseason pitchers, was injured and could not pitch again after losing the first game.

In a tough spot on the road, rookie Stottlemyre beat Bob Gibson to even the Series at a game apiece. Gibson had a 7–2 career record in three World Series with an E.R.A. of 1.89, but Stottlemyre was able to keep his team in the hunt.

Back at the stadium, Jim Bouton pitched the second complete game in a row for the Yankees. He finished the top of the ninth tied at 1–1, and the Cardinals manager, Johnny Keane, replaced Curt Simmons with knuckleballer Barney Schultz. Mickey Mantle hit Schultz's first pitch for a game-winning home run.

In the fourth game, Cardinals' starter Ray Sadecki was gone after ten pitches. Roger Craig, rescued from the New York Mets, arrived from the bullpen and stopped the bleeding. Craig gave up a run-scoring single as the Yankees went up 3–0, but New York would get only one more hit in the game. Ken Boyer hit a grand slam in the fifth inning, and that held up to even the Series for St. Louis.

Bob Gibson got his revenge in the fifth game. Gibson took a 2–0 lead into the bottom of the ninth. With two out and a runner on, Tom Tresh tied the game with a home run. In the top of the tenth, Tim McCarver hit a three-run shot to give the Cardinals the lead. Gibson then finished his work shutting out the Yankees in the bottom of the inning to preserve the win in the last World Series game played within the Stadium's original design. The Yankees would not get back to the World Series until 1976, and the showcase would then be dramatically different.

Mantle and Maris homered in the sixth game back in Sportsmen's Park in St. Louis to help force the seventh game. Jim Bouton won his second game of the Series, and, in 17.1 innings of work, posted an E.R.A. of 1.56.

An incident before the sixth game perhaps indicated how far out of its depth CBS was in its new role as owner of the Yankees. In his wonderful book, *October 1964*, David Halberstam describes Bouton's bewilderment that the players had been told to check out of their hotel *before* the game. If they won, they would check back in. If not, they would head to the airport. As Halberstam wrote, "That stunned Bouton; in the past the Yankees had always been both arrogant and parsimonious, but this was the first time he could ever remember their parsimoniousness outweighing their arrogance. It was, he thought, the work of people with a loser's mentality."[20]

The Yankees overcame the owners' timidity, but they faced Bob Gibson in the seventh game. The Cardinals broke out to a 6–0 lead, but the Yankees fought back. Mantle hit a three-run homer in the sixth, and Gibson was beginning to tire badly. Struggling into the ninth, Gibson held on to a 7–3 lead. He gave up solo homer runs to Clete Boyer and Phil Linz, but Gibson also got two strikeouts and a pop-up to secure the win. For the second consecutive year, the Yankees had lost the World Series, and they would be a while getting their next chance.

The ball club needed some changes, but it began with one it did not need. Yogi Berra was fired as manager despite a fine job in tough circumstances. The dismissal was thoroughly shabby. Johnny Keane, the Cardinals' victorious skipper, knew that he had been on thin ice in St. Louis.

The Cardinals' pennant win had required a complete collapse by the Philadelphia Phillies in the last week of the season. Had the Phillies held on, Keane would likely have been gone. Putting owner Gussie Busch in a very tough spot, Keane waited until a press conference at which Busch planned to announce Keane's new contract. Keane slipped Busch a note announcing his resignation.

Keane looked good to a lot of people. He had guided his club to a title while running from behind. He then took on the Yankees and beat them. To cap it off, he told his boss to go jump. He made himself a working-class hero.

Ralph Houk, who had managed the Yankees between Stengel and Berra, had developed doubts about Berra's managerial ability early in the season. Instead of being persuaded by the evidence before him, Houk moved to pick up Keane for the Yankees themselves. Long before George Steinbrenner arrived, anything short of winning the World Series could cost you your job with the Yankees.

Keane landed in the Bronx just in time for a total collapse. The Yankees fell to a sixth-place finish in 1965 finishing with a 77–85 record, and things were about to get worse. The 1966 season began with the Yankees dropping sixteen of their first twenty games. Johnny Keane was fired, and Ralph Houk returned to the dugout. The magic that had worked from 1961 to 1963 was gone because the players who had sustained it were gone. The Yankees crashed all the way to last place in 1966 and absolutely no one expressed any concern about the dominant power that CBS would have in baseball.

Whitey Ford retired after the 1967 season, and his great pal Mickey Mantle followed after the 1968 campaign. The other heroes were gone as well, and the Yankees became a team that every other club now looked forward to playing. They climbed up to ninth place in the old ten-team configuration in 1967. They soared to fifth place and a winning record in 1968. In 1969, the first year of divisional play, the Yankees were again fifth, but this time in a six-team division rather than a ten-team league.

The 1970 season showed promise. With Houk still in command, the Yankees finished second in the American League Eastern Division to the

Baltimore Orioles. Thurmon Munson had arrived to complement Bobby Murcer, Roy White, and Gene Michael, and Fritz Peterson won twenty games.

They slipped to a fourth-place finish in 1971, barely breaking .500. They stayed stuck at that level for the next two years as the city tried to renovate the Stadium and the network tried to unload the Yankees.

The CBS experience with the Yankees is perhaps best understood as a cautionary tale for some of the oldest concerns in the game. Owners, writers, and fans have been worried from the beginning that money can equate to dominance: "What chance will we have if we can't lavish money like the next guy?"

CBS did not run a productive franchise into the ground. The Yankees were in tough shape by 1964, and they needed serious help. The stars were in their final innings, and the farm system was thin. The situation may trace to Webb and Topping's decision to dismiss George Weiss after the loss to the Pirates in 1960, but that explanation may be too convenient. Weiss was replaced by good baseball minds who could recognize talent. Halberstam writes that Webb and Topping were cutting back on investments to make the books look good in anticipation of a sale, but the Yankees should have been marketable for their reputation alone.

The CBS experience suggests three conclusions. First, at least in the days before free agency, money was not sufficient for success on the field. Having resources helped, but it did not translate easily into championships because star players were tied through the reserve clause to teams that held them with below-market pay. Even now, any number of owners have picked up ball clubs anticipating that a spending spree will lead to champagne in the locker room, and most of those owners have been disappointed.

Second, the collapse of the Yankees may be the best illustration of how remarkable the dynasty was. The club had remade itself before, moving from Ruth to Gehrig, then DiMaggio, then Mantle. None of those transitions was easy. Ruth and DiMaggio were disgruntled when it was time to go. Gehrig was fatally ill, and Mantle was broken physically. Determining the time and manner of the hero's departure is an extremely difficult responsibility in any organization, and the Yankees had been successful at the task longer than most.

Finally, the CBS years corresponded with an interesting period in the business of baseball. We normally look to the aribitration decision by Peter Seitz, the Christmas present of 1975 that led to free agency for the players, as triggering a new age in baseball. The limitation of the reserve clause introduced obvious and important changes in the operation of baseball teams, but some of those changes had been brewing before Dave McNally and Andy Messersmith challenged the owners' reading of their contracts.

In the 1950s, George Weiss could treat Yankee players with disdain. He summoned even the stars to his office to be berated (often with good cause) for some late-night behavior that had made the newspapers. By 1970, the players, though not fully free, were beginning to change their status as hired help. Marvin Miller had been hired to head the players' union, and Curt Flood had filed a lawsuit challenging the stranglehold of the reserve clause. The players' liberation would eventually become a critical factor in the stadium game.

From the time CBS bought the Yankees in 1964 to the time that John Lindsay began to lobby Mike Burke in 1970 to let New York lavish money on the team, the political culture of America was undergoing a historic shift. At the time of the sale, the liberal confidence that government could solve social and economic problems was at its peak. Lyndon Johnson was persuading Americans that the strategies of the New Deal could be extended to every corner of the nation. No mountain hamlet was too remote; no urban neighborhood too damaged. Federal laws and agencies could redistribute money, regulate markets, and provide services that business withheld. The result would be a "Great Society," in Johnson's phrase, unprecedented in human history for its insistence that all would benefit. The ultimate test, liberals insisted, was that the nation's bounty would extend to its most marginal members.

In a few years, "The Great Society" would become a term of derision in American politics, referring to an exaggerated sense of government's possibilities, but, in the mid-1960s, the public was ready to share Johnson's dream.

By the time Lindsay approached Burke, the liberal ideal was in retreat. In 1964, Barry Goldwater was nearly a buffoon as the object of LBJ's scorn, and Richard Nixon was the epitome of a political loser—suffering a bitter defeat for the presidency in 1960 compounded by a humiliating loss for governor of California in 1962. But in 1970, Nixon was in the White House, Goldwater was a conservative icon back in the U.S. Senate, and Ronald Reagan—making virtually the identical argument that Goldwater had unsuccessfully advanced in 1964—was the governor of California preparing for his own presidency.

Bucking that conserative trend, John Lindsay was often packaged as the Republicans' Kennedy, a patrician with good looks who could walk the meanest streets in the hardest times. In the late 1960s, very few white men would dare to stroll through a black urban ghetto, but Lindsay was one who did. He had won the mayoralty in 1965 for the reason Republicans usually become mayor of New York: the Democrats that year were a mess.

Robert Wagner, the senator's son, was finishing his third term as mayor, and he tried to pass a sputtering torch to Paul Screvane. Abe Beame beat Screvane in the Democratic primary, but reform elements and some black voters defected to Lindsay in the fall while William F. Buckley Jr. drew some conservative support from Beame. Lindsay won the general election with less than 44 percent of the vote.

Hopes that the city had a mayor who was a budget hawk with a heart of gold quickly faded. Municipal unions challenged Lindsay for control of city services. Racial divisions continued to split both the city and the liberal coalition. Remnants of Tammany Hall plotted a return to power. In a most whimsical election in 1969, Lindsay lost the Republican nomination, but was returned to office as a Liberal Party nominee by an electorate that voted in the glow of the New York Mets' miraculous World Championship that year.

In the first year of his second term, Lindsay approached Mike Burke about Yankee Stadium. Lindsay offered to spend the same money on

Yankee Stadium that had been spent on the construction of Shea Stadium for the Mets. That figure was either $25 or $30 million, depending on the calculation. In a letter dated October 2, 1970, Burke expressed his appreciation, then emphasized some of his concerns. The letter was sent to Deputy Mayor Richard Aurelio, and it was more blunt than the August letter. Burke wrote, "Given the apprehension about personal safety that grips all citizens, it becomes imperative that sports fans be able to drive private cars with relative ease directly to Yankee Stadium and to park within full sight and easy walking distance of it."[21] Burke allowed that Shea Stadium was an ideal arrangment with ample parking surrounding the stadium, but in case that point was too subtle, Burke stressed, "Our location in the South Bronx and alongside Harlem makes this requirement for Yankee Stadium even stronger."[22]

By every account, Mike Burke was a thoroughly decent fellow — a hero of World War II, bright, energetic, and committed to the city of New York. For his part, John Lindsay was perhaps the first citywide candidate to take African-American voters seriously. They had become a vital part of his constituency, and his presence was welcome in the communities that Burke had dismissed. But for all that decency and commitment, Burke and Lindsay were in tacit accord that the resources of the mayor's office and the city should be focused on the creation of a *cordon sanitaire* around Yankee Stadium so that suburban fans would not feel troubled by the setting in which city children were being raised.

At no point did the Lindsay administration seem to pull back from an enormous commitment to the Yankees because of either the pressing needs of neighborhoods like Harlem and the South Bronx or because of the city's growing fiscal problems. At no point did the Lindsay administration puzzle aloud over the propriety of the city's providing a stadium upgrade, costing in the tens of millions of dollars, for the benefit of an entertainment conglomerate that could have afforded the repairs far more easily.

Further down in the October 2, 1970, letter, Burke pleads the Yankees' case for a lease with the city that is as favorable as the one the franchise had with the beneficiaries of John Cox: Rice University, the owner of the Stadium, and the Knights of Columbus, who owned the land. Burke concluded the point with the assertion, "As we understand it, the object of this renewal program is to ensure that the Yankees and the Giants [the National Football League franchise that also used Yankee Stadium] remain an integral and highly visible element of New York life, recognizing that the healthy and successful operation of the two teams attracts millions of dollars in revenue to New York."[23]

No evidence was offered about the actual financial benefit of the teams to New York. Given the $30 million of public funds that Burke was seeking, a detailed analysis of the returns on the investment might be expected, but no such study appears to have been made. As Burke's letter indicates, the Yankees were not the only sports franchise affected by the future of the Stadium. The Giants of the National Football League were also pressing for improvements in their own stadium arrangements and were being courted aggressively by the state of New Jersey, which was seeking to build a sports complex in the Meadowlands. The spectre of losing both the Giants and Yankees to New Jersey was an important factor in the negotiations because, among other things, it made palpable the risk of forfeiting the franchises if they were not satisfied with the city's final offer of stadium relief.

In March 1971, John Lindsay announced the administration's commitment to spending $24 million for acquiring Yankee Stadium, the property on which it stood, upgrading the facility, and leasing it back to the Yankees for thirty years. The mayor was clear that many hurdles remained. A detailed plan had to be drafted, along with specific estimates of the costs. The proposal then had to be approved by the two legislative bodies that were then part of the city government: the City Council and the Board of Estimate. The Board in particular was a critical actor, in many ways the most powerful unit of government in the city. It was composed of the mayor, the council president, the comptroller, and the five borough presidents.[24]

As soon as Lindsay made his announcement, some hard questions were raised. Dick Young wrote in his *Daily News* column, "I'm not the type who feels that everything else should stop while nothing is built but hospitals, schools and houses, because that kind of Utopian thinking is the first step toward big brotherism, but in this particular case it is simply a matter of placing priorities in their proper location."[25] Lest anyone think that the irascible Young was mellowing, he cleared that up when addressing the attractiveness of Yankee Stadium:

> The realistic truth is that people won't go there any more because it is not a nice place to go to. Not Yankee Stadium, but where Yankee Stadium is. It is a lousy Neighborhood [sic], particularly at night, and if that offends somebody, too bad.
>
> The way to improve that part of the Bronx is to make it a better place in which to live, and it can be done by tearing down Yankee Stadium and putting up some decent dwellings. If Mayor Lindsay does indeed have $24 million of the taxpayers money left, let him spend it in that direction, and let the fans drive across the George Washington bridge for their football and baseball, the way they drive out to Shea Stadium.[26]

Young concluded that New Jersey was simply a better location for New York sports than the Bronx had become, and that the reality of the matter should be recognized. The threat to move the Yankees to New Jersey has colored the future of Yankee Stadium. Under major league rules, owners are free to shift their franchises as long as they stay within their market. If they go outside their market, they need the approval of other owners. Moving a football team is far less complicated than moving a baseball team because going to New Jersey for a Sunday afternoon is a very different proposition than going on a Tuesday night for baseball.

In August 1971, the New York Giants announced that they were moving to the Meadowlands Complex to a new stadium designed for football. The loss of the Giants compromised the city's plans for the Stadium because a major tenant was leaving. At the same time, the loss of the Giants increased the pressure on Lindsay to make sure that the Yankees stayed put.

By the fall of 1971, Lindsay and Burke were taking distinctly different approaches to the Stadium problem. In a letter dated October 5, 1971, Burke informed Lindsay that an estimate by the firm of Praeger, Kavanaugh and Waterbury for modernizing the Stadium suggested that the budget was already blown. The cost of acquiring the Stadium and renovating it were pegged at $32 million. That took care of only one of the four points that Burke had insisted from the beginning needed to be considered as a package. Parking, road improvements, and helping a neighborhood in freefall would drive the price up considerably higher.

Burke noted that Lindsay was planning to go to the Board of Estimate shortly to ask for $3.5 million to acquire the Stadium and grounds from Rice University and the Knights of Columbus. That amount was about $1.5 million below what Burke thought would be needed. Lindsay then intended to go back to the Board in April for the balance needed to modernize the stadium. Burke posed his concerns: "I wonder about the wisdom of undertaking such a definitive step—asking for and spending money to acquire the Stadium—if the prospect of completing the total project is in doubt."[27] The Yankee president then offered a different approach:

> Before your program is presented to the Board of Estimate, especially
> if it were to carry an implied Yankee endorsement, I must present to
> my management for their consideration a clearly defined four-point
> program—Stadium, parking, traffic and environment—with a total
> cost estimate for all elements of the program, backed by appropriate
> guarantees that the program will be carried out and sound arguments
> that there is justification for it.[28]

In decision-making parlance, Burke was urging a rational-comprehensive approach while Lindsay was pursuing an incremental approach. Burke's strategy makes a lot of sense at the outset, and it is inevitably the one used in hindsight when a program is assessed. The piece-at-a-time technique is generally the one employed in government because it allows adjustments to political realities.

Burke implied that the Yankees' commitment to staying in the city was contingent on a serious effort by New York to tackle the Stadium issue as Burke had proposed. Looking realistically at the daunting prospect of winning approval of the ambitious renovation plan, Burke informed Lindsay that the Yankees needed to consider moving to Shea Stadium, the Meadowlands, or another city. He followed up a month later with a letter telling the mayor that the Yankees were exploring their options.[29]

Burke and Lindsay met, and the mayor was persuasive that his approach deserved a chance. Burke later announced, "He reaffirmed his total dedication for the project. And as for the political realities involved in obtaining approval, I got the impression that he was very bullish."[30]

As Lindsay pressed his case, not everyone was so impressed. The *Daily News* editorialized: "In his own slickster way, His Honor obviously intends to commit the city piecemeal to the stadium project without revealing the ultimate price tag. . . . Sentiment argues that New York should make every effort to keep the Yankees in the home they have graced so long with their presence. But a city that is broke cannot afford sentimental gestures, and hard facts make the stadium deal highly questionable."[31]

On December 7, 1971, the Board of Estimate heard testimony from Lou Gehrig's widow as Lindsay pulled out all the stops. The Board approved funds for an engineering study to determine the exact work that would be needed to bring the Stadium up to par.

Two days later, in an austerity move, Lindsay announced a moratorium on construction projects. He announced that "only the most urgent and fully ready new projects will be allowed to start construction during the moratorium."[32] Existing projects were allowed to proceed and, now forty-eight hours old, the Stadium deal was not subject to the moratorium. This exclusion saved the matter from being scrutinized thoroughly. The *Times*'s account mentioned that "the budget provides $24 million to acquire and renovate Yankee Stadium, but no funds for additional branch libraries."[33] A spokesman for the mayor expressed doubts about the value of more libraries.

The value of the Stadium was confirmed the following March when the Board of Estimate agreed to acquire and upgrade the Stadium "whatever the cost."[34] The Yankees agreed to a thirty-year lease that would keep them in the Bronx through the 2002 season. The deal maintained the fiction that $24 million would be enough to buy the Stadium and fix it. The work was scheduled to begin after the 1973 season, and it would be finished in time for Opening Day in 1976.

Deputy Mayor Aurelio had explained earlier to the *Daily News* the logic behind the original $24 million estimate, "It was simply a figure arrived at as a comparison amount to what the city laid out for the construction of Shea Stadium—and because of the mayor's announced determination to do as much for the Yankees as the city had done for the Mets."[35]

The comparison with the Mets is another point that greatly influenced negotiations over Yankee Stadium. Because the city had spent $24 million building Shea Stadium, Mike Burke approached the issue of equivalent spending on the Yankees as a matter of right. In his October 2, 1970, letter to the mayor, Burke described Lindsay's commitment to spend no more and no less than the city had spent on the Mets "immensely heartening."

The city never reexamined the spending on Shea Stadium to determine if it was a wise investment. They paid little attention to whether the same amount of money would yield the same outcome despite the greater costs of renovating compared to building anew. The administration left unchallenged Burke's argument that the neighborhood was a more serious problem in the Bronx than in Queens, but it assumed that the money would go as far anyway. It would not.

A year later, in April 1973, Mayor Lindsay announced that the cost of the Stadium renovation had increased by $7 million. The original contract included a provision that would cover a 15 percent increase in costs, but the first year of the deal saw the price jump by a third. Lindsay brushed off the increase as "routine—a moderate escalation." His casual reaction may have reflected his being in the final year of his second term. He told the *Daily News*, "By the time I retire the Stadium will be gutted and the project so far down the road it will be impossible to reverse it."[36]

John Lindsay knew that his city was in the grip of forces beyond its control. He may also have known that he and his predecessors had acted foolishly on occasion, so why did he stay committed to the Stadium deal? An answer is suggested in testimony by Ken Patton, Lindsay's Administrator of the City Planning Commission, making the case for Stadium renovation in October 1971. Lindsay sent the statement to Mike Burke on October 15, and promised to keep him apprised of the progress in navigating the budget labyrinth. Patton's statement offers two arguments that are often used to justify public financing of sports stadiums.

First, economic returns, it is alleged, will cover the investment. Patton claimed that the city received $3.4 million per year from baseball in the Bronx.[37] He broke that down as $356,000 in direct taxes on parking, tickets, concessions, and corporate revenues; $500,000 in increased use of mass transit; part-time jobs for 1,000 people, and full-time employment for more than 500; $670,000 from "peripheral activities which would vanish if baseball were lost"; $150,000 in spending by visiting teams; losses in advertising, television and related business if baseball were gone; and an estimated $800,000 from "benefits" to young people, old people, sandlot baseball, and public and school uses of the Stadium.

An accountant could poke at the numbers to see if they add up. An auditor could review them to see if they are all proper expenditures. An economist could put the figures in context by estimating opportunity costs or alternatives where the money might have been spent. These reviews could give us some useful information about the impact of Yankee Stadium on the city's economy, but they would all miss a fundamental point that Patton never addressed: Why does the city have to own the Stadium for these benefits to accrue?

If the Yankees owned their own facility or leased it from a private party, the same revenues would flow to the city. The same taxes would be collected. The same visiting teams would spend the same money on meals, lodging, and entertainment. The same number of people would use mass transit. The same "peripheral activities," whatever they are, would obtain. The same numbers of jobs would be required. The same advertising, television, and so on. The same benefits to kids and the elderly. In terms of the economics, everything would remain the same if the Yankees owned the Stadium as they had from 1923 to 1955.

Implicit in Patton's argument is the ominous assumption that, if the city does not take over the Stadium and renovate it, then the Yankees will not stay in the Bronx. Patton used the phrase "if baseball were lost," but why would it be lost?

The apparent answer is that, in October 1971, Burke was threatening to move the team to the Meadowlands or somewhere else. But how serious was that threat? The initiative for the Stadium's renovation was Lindsay's, not Burke's. In the summer of 1970, Burke had invited the mayor to an exhibition game between the Yankees and Mets. Lindsay brought up the subject of what the city should do to help the Yankees. No evidence suggests that the issue was a burning one for Mike Burke or CBS at the time. Once Lindsay committed, Burke took full advantage, but he had not been the one to raise the issue.

A second part of Patton's argument is the alleged non-economic impact of sports franchises. On this point, Patton offered bad poetry. He began his brief report:

Having baseball in the Bronx means so much to that neighborhood, that borough, and this city that I engage reluctantly in efforts to exhaustively dismantle this issue before you. Very simply, life in each would be much worse if baseball leaves as any resident of Brooklyn can confirm. It is a powerful integrating force, which motivates young, old, black, hispanic, white, male and female. It is an experience shared which contributes in large measure to the difference between being a community and just a place. It is part of the essence of a city.[38]

Patton was offering the old romance of sports, that it will help to bind a community in ways so mystical that they can hardly be put into words. We would appreciate this boosting from a public relations firm retained by the Yankees, but from a public official with obligations to the entire community the claim is beyond specious. For good measure, if the boosterism fails, the spectre of the Dodgers is brought into play.

The report continued in this vein:

The price of being without baseball is sufficient to drive every major city in the U.S., some in Canada, counties, and suburban towns, to seek it out, to tender daily competitive offers to baseball clubs and to invest, in the case of Pittsburgh, as much as $64.00 per capita for a new stadium, and in Cincinnati, $88.00 per capita. By comparison, Shea Stadium represents an investment of only $3.00 per capita. These commitments by others testify to the commercial and social importance of retaining professional baseball in a community.[39]

Patton's economics is shaky on its face. Not only does New York have far more residents over whom to average the cost of Shea Stadium, but Shea was built almost ten years before the stadiums in Cincinnati and Pittsburgh were constructed.

Probably without intending to, Patton reveals what was driving the Lindsay administration to fix the Stadium: Everybody else was doing it. In the 1960s and 1970s, building sports facilities was an indication of the economic strength and progressive force of a community. Atlanta and New Orleans were doing it to demonstrate that the South was no longer the backwater of the nation. Seattle was doing it to showcase the Pacific Northwest. Pittsburgh wanted to show that what was being called the Rust Belt still had life. Anaheim and San Diego were trying to prove that Walter O'Malley had not yet captured every dollar in Southern California.

The stadiums meant sports franchises, and that meant a city's name was in every major newspaper in America every day for months at a time. The publicity was presumed to attract business with jobs and other economic benefits too important to ignore.

Recessions hit the country hard in 1969 and 1973, but cities kept building their stadiums as a sign of confidence in the future. Those downturns were particularly hard on New York, but it too kept building. To do otherwise would be to admit that the city was in an especially grim position. Lindsay would have to admit that New York could not compete with the burgeoning cities of the Sunbelt, and he could not concede that.

Trapped in a snare of his own making, Lindsay did not see the powerful arguments that he might have used on his city's behalf. First, he should have waited for Mike Burke to come to him with any request about the Stadium. No doubt the call would not have been long in coming. With the stadium boom about the country, CBS would not have been content with fans having to peer around girders to follow a throw to the cutoff man. Still, Lindsay acted as an agent for CBS rather than as a servant of the people of New York. His near insistance that Burke meet with him to let the city match what it had done for the Mets put the Stadium issue on a level of fairness and justice rather than a handout that might have to be withdrawn.

Second, Lindsay needed to understand that moving the Yankees would not have been easy. The Meadowlands option that lured the Giants was not so promising in the Yankees' case. If anyone had done a serious market analysis, they likely would have found that Yankee fans on Long Island, in Westchester, and Connecticut would cut their trips to Yankee games dramatically. New fans would have been drawn from towns in New Jersey, but an awfully big market would have been abandoned by the American League. If the National League had responded with a second expansion team in New York, they might have kept the American League out of the country's biggest market indefinitely.

Third, Lindsay never looked to play the antitrust card over the Yankees, threatening baseball's exemption from that policy. He went to court in a futile attempt to keep the Giants from using their New York identification. Memos swirled about him concerning antitrust pressure that the city could apply to the NFL, but nothing about baseball because the administration never considered an option other than doing everything possible on behalf of the Yankees.

Antitrust threats worked wonders in generating expansion teams. Whenever an established franchise left for a new market, it was replaced in the original so-called bad baseball town in a few years to preclude a lawsuit. The NFL enjoyed a limited antitrust exemption, but baseball was the only major sport to have a blanket exemption. Both Congress and the courts had recognized the anomaly, but both had declined to lift it. Pressure from the New York congressional delegation to keep the Yankees at home could have been very persuasive on the other owners.

Lindsay also seems to have missed how vulnerable CBS was within the city. When Burke proposed in the fall of 1971 that the Yankees might have to move to another city, Lindsay could have threatened to lead a boycott of CBS sponsors in New York City. The threat would not have been hard to implement—it would actually have been popular among many in New York. And it could have been devastating for the network. As it was, the city cut a deal with CBS that was extremely generous to a corporation that did not need generosity.

In November 1973, Abe Beame, the City Comptroller, was elected mayor, and he immediately inherited the Stadium problem. On November 16, the Board of Estimate voted another $15.9 million for the Stadium project, bringing the total authorization to almost $40 million. Beame had estimated back in April that the final cost of the renovations would be in the range of $53 million. More risks lay ahead: The city had not yet actually acquired the Stadium, and, when contractors bids were opened in December 1973, they were $5 million above the architects' estimates.

Construction proceeded through 1974 and 1975. The next news on the cost of the project came in July 1975 when a contract was amended to allow the repair of concrete that was chipped when the old seats were removed from the Stadium. The repair was estimated to run $1,109,969, and it brought the total costs to just over $57,000,00.

By the end of 1975, in a clear expression of priorities, the city dropped its plans to spend $300,000 on neighborhood renewal, and directed that the money be spent directly on the Yankees instead. Instead of clearing deteriorating structures near the Stadium, the $300,000 was applied to buying features like a $215,000 tarpaulin for the field and $7,000 for carpet or terrazzo flooring for an office.[40] City officials whom the *Times* interviewed justified the expenditure on the grounds that the money had been promised to the Yankees, so, as they saw it, shifting the focus of spending directly to the franchise itself satisfied any moral problems with the changes in spending.

In December 1975, the *New York Times* published the findings of its own investigation into the Stadium project. It estimated that the direct costs of renovation had risen to about $75,000,000, and that indirect costs including interest, tax exemptions, and parking facilities "may add $150 million to the bill over the next 31 years."[41]

The article quoted Henry Gavan, an attorney for the city's Economic Development Administration who became project coordinator for Yankee Stadium in the Beame administration. He dismissed the original $24 million as "picked out of thin air."[42] He claimed that anyone who had used that figure as a serious estimate either was asserting "a deliberate lie" or else was guilty of "gross stupidity."

Lindsay was certainly not a stupid man, but Gavan's alternative explanation was supported by a memo that came to light in February 1976. Edward Hamilton, another attorney for the Economic Development Administration, wrote a memo after a meeting at City Hall in September 1973 in which the costs of the stadium project were put at $80 million dollars.[43] But three weeks later, when Lindsay broke ground in a public ceremony at the stadium, he stuck with the $27 million figure that he had been insisting was a fair estimate. Hamilton maintained the deception in an appearance before the Board of Estimate in November 1973. He avoided the economic arguments for the renovation, but insisted, "It is not a luxury. It talks to the pride of being a New Yorker."[44]

Gavan himself described the project as "a necessary luxury" that was crucial to the revival of the Bronx. The renovated Stadium would serve mostly as an inspiration, because the financial investment in the borough that had been promised had been put into the ballpark instead. Gavan remained optimistic. He told the *Times*, "The owners of those rundown businesses near the stadium are going to see that they are missing a chance to get the baseball crowds into their places, and they are going to do some painting and remodeling themselves."[45]

While financial pressures forced cutbacks all over the city, Mayor Lindsay had persisted with the stadium project, a transfer of wealth of approximately $100 million for the benefit of a baseball team that was owned by one of the richest corporations in the world. As its costs soared well beyond the original estimate, the only part of the original design that Lindsay gave up was the assistance to the neighborhood. The owners of small stores, the people who performed hard manual labor in the Bronx, the people who had their life savings invested in a family enterprise—they were told by the city's project director to put a coat of paint on their buildings, at their own expense. In the meantime, CBS had tired of the baseball business and had sold the Yankees without bothering to wait for the Stadium's reopening.

THE CITY AND
ITS STADIUM

CBS ended its dismal run with the Yankees on January 3, 1973, when the network sold the team for $10 million in cash to a twelve-member syndicate headed by Mike Burke and George Steinbrenner. The *Times* noted that the figure was several million below what CBS had paid Del Webb and Dan Topping; it was also roughly the same amount that less successful franchises were worth on the market.

Burke, who left CBS to pursue his new position full time, offered part of the explanation. He said that "CBS substantially broke even on the deal, taking account of investment and depreciation and things like that."[1] The mystery of how you break even when you buy for $14 million and sell for $10 million was revealed by Red Smith in a column on the sale.[2] Smith explained that the new owners might list their new investment as $1 million for the franchise, $500,000 for the office equipment, bats, balls, and other paraphernalia. The remaining $8.5 million is the value of the players, and that amount can be depreciated over five years at $1.7 million per year. If the team netted a $1 million gain one year, it could post a $700,000 loss on the books for tax purposes.

In the case of CBS, Smith continued, "Well, say the players represented $12 million of the CBS investment and they were fully depreciated over five years. The corporate tax runs about 50 cents off the dollar, so this would mean a saving of $6 million, reducing the total price paid for the club to $7.2 million."[3] In other words, the network had paid perhaps half of what it was thought to have paid for the Yankees, and, according to Smith, the news got even better. "Now say the Yankees lost $4 million during the eight years CBS owned them. That would be an actual loss of $2 million after taxes, bringing the CBS investment in the club to $9.2 million. Reckoned that way, $10 million from the Burke–Steinbrenner mob gets CBS out clear."[4]

Apart from the financial aspects, Burke indicated that the status that Bill Paley thought he was buying had not panned out. "I think CBS suffered some small embarrassment in buying a club at its peak and then having it fall from first place in the league to sixth and then to 10th. The Yankees no longer fit comfortably into CBS's plans."[5]

The accounts of the sale got its most important feature exactly backwards. George Steinbrenner 3d provided one of the most ironic quotes in modern sports: "We plan absentee ownership as far as running the Yankees is concerned. We're not going to pretend we're something we aren't. I'll stick to building ships."[6] He added, "I won't be active in the day-to-day operations of the club at all."[7]

Steinbrenner had no reason to lie, so his subsequent behavior is most likely the result of being bit by the baseball bug. He was one of the first owners to understand that the free agency the players gained in Steinbrenner's second year would change the way championship teams would be constructed. He acted decisively on the insight, and, when Yankee Stadium reopened for the 1976 season, the ball club was at the dawn of another championship era.

On April 15, 1976, Bob Shawkey again took the mound for the New York Yankees. The Opening Day pitcher in 1923 threw out the first ball in the renovated Stadium before a crowd of 54,010. Once again, the mayor was missing. John Hylan was too ill to attend the opener in 1923, and Abe Beame missed the ceremony this time. Plenty of celebrities more than filled the vacuum.

Governor Hugh Carey attended, as did U.S. Senator James Buckley. Governor Brendan Byrne of New Jersey came to see the team he had tried to induce to cross the Hudson River. Most impressive was eighty-seven-year-old James Farley, FDR's old hand, who had been at every Opening Day since the one in 1923.

In addition to Bob Shawkey, Waite Hoyt, Joe Dugan, Whitey Whitt, Oscar Roetiger, and Hinkey Haines represented the 1923 Yankees. Joe DiMaggio, Mickey Mantle, and Yogi Berra were some of the modern legends in attendance. Joe Louis reminisced about his second fight with Max Schmeling. Kyle Rote and Frank Gifford recalled some of the great football games played at the stadium. Actors, singers, and other notables filled out the glitter list.

One fan who might have been disgruntled was not. Alan Cohen was in charge of Madison Square Garden, which had been built for $50 million with private financing, and which was generating $3.5 million in taxes for the city. Cohen declared, "What makes cities great are places like Lincoln Center, Yankee Stadium, Madison Square Garden. If cities as we have known them are to survive, they must offer facilities that make men civilized—culture, sports, the arts."[8]

They also need budgets that work, and, on Opening Day 1976, New York City was broke. The news of the financial embarrassment had broken a little over a year earlier, about the time players were reporting for spring training in 1975. The state Urban Development Corporation (UDC), one of those government agencies designed to function with businesslike efficiency, was the first domino to fall. On February 25, 1975, it defaulted on over a hundred million dollars in short-term notes. Although a long-term plan to stabilize the UDC was already in place, two days later the domino fell on New York City.

The city tried to sell $260 million in tax-anticipated notes to a financial syndicate that was being represented for the first time by the law firm of White and Case. The attorneys were required by law to certify that the city had enough uncollected tax receipts, that they had not yet borrowed against, to cover the notes being sold. White and Case asked the city to do what had been avoided for years: Show these uncollected receipts.

City Comptroller Harrison Goldin protested that no one had ever asked such a thing before and that the elaborate accounting system used by the city precluded the rapid gathering of such information. White and Case persisted, and were given access to the city's books. The mess was examined through the dead of night, and on the morning of February 28, the city was told there would be no deal. New York City did not have the resources to justify additional borrowing. When their attorneys declined to certify the integrity of the city's accounts, the banks risked being completely responsible for the notes and refused to put themselves in that position.

Over the next few months, Governor Hugh Carey moved decisively to create new institutions that could earn confidence from the financial markets, then gradually transfer that trust to the city of New York. The Municipal Assistance Corporation (MAC) was designed to oversee the city's finances and provide the help that was genuinely needed. In September, another agency was created, the Emergency Financial Control Board. It had even more stringent controls over the city's budget than MAC did. It effectively controlled the city's budget, including authority to abrogate labor contracts. The Board consisted of the governor, state comptroller, mayor, city comptroller, and three business executives. It was an agency created in frustration at the slow pace of reform by the Beame administration, and it left the mayor of New York little more than a figurehead. Still New York City remained shut out of financial markets.

Another critical point was reached in mid-October when Mayor Beame was summoned from the annual Al Smith dinner to be told that the teacher's union was refusing to commit its pension funds to another of the last-minute deals. The city faced default and bankruptcy until the union relented. Desperate to find a more permanent strategy to save New York, Governor Carey pressed President Ford for federal loan guarantees.

Gerald Ford operated with the perspective, common in America, that New York's problems were largely self-inflicted. He drew analogies to families that spend beyond their means, and he reflected a fear that helping the city through its crisis would be the equivalent of helping a drug addict avoid the moment of truth. The president made his determination clear to the National Press Club on October 29 with his promise of a veto. New York got a measure of revenge when the managing editor of the *Daily News*, the aptly named William Brink, retaliated with a classic headline: "Ford to City: Drop Dead."

Significant progress followed the showdown. The potential ramifications of bankruptcy threatened the very banks that were declining to do business with the city. Gradually members of Congress from other regions of the country came to appreciate that banks back home were holding New York paper and that the financial security of their own states would be jeopardized if the city could not continue to function. Polls showed that nationwide the public did not support a draconian treatment of New York. In late November, in the season of Thanksgiving, a package to save New York finally developed.

Federal loan guarantees totalling $2.3 billion were extended in return for painful municipal reforms. The city income tax rate was raised. Labor unions continued to keep their pension funds available. City services were curtailed or eliminated. Thousands of city workers lost their jobs. With few exceptions, like Yankee Stadium, capital projects were deferred. In his history of the city, Oliver Allen concluded, "At long last, then, the city was suffering in concrete ways. The cutbacks touched virtually everybody in one way or another, and during the winter and spring of 1975–76 the atmostphere of pessimism was thick citywide."[9] Such was the state of the city in the months before the Stadium reopened.

The obvious question is: How could the city have been so negligent in taking care of its fundamental responsibilities while being so creative and determined in providing the Yankees with a modern stadium? Part of the answer is that the city was blindsided by forces beyond its control.

Ken Auletta wrote a masterful work, *The Streets Were Paved with Gold*, that reviewed various factors that played a role in the fiscal crisis.[10] In another analysis, Martin Shefter found a connection between the city's problems and cycles of reform politics.[11] Both Auletta and Shefter saw a disaster for New York in the growth of its suburbs. Transportation policies and low-interest mortgages encouraged people to leave the city. The National Highway Trust Fund was established in 1956, and it dovetailed with the expressways and parkways that Robert Moses had been building in New York to put people on the road. Beginning in 1944, the GI Bill of Rights offered veterans low-interest mortgages with no down payment. The Federal Housing Administration had been promoting home ownership since the 1930s. Tax policies that allowed interest deductions took the curse off mortgages that were not so generous as the ones obtained by those who had been in the armed forces.

The people able to take advantage of those policies often had job skills and a decent education. They just as often were replaced in the city by people who were coming to the city in need of both. Shefter found, for example, that federal policies encouraged the automation of southern agriculture after World War II, thereby sending a generation of poor African Americans in search of opportunities. He also found important effects in federal policies that let the states set levels of welfare benefits and ban union shops, meaning that more progressive states would attract a disproportionate share of people needing basic services. Complicating matters for the new arrivals, Shefter noted the policies of international trade that encouraged the development of low-wage manufacturing in other countries.[12] New York City became a haven for people displaced by these economic and social changes.

Compounding its ability to meet these challenges, New York City had made commitments that were increasingly difficult to keep. One such decision, as Auletta noted, was rent control. This policy dates to World War II when the city was concerned that tenants would be exploited during the emergency. The restrictions on rent increases were, of course, immensely popular; and, because so many of the electorate were renters, the controls proved next to impossible to lift. The effects, it is argued, include brutal cuts in maintenance as landlords try to keep their expenses lower than their limited revenue. The inevitable decline in the quality of apartments not only encouraged the development of slums, but it also limited the tax returns that the city could garner from that property.

Across the array of new responsibilities that New York was assuming, its public officials took very seriously the need to have competent professionals managing those responsibilities. If public authorities and other administrative agencies were staffed by political hacks, the very purpose for their creation would be defeated. To attract the kind of people who were needed for this work, government employment had to be made more attractive. Salaries were raised; benefits extended. The right to organize labor unions was recognized. Communities that made these kinds of adjustments were seen as progressive, and, in that regard, New York was as progressive as any city in America. Government policies to promote economic development combined with an interest in having a workforce as qualified as those of business corporations, and the unintended result was a slow-motion disaster for New York City.

The increase in labor costs was an undeniable factor in the problems that challenged the city. Municipal unions not only secured favorable contracts in Robert Wagner's administrations in the 1950s and 1960s, but Shefter contends that they also used their political muscle effectively in Albany. "In return for campaign assistance, members of the city's delegation to the state legislature supported bills benefiting civil servants—in particular, increasing pension benefits—that were extremely costly to the municipal treasury."[13]

As the disparity grew between the city's responsibilities and its ability to meet them, several officials resorted to gimmicks to hide the problem. To float its bonds, the city is required to produce collateral that shows resources sufficient to cover the loan that it seeks. The nature of that collateral changed radically during the 1960s.

Despite the new realities, the old appetites for expansion remained, and financial gimmicks put a fig leaf over the spending that revenues failed to cover. Auletta noted, "When he foreboded that the city was living beyond its means, Democratic gubernatorial contender Howard Samuels was assailed for being 'anti-New York.' Such was the temper of the times. Critics were bucking the sixties—the age of good intentions, limitless optimism, when candidates vied to outspend their rivals and promised new ideas, new programs, new solutions."[14]

In 1965, faced with another budget deficit, Mayor Wagner and Governor Rockefeller worked to amend the state's local finance law. As described by Ken Auletta, "Instead of requiring that all revenue anticipation notes (RANs) be pegged to the previous year's actual receipts, from now on they would be pegged to the mayor's own estimate of the next year's revenue."[15] Whatever mischief might have come from a determination of past revenues was compounded to an incalculable degree by basing collateral on an elected official's prediction of a rosy future. This particular dodge came five years after another Rockefeller concoction. In 1960, the state of New York established the State Housing Finance Agency, whose purpose was to evade two impediments to the state's incurring more debt. To that point, bonds required voter approval and were limited to projects that were "self-sustaining"—that is, they would generate revenue that would retire the bonds.

The State Housing Finance Agency was authorized to float "moral obligation" bonds. Voter approval was not required, nor did the projects have to pay for themselves. The designation of moral obligation came to be the bitterest joke of the fiscal crisis. The most basic fiduciary responsibilities were ignored to generate income.

The urgency to find money to cover government operations led Wagner and Rockefeller in 1964 to begin to charge expense items to the capital budget. As with the other tricks, a short-term problem was solved, but the price was a far more serious matter that would arise down the line. Not only had the original bill not been paid, but essential capital projects were ignored because those funds were being diverted to items that should have been paid for through annual tax revenues.

Lindsay railed against these tricks in his 1965 campaign, and he resisted them for a couple of years after he was elected. In time, he would use the gimmicks himself. Abe Beame, the City Comptroller in Lindsay's second term, knew better than anyone the fiscal standards that the city should apply, yet he himself broke them both in Lindsay's administration and in his own.

New York also persisted in its decision to renovate Yankee Stadium in part because of a powerful assumption that, of all the kinds of spending that government engages, money committed to economic development is well spent because it will be returned many times over. This belief traces back to the New Deal, the administrations and policies of Franklin Roosevelt, who had rejected both the Republicans' confidence in the outcome of free markets as well as the kind of economic intervention favored by Tammany Hall.

The New Deal model of public works provided not only infrastructure in undeveloped parts of America, but it also built post offices, libraries, municipal buildings, and other civic projects. A museum was a less imposing structure than a dam, but its construction offered jobs to people who had been unemployed perhaps for years. That economic impact held a political appeal beyond Democratic administrations. The interstate highway program connected the nation during the Eisenhower administration, and both Republican and Democratic administrations pressed the space program. Defense spending, along with river and harbor projects, were other staples that rested on strategies of economic development and national security without regard for ideological purity.

In time, cultural institutions were added to the list of projects worthy of governmental support. Museums, symphonic halls, and theaters were justified as attractions that could draw audiences with money to spend. Ripple effects in local restaurants and retail stores were anticipated, so some public subsidy to the opera or ballet was justified as a worthwhile investment. The next logical step reasoned that sports represented a cultural interest even more popular than Puccini, so stadiums joined the roster of public goods.

The public money that was used to acquire and renovate Yankee Stadium fits a pattern of stadium construction that was dominating the financing of these facilities since the 1950s. The commitment to this kind of investment crossed all barriers of political ideology, and it became the foundation of the stadium game as it was played most places from the 1950s to the 1980s. Many conservatives were stadium boosters because they were not really in favor of laissez-faire so much as government policies that facilitated enterprise, a Hamiltonian conception of the purpose of the state. Liberals expected government to play a major role in the economy, and they supported stadium projects so that the enterprise might conform to their notion of the public interest.

If the right approved of government's promoting the interests of the rich, the left countered that the nation's bounty should reach all segments of society so that more people could press their needs and desires on the economy and stimulate growth through ever-increasing demand for goods and services. The stadium game allowed both camps to be satisfied: The teams were owned by the wealthiest people in a community, and the construction or renovation provided jobs and contracts that might be steered to struggling economic interests.

Stadiums became part of a political economy that had been developing in America since the New Deal. Alan Brinkley describes its central characteristic as a fundamental shift in the focus of liberalism that he dates to the second administration of FDR.[16] Instead of pursuing the Progressives' aims of restructuring the American economy to control corporate power, Brinkley argues that the fundamental features of modern free market capitalism were accepted so long as more and more people were able to acquire the products of that system.

He writes that liberals "had reached an accommodation with modern capitalism" that shaped the modern political economy:

> They had done so by convincing themselves that the achievements of the New Deal had already eliminated the most dangerous features of the corporate capitalist system; by committing themselves to the belief that economic growth was the shortest route to social progress and that consumption, more than production, was the surest route to economic growth; and by defining a role for the state that would, they believed, permit it to compensate for capitalism's inevitable flaws and omissions without interfering very much with its internal workings. They had, in effect, detached liberalism from its earlier emphasis on reform—its preoccupation with issues of class, its tendency to equate freedom and democracy with economic autonomy, its hostility to concentrated economic power. They had redefined cit-

izenship to de-emphasize the role of men and women as producers and to elevate their roles as consumers.[17]

After World War II, Americans would become consumers of all the material goods of a modern industrial economy. They would buy new homes out of the old neighborhood. These homes had gardens in which flowers rather than food would be grown. They also had garages to accommodate the cars that would be acquired. The bounty would stem both from a powerful economy that could turn from the needs of war to the desires of peace and from government policies that were driven by a fear that a failure to stimulate that economy could lead to a return to the Great Depression.

While New York struggled with the challenges of postwar America, major league baseball was having its own problems with some of the same factors. The rush to suburbia stripped eastern cities of a sufficient fan base to support two teams. Television gave people an incentive to stay home for their entertainment during the summer or air-conditioned theaters induced them to the movies.

At the very time the ballpark needed to be its most attractive, the World War I generation of facilities were showing their age. Maintenance was becoming increasingly expensive. Cramped, inner city neighborhoods could not accommodate more than a few hundred cars. Girders that obstructed views became as much a nuisance as a necessity. New ballparks were needed, and the question of where to put them was very much in the air.

When Milwaukee lured the Braves out of Boston with a publicly financed stadium, a new relationship between baseball franchises and their stadiums was forged. The right deal could liberate the club from maintenance expenses while allowing it to keep a substantial part of the revenue stream. Some kind of rent would be paid for the facility, of course, but that might be comparable to the taxes paid on a ballpark that no longer served its purpose.

The Milwaukee model suddenly shattered the hold of many cities on their historic ball clubs. The Browns and Athletics quickly bolted for Baltimore and Kansas City. The Giants had a choice between Minneapolis and San Francisco, and chose California to maintain the rivalry with the Dodgers, who were leaving under a stadium model now unique to them and Los Angeles.

Cities that had been on the map in 1930 as cowtowns, military bases, or tourist spots had become major population centers and urban economies by the 1970s. They were, in the minds of their boosters, "big league" in every sense but the literal one, and, to crown the achievement of their growth, they would be looking for their own sports franchises. When they did, agencies like the TVA became models for the type of organization needed for this purpose. Public authorities, government corporations, boards, and special districts were created for the stadium game as end runs around Madisonian impediments of separation of powers and checks and balances.

When communities decided to secure an existing major league team or gain an expansion club, they built public facilities in lucrative deals for the ball club. From the time the Dodgers and Giants left to the period when Yankee Stadium was renovated, new facilities were built with public money in Anaheim, California (1966); Arlington, Texas (1972); Atlanta (1966); Cincinnati (1970); Houston (1965); Oakland (1968); Philadelphia (1971); Pittsburgh (1970); St. Louis (1966); San Diego (1969); and Washington, D.C. (1962). New York itself had joined the list when Shea Stadium opened for the Mets in 1964, and it quickly became a reference point for what the Yankees were due.

For two seasons, the Mets played in the Giants' old park, the Polo Grounds, while Shea Stadium rose in Flushing, Queens. Robert Moses, who had resisted Walter O'Malley's petitions to help in building a privately financed stadium in Brooklyn, had no hesitation about providing the land for a ballpark that the city would own. The promise of Shea Stadium allowed National League baseball to return to New York through a stadium model that was becoming acceptable to every major city in America. When newspaper editorials detailed the cost overruns and opportunity costs associated with Yankee Stadium's renovation, a curious notion of justice maintained its hold on John Lindsay and his administration. We did this for the Mets, the argument went, we have to do the same for the Yankees.

Through the 1960s and into the 1970s, the public stadium model transformed the architecture of major league baseball. In most cities, economic efficiencies dictated the construction of multipurpose facilities that could serve both baseball and football. The stadiums became virtually indistinguishable as charm was exchanged for efficiency.

The improvement in the economic aspects of their stadiums came just in time for the major league owners. On December 23, 1975, major league baseball entered a new age. Ruling on the legitimacy of the owners' historic interpretation of the reserve clause, Peter Seitz cast the deciding vote that ended the owners' right to renew a player's contract indefinitely and unilaterally. An infusion of talent was available to any club willing and able to adjust to the new financial realities. At the head of that line was George Steinbrenner.

Steinbrenner was part of the owners' chorus that chanted about the ruin of baseball that free agency was causing, but, as Marvin Miller, the head of the Players Association at the time, has noted, the Yankee owner's behavior varied from his rhetoric. "When Richie Zisk signed with Texas for $2.7 million over ten years, Steinbrenner said: 'Brad Corbett's crazy. He's ruining baseball.' George neglected to mention that from 1975 to 1977, Yankee home attendance jumped from 1,288,048 to 2,468,092, bringing an increase in revenue of roughly $10 million a year. And that didn't include the additional millions of dollars from the playoffs and World Series, and from the vastly increased television and radio payments."[18]

To his credit, while other owners were paralyzed by the players' new freedom, Steinbrenner understood that it represented a potential bonanza for the Yankees. They would have the inside track in terms of money and prestige to attract the best stars in the game to New York. Catfish Hunter arrived in 1975, the year that Billy Martin began his first term as Yankee manager. Hunter was one of the first players to test the weak links in his contract. He escaped the Oakland As only because owner Charlie Finley failed to meet one of the terms of Hunter's contract, but the star pitcher was an omen of how the game would change after the Seitz ruling. Under Martin's guidance, the Yankees finished third in the American League East, twelve games behind the Boston Red Sox.

In 1976, the Yankees won their first pennant since 1964. Roy White, Graig Nettles, Chris Chambliss, and Thurman Munson formed the core of regulars who responded to Martin's direction. Even though they were swept in the World Series by the Cincinnati Reds, nearly all the elements of the Yankees revival were in place. The final piece was Reginald Martinez Jackson who arrived for the 1977 season.

In a twenty-one-year career, Jackson spent only five seasons in the Bronx, but they were extremely memorable ones. He had his battle with Martin in Fenway Park during his first season. In the World Series that year, he finished with three home runs in the final game that beat the Dodgers and gave the Yankees their first World Series title since 1962. Jackson was one of the clubhouse forces that stabilized this remarkable team while the management of the franchise was in chaos. Steinbrenner fired Martin for the first time in the 1978 season, and the Yankees overcame a tremendous lead by the Red Sox to catch Boston. They won the pennant in a terrific playoff game on Bucky Dent's historic home run over the Green Monster in Fenway. The Yankees again beat the Dodgers in six games, and remained atop the baseball world.

The Yankees' return to prominence coincided with the city's recovery of confidence. Ed Koch's election as mayor in 1977 restored a brashness to city government that had been lost in the fiscal crisis. Koch's election was another turn in New York politics. He had begun his career as an anti-Tammany reformer in Greenwich Village in lower Manhattan, but by 1977 had established his independence from the more liberal elements of New York's Democratic Party. He was challenged with a transit workers' strike in 1980, and his enthusiastic rallying of New Yorkers to go about their normal pursuits despite the inconvenience dispelled any sense of paralysis or self-doubt at City Hall.

Koch's success was achieved amid an apparently conservative shift in American politics. Ronald Reagan's victory over Jimmy Carter in the 1980 presidential election was characterized as a revolution away from the liberal trend that had prevailed since FDR. Whether Reagan's victory was that fundamental is questionable; nevertheless, the liberalism that had dominated New York City politics was arrested, if not reve sed.

When Koch was reelected in 1981, he faced a second term challenged by serious cuts in federal social spending. The city enjoyed an economic resurgence in the 1980s as the pro-business policies of the Reagan administration were beneficial to financial interests in the city. Real estate, Broadway, and businesses ancillary to Wall Street reaped subsequent rewards, but a great part of the city remained locked in poverty. An epidemic of drug addiction and the impact of AIDS kept much of the city in a bleak state while the ebullient mayor championed its revival.

No one ever accused Ed Koch of being a baseball fan. He himself later wrote that "as mayor, I dutifully attended both Yankees' and Mets' opening days, staying for one or two innings and leaving my staff to enjoy the rest."[19] The involvement of his administration with the Yankees was limited generally to annual wrangling about how much rent the Yankees owed and whether the city had met its obligations under the Stadium lease. From time to time, the city negotiated with the Yankees to extend their lease and secure the team's future in the Bronx, but the prospects always seemed poor.

In the summer of 1987, in the middle of Koch's third and last term, negotiations for a lease extension became serious. On November 1 of that year, an agreement was announced at the Stadium that would have secured the Yankees in their historic home until the year 2032. The terms of the deal included the construction of a Metro-North train station at the Stadium, a new 3,200 space parking garage, improved highway access, and improvements within the Stadium. The Yankees were given three months to select one of four options for rent payment.

For the city, the new agreement was an improvement because, under each of the four options, the Yankees would no longer deduct maintenance costs from their rent. Despite that adjustment, the great advantage that the Yankees held in the negotiations remained evident. The financial obligation for the work was the responsibility of the city and the state Urban Development Corporation (UDC), but the *Times* reported that "the Yankees had 'agreed to consider' financing some work under the plan. 'However, if they choose not to exercise that option, the public sector will undertake construction' according to a statement from the Mayor's Office and the Urban Development Corporation."[20] We can imagine the Yankees' consideration of paying for renovations themselves or having the public do it for them.

Through the months after the initial agreement was announced, a sticking point developed over the amount that the Yankees would pay the city based on cable receipts. As Sam Roberts reported in the *Times*, "The city wanted to continue to collect a percentage of cable television revenue. The Yankees preferred to pay a flat rate. 'If I could get one figure, I'd extend the lease,' Mr. Steinbrenner insisted."[21] The city had been advised that the cable business was too unpredictable to risk settling for a fixed fee.

The warning was sound because the Yankees would secure a new television arrangement that transformed the financial structure of major league baseball and changed the nature of Yankee Stadium as well. When it was built, the Stadium was the primary source of revenue for the franchise. The cable television deal that was reached in 1989 between the Yankees and the Madison Square Garden Network would add half a billion dollars to the Yankee treasury over its twelve-year term. The Yankees would begin the decade of the 1990s with an annual revenue stream of more than $40 million from cable alone. The New York Mets received $38.3 million in 1990 from all radio and television sources, and they took in more than any club other than the Yankees. When radio and broadcast television receipts were added to the Yankees' cable package, the total revenues from those sources totaled $69.4 million in 1990.[22]

The cable deal was made when the Yankees were almost as bad as they had been in the CBS era. In the late 1980s, managers seemed to come and go like relief pitchers. The 1988 season began with Billy Martin in his last of five terms as manager. He was replaced by Lou Piniella, who himself had been replaced by Martin after the 1987 season. Piniella gave way to Dallas Green for 1989, but Green could not complete the season. He was replaced by Stump Merrill; he was able to start and finish the 1991 season while the team went 71–91 in a fifth-place finish.

During these miserable performances, attendance dropped below 2,000,000 in 1991 and 1992. The fans could vote on the team by staying away, but the cable deal meant that enough money would flow to the Yankees to sustain the operation even when attendance was down. When the Yankees began their resurgence under Buck Showalter in the early 1990s, the crowds returned—and they have remained. The brimming attendance obscures an unsettling notion: Even if people stopped coming to the games, Yankee Stadium would still be a profitable television studio.

Much of the nostalgic treatment of teams and their ballparks reaches a point of romantic blather rather quickly, but the assumption of emotional ownership has led to the most practical consequences: The real owners have been able to induce the public to become partners. Those who have resisted the charms of sports may think that the energy that fans expend is silly or childish. Nonetheless, people who have never been to a professional game may be partners in the enterprise through their tax support of the ballpark. This phenomenon operates nationwide, but its development in New York offers an intriguing look at how a sentiment for a ball club evolved into a transfer of wealth from the middle class to the wealthy and privileged.

With special responsibilities as the economic center of the nation, New York City pursued public works and personnel policies that had unanticipated and damaging effects. It put itself in increasingly difficult straits to meet its most basic responsibilities. It finally reached a point of national humiliation in its inability to pay its bills. Across America during this time, the business of major league baseball was building an argument that public treasuries were the proper source of funding for new stadiums. Driven by their own profligate spending habits, the owners became increasingly desperate to get the public money so that they could stay at the table competing for free agents. Through its participation in the stadium game, New York City was bankrolling that competition.

THE STADIUM GAME
IN NEW YORK

With the cable fortune in his pocket, George Steinbrenner turned his attention to securing a new Stadium deal. In 1993, David Dinkins, Koch's successor, was in a tough re-election fight with Rudoph Giuliani, the man he had narrowly defeated in 1989. In June, Steinbrenner was reported to be considering an array of sites for a future stadium for the Yankees.[1]

In addition to the existing location, Steinbrenner was said to be looking at Van Cortlandt Park (also in the Bronx), 32nd Street and 11th Avenue on Manhattan's West Side, Coney Island in Brooklyn, the Meadowlands in New Jersey, Staten Island, three locations in Queens, and the Yonkers Raceway. The specification of these sites introduced an important twist to the stadium game in New York, since the threat to move had always been vague. Somewhere—usually New Jersey—was an option to staying in the Bronx. The move of the NFL's Giants to the Meadowlands had made the threat more credible, but keeping a future move indefinite put the focus on improving the Yankees' home in the Bronx.

By identifying possible locations for a new stadium, attention could shift to considering how suitable each would be. When the Lindsay administration renovated the Stadium in the 1970s, the role of government was to acquire the existing property and pay for its upgrade. The Yankees were indicating in 1993 that they might require an entirely new exercise. The city might be asked to locate and make available a suitable piece of property for a new stadium. This prospect would inevitably mobilize neighborhood groups that would resist the impact of traffic, noise, and commotion from major league games. Van Cortlandt Park has a citizens' group dedicated to its improvement and they might not favor the introduction of a baseball stadium. Environmentalists could be assumed to raise questions about the impact of construction from any project this size. The Meadowlands is adjacent to wetlands that would attract an entirely separate set of concerns. Virtually any location would likely trigger a group of citizens who would be prepared to apply the familiar instruments of deliberation to frustrate such a project.

This 1993 gambit did not lead to serious negotiations, but it sharpened the focus on the future of Yankee Stadium. If the city was going to continue to play the stadium game, it would need to commit even more money than it had in the 1970s. But now, officials knew that they might face a task even more complex than spending over a hundred million dollars of taxpayer money. They might have to acquire a stadium site, and the implications of that exercise were daunting.

Dinkins lost his rematch with Giuliani, and, in the new administration, the Yankees began to return to their familiar place in baseball. They won their division in 1994, and, from a wild-card position, lost a thrilling playoff series to the Seattle Mariners in 1995. The last bump before their current excellent run was the departure of Buck Showalter following that series. He was credited with restoring the Yankees to prominence, and his replacement with Joe Torre caused a firestorm of calls to sports radio.

Torre, who had the same kind of lackluster managerial record that Miller Huggins and Casey Stengel had brought to the Bronx, took care of the critics with dispatch. The 1996 season was one of the greatest years the franchise had ever enjoyed. The Yankees won their division by four games with a 92–70 record. They cruised through the American League playoffs, then met the Atlanta Braves in the World Series. The favored Braves won the first two games at the Stadium, but a dramatic third-game home run by Jim Leyritz reversed the momentum. The Yankees won the last four games to capture their first title since 1978.

Steinbrenner raised the Stadium questions in the wake of the celebrations of the World Series. He focused attention on attendance, noting that the Yankees had been outdrawn by the Seattle Mariners. Elected officials scrambled to placate the Yankees' owner, and the stadium game was again afoot.

Jim Dwyer of the *Daily News* wrote a column to put stadium negotiations into some perspective.[2] He pointed out that, a few years before, the Yankees had included an engineer's salary as part of their maintenance expenses that could be deducted against rent. The engineer was paid for 168 hours of work per week. Dwyer did the math, and announced that the engineer was being paid for twenty-four hours of work, every day, seven days per week. After the administration challenged the Yankees' claim, the deduction was reduced to sixteen-hour days, seven days per week. Dwyer concluded, "That is the history of the Yankees, in one short course."[3]

In March 1996, the architectural firm of Hellmuth, Obata and Kassabaum (HOK), perhaps the leading stadium architects in the country, published a study of four alternatives for the Yankees. The options were (1) Van Cortlandt Park in the North Bronx; (2) Pelham Bay Park in the East Bronx; (3a) a renovation of Yankee Stadium or (3b) a new Yankee Stadium adjacent to the current site; and (4) the West Side Rail Yard on the Hudson River in midtown Manhattan. The sites were compared on five criteria: transportation; environmental and land use impact; schedule; construction cost; and economic impact.

The study eliminated Van Cortlandt Park and Pelham Bay Park fairly easily. Both were described as failing the transportation test, costing in the neighborhood of $1 billion, requiring the loss of 140 acres in Van Cortlandt Park and 190 acres in Pelham Bay Park, and likely to attract litigation. A renovation or new stadium at the current site was estimated to cost under $1 billion, but the economic effects were said to be negligible. The Executive Summary enthusiastically embraced the West Side Rail Yard option:

Transportation: Best alternative due to significant transit opportunity and existing parking resources. Additional study warranted.
Environmental Impact: With limited new parking construction—environmental impact may be mitigated. Additional study warranted.
Schedule: Opening 2004 with aggressive approvals & construction sequencing.
Construction Cost: Baseball—$850 million; Multipurpose—$1.1 billion.
Economic Impact: Likely beneficial economic impact due to existing commercial diversity. Preferred location of event promoters.[4]

The report was received eagerly by Steinbrenner and Giuliani. The familiar claims of economic stimulus were offered with confidence. Obstacles were dismissed, and a glorious new day for New York baseball was predicted. But, on its face, the study made no sense. For one thing, it neglected the costs of site acquisition. Perhaps the architects thought that government is government, but the Metropolitan Transit Authority (MTA) would not release such an asset without compensation any more than a private party would. The MTA in fact had plans to develop the site, and use the revenues to finance capital improvements for public transportation.[5] The $1.1 billion figure was completely inadequate on the day the HOK proposal was announced.

An additional complication was that the city had only recently failed in an attempt to build Westway, an extensive highway and park system along the Hudson River in Manhattan. The project died through protracted opposition that challenged every permit, license, variance, and exception that the developers needed. Many construction projects nowadays are defeated, not on their merits, but by administrative and judicial filibuster, endless deliberation in administrative agencies and the courts that ultimately makes the costs of the projects prohibitive.

Ed Koch later recalled the final blow to Westway: "There the environmentalists alleged the rotted Hudson piers—which would have been removed to build Westway—were needed to help the striped bass propagate. I offered to build the fish a motel in Poughkeepsie to assist them in their assignations, but the federal court found for the fish."[6]

HOK never mentioned the striped bass in their report, and their description of the site as having a "significant transit opportunity" is a puzzle. Westway had been blocked because of fears about the resulting congestion. Now a building would be constructed whose purpose would be to attract over three million people to a single city block in a six-month period each and every year. Subway extensions were considered, but they would be guaranteed to trigger the fury of other commuters who would want the resources committed to alleviating the burden of being packed into overcrowded cars during rush hour every day. Litigation would have been certain, meaning that the $1.1 billion proposed costs would have an additional and unpredictable expense even after the site acquisition fee had been determined. New York City could repeat the fiscal fiasco of the Lindsay and Beame administrations.

Richard Sandomir reported additional problems in the *New York Times*.[7] Debt repayment would either require unrealistic taxes or significant channeling of the revenue stream that, one assumes, had attracted Steinbrenner in the first place. The dilemma for the West Side stadium advocates was that the crowds that would be needed for Yankee games, football games, and other events would have to be so great that they would create the very traffic problems that had so many people already alarmed.

The HOK report had been gathering dust for a couple of years until April 13, 1998, when a beam gave way at the Stadium, crushing the seats below. A tragedy was averted because no game was under way and no one was near the site of the accident. The participants in the stadium game had been preparing to play again, and the accident drew public attention to the issue. Mayor Giuliani revived the idea of a new stadium for the Yankees on Manhattan's West Side, but opponents were ready.

On the very day that the beam fell, Fernando Ferrer, the Bronx Borough President, offered his counter to the HOK proposal. Ferrer called for a new Metro North station, more parking, better highway access, and a kind of theme restaurant and sports district that would serve as an economic engine for the area. The old Bronx Terminal Market would be sacrificed in the venture. This "Yankee Village" plan would cost $488 million, of which $372 million would be provided by New York City, $25 million by the federal government, $19 million by the state, and $72 million from private sources.[8] The report's recommendations were dismissed out of hand by Mayor Giuliani, who, at the time, was still committed to the West Side proposal.

In terms of Yankee Stadium and the public interest, New Yorkers were offered two choices: (1) a plan that would commit over $1 billion from unknown sources to build a stadium on land that had not been acquired in a venture of unlimited possibilities for litigation; and (2) spending $372 million of city tax money to upgrade the existing site in the Bronx.

The New York City Independent Budget Office released a report, *Double Play: The Economics and Financing of Stadiums for the Yankees and Mets*, shortly after the accident at the stadium. The eighteen-page report concluded that the city was in a good position to negotiate a sensible stadium deal with both its major league franchises because of its preeminence as a media center. It further concluded that suburban fans who visited Shea and Yankee Stadiums provided a small contribution to the city treasury, but that the amount of money they represented did not justify more than a very limited commitment of public funds to any stadium project. Finally, the report noted that a national trend in stadium construction was relying increasingly on substantial contributions from the ball club to pay for a new stadium.

At City Hall, Comptroller Alan Hevesi pledged to block the sale of city bonds if they were to be used to pay for a new stadium in Manhattan. He told the *New York Post* that new stadiums for the Yankees and Mets were legitimate undertakings because of the money that is generated for the city. "Having said that, when I hear a billion-dollar figure being floated, my eyebrows become raised. A billion dollars for the city is very problematical because that is a huge amount of debt. The city's annual debt service is higher than it is supposed to be, and we have huge capital needs, including a school-overcrowding problem that hasn't been adequately dealt with."[9]

In Jack Newfield's column in the same issue of the *Post*, he added more reasons why the West Side stadium proposal should be rejected. Newfield referred to a recent poll that found over 80 percent of the public wanted the Yankees to remain in the Bronx. He added that the city had more pressing needs for the money, that environmental issues would delay the project endlessly, and that it lacked the needed political support.

George Steinbrenner finally weighed in. The Yankees were back from a 7–1 road trip that brought their record to 25–7 in the middle of May. A crowd of 16,006 made it to the Stadium on a Tuesday night to see the Yankees play the Royals, and Steinbrenner took the opportunity to hammer his point to the *Daily News*. "Why should we be sixth in the American League in attendance? You can't say we haven't put a good product on the field. I don't know if Mr. Ferrer was there Tuesday night, but maybe he can explain why we're drawing bigger crowds on the road than we are at home."[10]

Clint Roswell, a spokesman for Ferrer, offered the explanation: twelve straight days of rain that flooded the city and temperatures in the forties. Roswell added that attendance picks up when the weather warms, school ends, and the pennant races heat up.

In Steinbrenner's analysis, only one explanation was possible for the lagging attendance. "If I didn't put a good product on the field, then I'd take the blame. The fact is we have a $72 million payroll, we paid another $8 million in revenue sharing and we spent $24.5 million in scouting and player development this year. If it's not the Bronx, then what is it?"[11]

Dean Chadwin offered another explanation in his book, *Those Damn Yankees*: For the attendance figures that Steinbrenner wants, his ticket prices are too high.[12] Chadwin compared the Yankee ticket scale with that of the Dodgers after they were acquired by Ruppert Murdoch. The top price at Dodger Stadium in 1998 was $14 for a field box seat. The equivalent seat in Yankee Stadium was $45. A loge box seat went for $12 in Los Angeles, but it too was $45 in the Bronx. Most other types of seats were at least twice as much at Yankee Stadium, with only the bleachers being comparable. As Chadwin concludes, "Steinbrenner clearly does not want to maximize the number of people at the games, and he has no right to complain when raw attendance data shows he's losing to his competitors. Those numbers mean nothing out of context. Given a ticket price more than twice as high, Steinbrenner drained much more money out of the pockets of Yankee fans than Rupert Murdoch sucked from Dodger faithful during 1998."[13] All of that in the middle of a twelve-year half-billion-dollar cable deal.

As spring turned to summer in 1998, the stadium game centered on two issues. One was the charge that Yankee Stadium was inadequate to the needs of the historic franchise that was playing perhaps its greatest season. Closely related but critically distinct from that charge was Steinbrenner's insistence that the fundamental problem with the Stadium was its location. In other words, the city could make the Stadium as splendid as it wanted, but people might still stay away because going to a Yankee game meant taking a trip to the Bronx.

As the stadium game was played in New York, Steinbrenner's harshest critics were ready to lavish nearly $400 million of the public's money on the Stadium, so the debate about public policy and the Stadium would not be about the propriety of taxpayer money subsidizing this business. The argument instead would involve the proper location for Yankee Stadium, and that was an issue that worked against Steinbrenner and Giuliani.

The tactic that focused the debate was a proposal by City Council Speaker Peter Vallone to put the HOK proposal on the ballot in the November elections. Vallone would be the Democratic candidate for governor that year, and the referendum was a way to boost his campaign with the popular position of keeping the Yankees in the Bronx. Giuliani employed an old trick of New York governing: dueling charter commissions. Under New York state law, in the event that a city legislative body proposes ballot referenda, the proposals are rescinded if a mayoral charter commission proposes measures of its own. Giuliani denounced Vallone's efforts as a political stunt for his governor's race. He also decried the complication that a referendum would represent. "I think the calculation was he felt he would get 100,000 more votes if he put this on the ballot. So to create a difficult problem in a very sensitive negotiation which this will no doubt do, for a city that has had a terrible record of keeping sports teams, just in order to get yourself 100,000 votes on the ballot seems to me the wrong thing to do."[14]

Vallone rebutted that the taxpayers had a right to determine how their money is spent. He wrote in the *Daily News*, "I believe that the prospect of moving the Yankees to another borough, particularly Manhattan, raises so many complex issues—from basic quality of life to traffic to financing—that the city must give the taxpayers a chance to have a say."[15]

The ballot referendum has become increasingly important in the stadium game. If voters approve the financial plan that spends their money on stadiums, we must assume that the public interest has been served. Perhaps the voters made a mistake, but it is *their* mistake, not that of their representatives. And referenda are not easy to come by in New York. The state never entirely embraced the Progressive Movement of the late nineteenth century, especially reforms that put governing power directly in the hands of the people. Referenda are possible in New York, but only if elected officials promote them. The additional tool of ballot initiative—citizens themselves putting referenda on the ballot—is not available in New York, so, if the taxpayers are to protect themselves against a second stadium deal that breaks every budgetary constraint without securing the Yankees, elected public officials will have to agree to let them.

In the case of Yankee Stadium, the battle over the proposed referendum wound up in court and, in the middle of the litigation on July 12, 1998, Steinbrenner graced the front page of the Sunday *Daily News*. A combative photograph accompanied the headline "The Boss Warns City: Don't Force Me Out." Steinbrenner compared his situation to that of the Brooklyn Dodgers and he warned that the city would lose the Yankees if they were singled out for a ballot referendum on public assistance for a new stadium.

Through a phone interview from his home in Tampa, Steinbrenner grimly noted that sports history might be repeating itself for New York. He lumped together the Dodgers, Giants, Jets, and NFL Giants, as if all the franchises had left the city for the same reason. When informed that polls indicated strong public support for keeping the Yankees in the Bronx, Steinbrenner replied, "Time and time again these polls have been run, and people have left New York."[16] He took exception to being singled out in the poll while the Mets were also looking for a new stadium, but the HOK proposal was itself limited to a new home for the Yankees.

He specifically warned Vallone that he could suffer electoral retribution if he were identified as the man who lost the Yankees. Steinbrenner insisted that this was not a threat, merely a reading of sports history, and again recited the litany of lost franchises.

Jim Dwyer covers city politics for the *Daily News*, and he took on the comparison that Steinbrenner drew with Walter O'Malley, "If George Steinbrenner wishes to stand up today and say I, like the Brookyn Dodgers, am willing to use my funds to pay for this thing, then the whole discussion is over. He can build any place he wants. He has no intention of spending his own cash because he has been spoiled rotten for the past 26 years. He is more dependent on government than all the welfare mothers in New York."[17]

Mike Lupica of the *New York Daily News* may be the most widely read sports columnist in town, and he regularly has blasted George Steinbrenner and Mayor Rudolph Giuliani for their eagerness to build a new stadium for the Yankees at public expense. Lupica reacted to Steinbrenner's interview in his column in that same edition. "Why does he want a new ballpark? He is exactly like Giuliani in this regard: He wants what he wants when he wants it. This has nothing to do with the Yankees, or the future of the Yankees, or their ability to compete, or the quality of life in this city. This is about the greed of the Yankee owner and the arrogance of the mayor. They have pushed people around their whole public lives and don't stop now."[18]

The *Daily News*, the *Times*, other newspapers, and electronic media have made a lot of money over the years covering the Yankees, but they have not rolled over and performed as boosters for the new stadium. They analyze the reports of economists about the poor public returns on taxes invested in stadiums, set the record straight on the Dodgers' move, and remind their readers and viewers about other needs that the city faces.

New York City has thriving sports media in every aspect of the industry. Teams are represented in every major sport, and the tradition of journalists as stars in their own right traces to Damon Runyon, Haywood Broun, and other scribes of the early twentieth century. To its credit, the media have been remarkably thoughtful about the stadium game in the case of the Yankees. In that vein, Lupica bluntly offered an assessment of Steinbrenner's tactic:

This is all a con, here and anywhere else where Steinbrenner goes to run it up the flagpole. And you have to call him out on it, every time, even when the material isn't worth the ink.

Because if you believe that anybody is forcing Steinbrenner to do anything, if you believe this is about anything but his own greed, then you are exactly the kind of sucker he is looking for. Steinbrenner is trying to play the whole town for a sucker and so is Rudolph Giuliani, the mayor of Steinbrenner.

They want you to believe that building a new ballpark for George Steinbrenner is the civic duty of all good New Yorkers. And it certainly is not.

Don't force me out? Is he kidding? He is going to break the all-time Yankee home attendance record this year. He has one of the great Yankee teams in history, and one of the most expensive. He is running away from the rest of baseball. He has taken a $2 million investment of his own money 25 years ago and has parlayed it into a ballclub now conservatively worth $500 million.

He has the biggest local television contract in the history of the known universe, one that will only get bigger when the Yankees become a television free agent. This guy acts as if he is the one facing Armageddon here, when he is flush. This is all phony even for him.[19]

When Randy Levine, former advisor to the major league owners, left his position as Deputy Mayor under Giuliani to become president of the Yankees under Steinbrenner, Lupica wrote, "It is now completely official that Steinbrenner's private box at the Stadium has become an annex to Giuliani's City Hall."[20] He added in the none-too-gentle style his readers love: "Levine was barred from city dealings with the Yankees or Mets, both of which are looking for hundreds of millions in taxpayer handouts to build new stadiums. Apparently, this meant that Steinbrenner could bounce Giuliani on his knee during Yankee games, but not Levine."[21]

Lupica's writing is a great example of a sports column in modern times. He flays the powerful and privileged when they get too full of themselves, and does it in a style that is sure to please the fans who love the games and have to struggle to pay to see them. Lupica's approach complements the work that Richard Sandomir and others had been doing at the *Times*. As Dick Young and other writers did in the 1970s, Lupica, Dwyer, Sandomir, and their colleagues do now: They put the stadium issue before the public in unvarnished terms.

In a review of the Stadium negotiations in December 1999, Sandomir proclaimed the West Side project dead and suggested that the ideal moment for the Yankees to strike a deal may have passed.[22] The assumption had been that Steinbrenner would get his best offer from the Giuliani administration. The mayor's attention was first deflected by a brief run for the U.S. Senate, then by health and other personal problems. The one bold initiative for the Yankees appears to have been the HOK proposal that never had a serious chance.

The New Jersey threat receded when Governor Christine Todd Whitman declared that her state would not contribute public money to a new baseball stadium. Her determination was supported by polls that indicated a decided lack of enthusiasm among New Jersey residents to lure the Yankees across the Hudson River. New York was left negotiating against itself, and the advocates for the West Side site were hopelessly outnumbered.

Sandomir concluded that Steinbrenner could exercise one of two five-year options under the current lease. That may happen, but it is a long way from resolving the outstanding questions. Steinbrenner is seventy years old, and he has his hands full reconfiguring the ownership of the Yankees. After resisting a strong ownership bid from Cablevision, Steinbrenner improved his position in 1999 by forming a holding company consisting of the Yankees and the New Jersey Nets of the National Basketball Association. The *Daily News* reported that "the new YankeeNets could spark a bidding war that could pull in $1 billion for ten years for cable rights—especially if they buy a hockey team as well, some analysts estimated."[23]

Although the Wrigleys and the O'Malleys eventually found family ownership imprudent despite their location in large markets, Steinbrenner appears determined to keep control of the operation. His expansion into other major professional sports, and possibly the creation of his own television business, could expand his base of operations to withstand any commercial reverses. When the ownership questions are settled, when the various responsibilities are determined for running the different franchises, Steinbrenner will likely return to the stadium game for one last attempt to secure that part of his legacy.

Sandomir concludes that the next mayor is likely to be a Democrat and "unlikely to be as generous with the Yankees" as Giuliani has been.[24] But the history of the Stadium tells us that it was the liberal John Lindsay, who wound up a Democrat, who fashioned the public renovation of the 1970s. Governor Mario Cuomo, a great Democratic hope during the Reagan years, was one of the first to propose the West Side site in 1993. And Democrats on the City Council had no hesitation to extend an important indirect subsidy to the Yankees just in the past few years.

Although hardly in a position to need financial help, Steinbrenner received some anyway from the city of New York. In 1999, the City Council, including Speaker Vallone, voted to spend $76 million to build a minor league ballpark in Staten Island for a Yankee farm team. Jim Dwyer pointed out that "the city will spend more money on this one palatial ballpark than has been spent for all public school sports for the last 10 years put together."[25] He characterized it as "a $76 million summer jobs program for Hal (Son of) Steinbrenner and 25 teenagers from Arizona and Florida."[26]

The vote in the City Council was 39 to 5 in favor of the project. Michael Carey, son of the former New York governor, presented the measure to the Council on behalf of the Giuliani administration, and he assured the legislators that the project would "more than pay for itself." The Yankees' lease runs only three years after which, they could leave; then, under the rules of major league baseball and its antitrust exemption, the Yankees could bar any other minor league franchise from using the facility.

The Staten Island deal indicates that the political culture of New York has no problem with subsidizing the Yankees with taxpayer money. Many financial experts may have found no way to make the numbers add up on the West Side, but the concept of transferring money from middle-class entrepreneurs and blue-collar workers to an immensely profitable entertainment business does not offend the city's sensibilities. Anyone who reads the sports sections of the daily newspapers would have all the necessary information to make an informed judgment, so one can only conclude that the largesse is in accord with public opinion.

The Staten Island stadium and one proposed for Coney Island for a Mets' minor league are relatively small facilities that are unlikely to create the kinds of traffic nightmares that helped frustrate the HOK proposal. They represent, nevertheless, a sizeable indirect subsidy to businesses that manifestly do not need them. In that respect, these transfer payments are a puzzle in this political age.

Both political parties have insisted that only people in dire circumstances, not of their own making, have a legitimate claim on the public purse. People who milk public assistance have been disdained from the time the programs were first created, and they now face serious restructuring of many of those same programs to protect the treasury from un-warranted claims. At the very point that our patience is exhausted at the prospect of giving people money that they do not deserve, we continue to lavish hard-earned money on sports owners so that they can continue to disguise their hobbies as businesses and run them in thoroughly reck-less ways.

STADIUM WELFARE, POLITICS, AND THE PUBLIC INTEREST

T he history of Yankee Stadium leads to several important conclusions about public policy and the business of professional
baseball. These lessons can help New Yorkers and taxpayers in
other cities to determine if their public officials are effectively representing their interests.

The first point that can be held with near certainty is that an economic investment in a stadium will not be returned. Like other cities in
America, New York has taken the responsibility of financing baseball
stadiums for its major league teams on the grounds that the investment
will be returned through the economic stimulus that the games will
generate. This argument has been applied in every city that has spent
money on stadiums, but it remains unpersuasive to the economists who
have studied the returns on stadiums.

In classic public works projects, government invests capital in enterprises that subsequently serve many individual firms. The Erie Canal,
Hoover Dam, and the Saturn rocket all lacked a single economic actor
with an incentive to invest massive resources in the expectation of a
profitable return, but those projects promised widespread economic

prosperity and opportunity to the community or an important intangible benefit like a symbolic victory in the Cold War. Publicly financed stadiums have been promoted as public works, but one economic study after another has failed to find the promised commercial returns.

Andrew Zimbalist and Roger Noll are economists who have studied the effects of publicly financed stadiums. They have compiled the work of a number of their colleagues in sports economics and have added their own helpful analysis.[1] Their work removes any inclination to think that New York's stadium follies are unique to that city. Admittedly, New York received a pounding in the national media during the fiscal crisis for its allegedly irresponsible spending programs, but the economic analyses of independent scholars demonstrate that the stadium game often is played badly, even in the cities that scorn New York.

Zimbalist and Noll focus on the same point that Alan Brinkley raised about the shift to an economy that grows through consumer demand. They conclude that, from an economic perspective, the impact of a stadium and sports franchise is not insignificant. They write that "a classic example of an investment that can provide valuable public consumption benefits is a park."[2] They explain that parks serve a dual purpose of providing recreation or entertainment for their visitors while also preserving a place of natural beauty or cultural significance. They add that the argument for sports facilities is similar to that for parks because, apart from economic returns, many people value having a sports franchise in town, so the authors maintain, "the notion that a sports team provides significant public consumption benefits is not frivolous."[3] They persuasively establish that the sports franchise has a relatively small economic impact on its community, falling far short, for example, of the economic benefits of a private university. "Nevertheless," they claim, "it would be inaccurate to conclude from these figures that major league team sports are unimportant."[4]

Noll and Zimbalist point out that sports attract many consumers who follow the games without necessarily attending them. Newspaper, cable, satellite, and broadcast coverage allow many people to develop an allegiance to a team without "consuming" the entertainment by paying for it. The authors stress that comparing tangible economic costs against amorphous benefits is a very uncertain proposition, but they acknowledge that enough people may be sufficiently enthusiastic about having a team that a public subsidy will be politically popular.

Their analysis stretches the comparison between parks and stadiums too far. An obvious distinction is that park rangers are not paid millions of dollars a year. Baseball, like the rest of the sports industry, generates enough revenue to pay for its own facilities, but that money does not go to finance a modern stadium. Instead, the revenues pay player salaries. In a reprise of Lindsay economics, money that could pay for capital improvements is diverted to operations.

Dennis Zimmerman has examined stadium financing in terms of the tax implications of the investment. This perspective focuses indirect costs such as the deductions on federal income taxes that bond holders are allowed. Zimmerman also describes the intricate ways that stadium boosters have tried to elude several attempts to limit public financing of stadiums. Addressing the propriety of the current tax structure, he has written:

> The benefit principle of taxation requires that those who benefit
> from a public expenditure should pay for it. The studies by propo-
> nents of publicly financed stadiums emphasize the income that a sta-
> dium generates. These benefits are vastly overstated as net benefits to
> the community, but they do represent rough approximations of the
> gross benefits to businesses associated with sports: the team, the con-
> cession suppliers, some nearby local businesses, and businesses that
> buy season tickets as a means of increasing their own sales.[5]

Zimmerman concludes that the benefit principle of taxation is ignored in the case of stadiums—meaning that the burden is not borne by the beneficiaries. Making matter worse, tax-exempt bonds require some kind of compensating levy on the general population to offset the revenues lost through the bonds.

Zimmerman's point is especially important because it establishes that the public subsidy is a fundamentally different type of consumption than we would see in a stadium that is privately financed. To say that Walter O'Malley, for example, paid for Dodger Stadium himself is not entirely accurate. Ultimately, the public paid for Dodger Stadium, but it did so voluntarily through the purchase of tickets, concessions, parking, and products that were advertised on Dodger broadcasts. The money that O'Malley advanced was his own, but he did so in the full expectation that it would be returned many times through the team's fans. The Dodgers owner had to compete with the rest of the entertainment market in southern California and that helped to improve the product that fans consumed.

As Zimmerman demonstrates, the people who benefit most directly from stadiums financed through government do not bear the burden of paying for the facility. The public that picks up the tab does so through the compulsion of taxation rather than the free choice to go to a ball game instead of the movies. This compulsion by law raises serious questions about the propriety of the stadium game. At their worst, publicly financed stadiums represent a luxury for the privileged, paid for largely by the middle class, in communities that often neglect essential needs of the helpless. Even limiting the impact to more fortunate members of society, sports fans who support or permit the public financing of stadiums may price themselves out of the building. The current meaning of obsolescence as applied to sports facilities is that the building lacks a sufficient number of luxury boxes. By cooperating with the construction of a replacement facility, taxpayers may limit themselves to watching games on television.

Among the alleged beneficiaries of stadium subsidies that Zimmerman counts are businesses in the vicinity of the stadium: bars, restaurants, and souvenir stands are the obvious examples. Robert Baade and Allen Sanderson, leading economists of stadium effects, put that impact in perspective. "Individuals and families have limited leisure budgets, defined in terms both of time and money. Money spent on watching professional sports events is money not spent on other leisure activities. In practice, many subsidy supporters have neglected, in some instances ignored, this substitution effect, with the result that estimates of the benefits to having a team or the costs of losing one are in many cases biased."[6]

Baade and Sanderson's work shows that stadiums actually can have a negative economic effect on parts of a community. The restaurant near the movie theater can lose customers who pass up a film to take in a ball game. Another restaurant may benefit, but wealth is not being created by the stadium so much as it is being diverted from one place to another.

This point is supported by James Quirk and Rodney D. Fort who write that "any money spent on attending a sports event means there is less available to spend on alternatives, such as movies, plays, concerts, VCR rentals, and the like. And decreases in spending on these other activities produce direct and indirect expenditures losses for city businesses to offset in part or in whole any expenditures benefits associated with the team or the facility."[7] In other words, in making the case for public financing of stadiums, counting only the economic gains in the immediate area of the stadium is inaccurate. At least some losses will occur elsewhere in the entertainment economy of the city, and, even though such losses are difficult to quantify, they are just as real to the community as the benefits.

Financial analysts have argued the details of the Yankees' lease obligations with the city of New York, but a lesson from Sherlock Holmes may be more instructive. The dog who didn't bark in this case is the person with compelling information that the city has benefited from its investment of thirty years ago. No such person has been heard from in the time since John Lindsay cut his deal with CBS. As the lease nears its expiration, we hear how important it has been to the city that the Yankees have been here, but we have no clear evidence that spending over $100 million of the public's money has been a prudent investment that has been returned to us in economic growth.

If New Yorkers will not enjoy an economic return on their investment, what should they look for as the basis for entering another public stadium deal with the Yankees? The real reason New York and other cities pursue these stadium ventures is a sense of civic pride. Economic arguments are trotted out for public consumption, but not in a way that is persuasive. When pressed by critics for solid data on the stadium's financing or when asked about the urgency of competing claims for public resources, the boosters quickly shift their stance.

These advocates retreat to vanity: We are a major league city, and we need a major league sports franchise to demonstrate that fact. Mark Rosentraub of Indiana University has studied the stadium game and he addresses its civic dimension bluntly. "Why do citizens accept and support the subsidies provided to teams? The emotional attachment to sports, cultivated by institutions that also profit from sports, has clouded their judgment and established a set of unrealistic priorities."[8]

Rosentraub does not condemn sports as frivolous, but he is persuasive that, at the professional level, teams profit by marketing a variety of cultural echoes. Our language, politics, and mythology celebrate the games as opportunities for displaying virtue. In addition, sports often offer compelling entertainment, especially when played by world-class athletes. Propelling the enthusiasm, a very popular communication industry has grown up around the games. Sports programs marble together news, entertainment, and opinion. In the format of call-in radio: Report the essential facts of an upcoming game; intereview a coach or athlete about the contest; open the phone lines for the furious reactions of fans.

This passionate commitment to the home team is what Rosentraub describes as clouded judgment. As communities, we become convinced that we simply must have the games, that we are a poorer place without them, that the rejection of our fair town by a sports owner is an indictment of the very place in which we raise our children. Because the number of teams is artificially low, we become ever more desperate to secure one of the scarce franchises and we make a public choice that may not serve our public interest.

Data from the Board of Education for New York City indicate that, during the five years from FY 1994 through FY 1998, the city spent a total of $59,949,541 for high school sports.[9] For some high school football players, the money falls short of even basic requirements. The *Daily News* reported that the Manhattan Center High School team practices at a neighborhood park that must be cleared of dog feces before they can practice.[10] They play their home games at Adlai Stevenson High School in the Bronx, but a sinkhole developed in a game there. The *News* reports, "School officials acknowledge that many high school fields are in poor shape, but they say they must contend with more pressing problems such as overcrowded classrooms and leaking roofs."[11]

Public budgets are perhaps the most tangible expression of the values of a community. If money is available to subsidize professional teams that are enormously successful, how can it not be available to provide safe and decent facilities for teenagers who play for the city's schools? As long as the city loses money in its operation of its stadium business, the inevitable conclusion is that schoolchildren subsidize professional athletes and owners by playing under substandard conditions while professional playgrounds are maintained to the highest standards.

If the stadium game is bad economic policy and a bad public choice, it also represents a public policy that has become almost thoroughly discredited across the political spectrum. Welfare is a term with strong negative connotations and all of them fit the public assistance that has poured into Yankee Stadium. We normally think of welfare as aid to poor people, some of them deserving of help and others not. If we broaden the concept to think of welfare as the transfer of money from one social class to another, we can see how the pathologies that are ascribed to welfare fit the renovation of the Stadium.

This indictment is summarized by Milton and Rose Friedman in their very popular book *Free to Choose*, a work published in 1979, a year before Ronald Reagan's rout of Jimmy Carter:

The defects of our present system have become widely recognized. The relief rolls grow despite growing affluence. A vast bureaucracy is largely devoted to shuffling papers rather than to serving people. Once people get on relief, it is hard to get off. The country is increasingly divided into two classes of citizens, one receiving relief and the other paying for it. Those on relief have little incentive to earn income. Relief payments vary widely from one part of the country to another, which encourages migration from the South and the rural areas to the North, and particularly to the urban centers. Persons who are or have been on relief are treated differently from those who have not been on relief (the so-called working poor) though both may be on the same econonic level. Public anger is repeatedly stirred by wide-spread corruption and cheating, well-publicized reports of welfare "queens" driving around in Cadillacs bought with multiple relief checks.[12]

The Friedmans' outrage approaches hysteria, and the remark about "welfare queens and Cadillacs" is embarrassing for its racial overtones. The critique, however, cannot be dismissed entirely. Milton Friedman is a Nobel Prize winner in economics, and his public arguments have been a significant part of the country's discussion of domestic policy. The target of the Friedmans' attack was welfare as it is traditionally understood, aid intended to help the poor but that often corrupts or is taken by those who do not need the help. Stadium welfare fits the accusation better than any abuse of food stamps ever did, and we see this when we take this conservative attack on welfare point by point as it applies to the Yankees and major league baseball.

The Friedmans begin by asserting that welfare grows despite a strong economy. The public assistance that the Yankees received has been spread over thirty years of unprecedented prosperity for the franchise. George Steinbrenner and his partners bought the Yankees for $10 million in 1975, and in 1999 they could have sold the team to Cablevision for somewhere between half a billion and a billion dollars. Attendance finally reached 3,000,000 in 1999 despite a drumbeat of negative news about the Bronx coming from the Yankees themselves. The television package is unprecedented in the sport, yet the Yankees demand that the city government compel its citizens to subsidize a new stadium.

The Friedmans claim next that public officials focus on the dance steps of process rather than the public interest. They object to bureaucratic paper-pushing, and the comparable point in the stadium game is the incredible opportunity costs of having public officials so engaged.

The paper trail in the Lindsay administration indicates that virtually every major official in the city was in the loop on the renovation of the Stadium. Significant time has been committed in subsequent administrations to figure out how to keep the Yankees happy after the lease expires in 2002.

All these resources of time, energy, and imagination were diverted from other public needs. Stabilizing the city's finances, reversing a growing crime rate, stopping the loss of entry-level jobs, adjusting the school system to account for new challenges, promoting new capital projects in transportation, devising ways to alleviate the growing racial tensions—all these issues became acute problems in New York City during the years its government figured out how to rebuild Yankee Stadium at public expense.

A third count in the Friedmans' indictment is that welfare promotes dependency. At no point in the renovation of Yankee Stadium is there any evidence that CBS or George Steinbrenner ever considered assuming responsibility for the stadium. Jake Ruppert never seems to have thought that the city owed him a stadium. Not even Jimmy Walker could stretch his imagination for the irresponsible that far. In the middle of the Roaring Twenties, Walker never did what Lindsay did during the growing fiscal crisis: approach the Yankee owner with an offer to buy the facility and maintain it in prime condition. Nothing suggests that Ruppert would have been open to such an offer. Like Walter O'Malley, Ruppert saw the Stadium as an essential part of his business, not an expense related to his hobby. Now, as the lease expires, Yankee officials insist on their need for a new facility, but they never discuss satisfying the need themselves.

Fourth, the Friedmans contend that public assistance divides society into providers and recipients. This point has never quite matured in the various complaints about the stadium game, but it is a critical one. Simply put, in 1970, the Yankees were in exactly the same situation that confronts most businesses at one point or another: Their shop was in need of repair or replacement. All over the city, business owners have been faced with the same problem. The difference between the Yankees and these other entrepreneurs is the city's reaction.

In some cases, the city will try to lure businesses with tax breaks or other considerations, but the Yankees are unique for having the city offer to buy their facility, renovate it at public expense, and lease it back on extremely favorable terms. The help that the Yankees received is not offered to small businesses that struggle with limited or deteriorating storefronts. Those business owners are expected to overcome through their own wit and initiative or be ruined by pitiless market forces.

Fifth, the aid corrupts by sapping the work ethic. Welfare becomes morally corroding when recipients forgo employment for public assistance. This effect can be one of the most disheartening and frustrating of all the problems commonly associated with welfare. Does even this corruption appear in baseball? Indeed it does. The evidence can be found in player salaries, the reaction of the owners to them, and in the purposes for which owners acquire franchises. In today's business, the people in the front offices work very hard under great pressure to keep payroll down and generate revenue wherever possible, but one factor has changed considerably. The stadium game means that the front office is playing with house money.

Next, welfare encourages instability by inducing movement to more generous communities. The Welfare Reform Act of 1996 reflected such alarm about people coming to America to secure public assistance that it barred immigrants from receiving aid. Similar concerns have sparked resentments in American cities about "outsiders" moving in to enjoy the bounty that had been intended for the deserving neighbors.

Of all the major sports, baseball has been the most stable in the past few decades. Franchise movements have been discouraged as clubs are sold rather than uprooted, but the Yankee case shows that actual movement does not exhaust the story. The *threat* to move has been important in the Yankees' dealing with the city. The club has not actually moved since it left Baltimore in 1903, but the threat has served the purpose of generating public assistance in the 1970s with the promise of additional help today.

Cities do not foster rivalries over the quality of their homeless shelters, libraries, health clinics, and subways. Instead, they attract millions of dollars of media coverage establishing themselves as superior communities because of the performance of one of their private entertainment businesses over a short season or a single championship day.

Finally, it is argued that the public becomes disgusted and cynical about the abuse of their generosity. The Friedmans invoke the noxious stereotype of the "welfare queen" and they are correct that the public fiercely resents the abuse of its assistance. In New York and other cities, fans may be connecting the dots to discover that their disgust with strikes, lockouts, obnoxious players and owners, assorted lawsuits, and other pollutants of the sports pages ultimately reflect, to some degree, the infusion of hundreds of millions of dollars of public largesse that neither players nor owners have earned.

Applying the term *welfare* to the public support of stadiums can seem inflammatory because of the intense emotions that surround policies that fit this type of public spending. Transfer payments flowing from the prosperous to the needy have been hailed as humane and wise investments in our future; they have also been condemned as handouts to the lazy and irresponsible. Few domestic issues generate as much furor as the public responsibility to the poor.

The sources of this powerful emotion are worth a brief look because they suggest that the contention about the issue is not likely to abate. Max Weber, among others, has argued that important links can be found between Protestantism and the essentials of capitalism.[13] Self-reliance, sacrifice, prudence, determination, honesty, thrift—these are moral values that can lead to wealth. The so-called work ethic is widely celebrated in the American economic tradition. In some cultures, begging is an acceptable way to make a living. In the United States, the practice is a scandal that, depending on the passerby, invites scorn for either the beggar or those believed to be responsible for his or her condition.

When applied to sports, this ethic assumes even greater significance. In Carl Prince's study of the Brooklyn Dodgers, he pointed to the implicit sexual themes in baseball. "Physical challenge and response, redemption of the male ego, attempts to intimidate, to provide a failure of manhood."[14] These qualities of toughness, self-reliance, and giving no quarter are part of the culture of business as well as sports. Yet the public financing of stadiums corrupts that standard by removing the threat of ruin from a privileged group of business owners, the very factor that compels them to do their best.

The flip side of the work ethic is that people who are poor are themselves to blame. They are lazy, shiftless, self-indulgent, inclined to drink, take drugs, or be sexually promiscuous. The constant image is of fat, stupid, lazy, dissolute adults surrounded by a swarm of doomed children. The details of this image vary little by ethnicity. Thomas Nast drew the Irish this way in the nineteenth century, and various media have passed the stereotypes through other ethnic and racial groups down to our own day.

The Depression forced a limited suspension of this moral derision. With so many people impoverished, the weak individual explanation was overwhelmed by the masses in need. Economics and sociology replaced morality as the means for explaining the crisis. For the first time in American history, care for the poor became a permanent federal or national responsibility.

The economic crisis of the 1930s was sufficiently grave to force new policies, but it could not completely lift the stigma that attached to asking for help. Simply put, welfare was shameful. To be on relief was to admit the most profound and personal kind of defeat. Many Americans had become accustomed to some kind of confession in their religious practices, but admitting sin in a community of sinners was a different proposition from admitting failure in feeding oneself and one's family. As Roosevelt historian William E. Leuchtenburg has written, "To be unemployed in an industrial society is the equivalent of banishment and excommunication."[15]

Tammany welfare operated as a kind of market: You traded your vote for economic help. The Depression forced a new exchange, one far more bitter. As Leuchtenburg has noted,

> The failure of the First National Bank in one Midwestern town forced twelve families on the county. When the bank collapsed, one woman, shouting and sobbing , beat on the closed plate-glass doors;

all of her savings from a quarter of a century making rag rugs had vanished. A woman who had taught the fourth grade for fifty-two years lost every penny she had set aside for her old age. Thousands of hardworking, thrifty people now had no alternative but to make their way to the relief office. "It took me a month," said an Alabama lumberman. "I used to go down there every day or so and walk past the place again and again."[16]

The new exchange demanded self-respect for public assistance. No economic or social theory could alleviate the shame that most people felt in asking their neighbors for help in this thoroughly impersonal way. Nothing but the most desperate economic conditions could compel the application for relief. Experience with a welfare state in Germany, England, and other nations only made the embarrassment more acute. Relief was understandable in the land of one's forebears, but, by that very fact, it was effectively un-American.

Studs Terkel's oral history of the Depression includes other descriptions of the price of asking for help:

I finally went on relief. It's an experience I don't want anybody to go through. It comes as close to crucifixion as . . . You sit in an auditorium and are given a number. The interview was utterly ridiculous and mortifying. In the middle of mine, a more dramatic guy than I dived from the second floor stairway, head first, to demonstrate he was gonna get on relief even if he had to go to the hospital to do it.[17]

Another of the people that Terkel interviewed remembered:

I didn't want to go on relief. Believe me, when I was forced to go to the office of the relief, the tears were running out of my eyes. I couldn't bear myself to take money from anybody for nothing. If it wasn't for those kids—I tell you the truth—many a time it came to my mind to go commit suicide. Than to go ask for relief. But somebody has to take care of those kids.[18]

The shame that tortured so many of the recipients of welfare stemmed from their sense that they were violating one of the basic American tenets: self-reliance. Terkel's interviews, including some with social workers, indicate that public assistance generally was granted only after an embarrassing inquiry into the merits of a plea. Why can't you make it on your own? Why are you out of work? Why don't you sell something? Why doesn't your family help you? Homes were visited. Closets inspected. The most personal and intimate aspects of life were scrutinized—all to determine that the public's money was not being spent on people who had resources of their own.

While the Giuliani administration has worked to help the Yankees, recipients of other forms of public assistance have seen a different face of city government. In December 1998, the Giuliani welfare strategy was the focus of a front-page article in the *New York Times* Magazine. In establishing his core principles on the subject, the mayor is quoted that "from 1960 to 1994, the work ethic was under attack in New York City. New York City viewed welfare as a good thing, as a wonderful thing. They romanticized it and embraced a philosophy of dependency, almost as if it's better to have somebody on welfare than to help somebody to work."[19]

The mayor's determination to move people to some kind of employment is described in the article as total. "What Giuliani does mean in a surprisingly literal sense is that the obligation applies to *everybody*: the armies of women with pill bottles and doctor's letters, immigrants who speak only Spanish, addicts in treatment programs. Whether they can sit but not stand, or stand but not lift, Giuliani is vowing to put them to work—if possible in a private job, if necessary in a workfare position tailored to their needs."[20]

The strategy is implemented by Jason Turner, the mayor's welfare commissioner. Turner is described as accepting the difficulty that some welfare recipients will face in the new regime, but that the reforms will serve them well in the end. He concluded a session with workers in one of his offices with the directive: "Let me leave with this one thought, I don't want our agency to own every circumstance and problem a client faces. That's part of empowerment."[21] Asked by a caseworker if recipients could get money-management courses, Turner replied that it might happen, but that more would be achieved by following the dictum, "Live on what you get, and if you run out, figure out what to do until your next paycheck."[22]

In speculating about the end of stadium welfare, Roger Noll and Andrew Zimbalist wrote that "if teams had to pay for their own facilities, stadiums would have to be much smaller and much less elaborate."[23] Quite possibly, revenue streams would be smaller. Front offices would have to scramble to adjust. Player salaries might be reduced, with aggregate payrolls declining.

As things stand in New York City, we will never know because stadium welfare is calculated independently from other forms of public assistance and the debate over what the Yankees will receive from the city is one of amount rather than legitimacy.

The ultimate irony of the stadium game may be that it confounds the baseball business as much as it complicates public policy. A so-called Blue Ribbon Commission was assigned by the major league owners with the task of analyzing the economic state of baseball.[24] The commission was led by Richard Levin, the president of Yale University, former senator George Mitchell, former chairman of the Federal Reserve Paul Volcker, and political columnist George Will, and it serves as a foundation for the owners' strategy in negotiating with the Players Association when the current Basic Agreement expires at the end of the 2001 season.

The Commission proposes, "Despite impressive industry-wide revenue growth over the past five years, MLB [major league baseball] has an outdated economic structure that has created an unacceptable level of revenue disparity and competitive imbalance over the same period."[25] The goal of the study is to contribute to a standard in which "a well-managed club that demonstrates baseball acumen should allow its fans a reasonable hope that their club will be able to play and win in the postseason."[26]

The barrier to this objective is the gap in local revenues among the major league franchises. These funds accrue from "ticket sales, local television, radio and cable rights, ballpark concessions, parking and team sponsorships."[27] For the period 1995–1999, the average local revenue per club ranged from Montreal with less than $20 million per year to Baltimore and Cleveland in their new ballparks at about $100 million per year. Then, off by themselves, the New York Yankees topped the major leagues with $130 million in local revenue per year.

The trend is even more ominous for competing franchises. In 1999, the Yankees took in $176 million in local revenue, so even their $100-million payroll left them with a sizeable profit.[28] Several other franchises outdraw the Yankees in terms of home attendance, but no club comes close for local broadcast revenue. And, at the very time that the Basic Agreement is expiring, the Yankees' cable deal is also up for renewal.

The Yankees received up to $48 million a year from the Madison Square Garden (MSG) network under the old cable agreement. That amount was far greater than that garnered by any other major league franchise, but the new agreement promises to move the advantage significantly. Cablevision now owns the MSG network as well as the Fox Sports New York network, but the Yankee merger with the New Jersey Nets creates the potential for the ball club to start their own cable system with almost year-round sports programming. *Crain's New York Business* concluded that the Yankees might double their cable revenue in a new deal with Cablevision to a tune of $100 million per year.[29]

Major league baseball is also facing the nightmare of another strike or lockout when the basic agreement expires in 2001. The strike of 1994 seriously damaged the business of baseball, and the drama of Cal Ripken's streak and the home run barrage of recent years barely cleared that damage. Another work stoppage could be devastating, but the owners are determined to force the issue because of the financial pressures on them to compete with the most successful clubs. At the very point that the labor wars could resume, the Yankees could move to an annual revenue level that some clubs cannot match in a decade. And, at that very point, the city of New York is contemplating handing hundreds of millions of dollars of taxpayer money to the Yankees.

Perhaps the Blue Ribbon Commission should have concluded that the Yankees along with some other clubs have outgrown the major league structure that dates to 1903. The most sensible course for professional baseball very well may be to let the Yankees and clubs with adequate ownership and markets separate from their colleagues who are not so blessed, and form a kind of super major league. Some interleague play or postseason meetings could revive the memories of the twentieth-century game.

Whether such a drastic step should be taken, major league owners can hardly ignore that new stadiums in Milwaukee, Seattle, Cincinnati, and a few other smaller markets are short-term fixes. The new ballparks may make those franchises competitive in the short run, but the dominant teams in the sport—the Yankees, Red Sox, Mets, Dodgers—could secure new facilities that could take them well past the heights that the Brewers and Mariners have recently and painstakingly climbed. What would be the remedy for the rest of baseball if New York put half a billion dollars of taxpayer money into the Yankees' treasury at the very point that most of the other major league franchises were struggling to keep pace?

Another way in which stadium welfare defeats the business of baseball is in development of future markets. When money is diverted from playgrounds to stadiums, children have an incentive to play somewhere other than muddy or rock-strewn fields. Some of baseball's marketing experts fear the loss of future fan bases to basketball, football, soccer, or some other sport. More likely the kids will be lost to computer games or some other engaging sedentary pursuit. The game will not be deprived of great players—they seem to find a way to the top despite obstacles. But where will the fans learn this beautiful and intricate game if diamonds are neglected and coaches cut from school budgets? Even if great players continue to develop, will the fan base materialize from a city that diverted its resources from the poor and middle class to the most fortunate?

Sometimes economists, public officials, and baseball executives seem to assume that public money flows to stadiums as if by an immutable force of nature, but this form of corporate welfare reflects the political choices of a community. Subsidies for sports franchises can be reduced or eliminated altogether if the taxpayers choose to do so and can enforce that decision on their public officials.

Ten years ago, New Jersey governor James Florio actively courted the Yankees, giving George Steinbrenner tremendous leverage to use against New York. Florio was defeated by Christine Todd Whitman who has reformed welfare for the rich as well as the poor, and she effectively has closed the New Jersey option for the Yankees.

John Lindsay was eager to spend public money on the Yankees in the 1970s, and Rudy Giuliani is such a fervent fan that his usual keen ability to spot welfare abuse is lost when the practice involves his favorite franchise. On the other hand, Ed Koch could barely sit through a few innings on Opening Day, and David Dinkins—tennis fan—worked out a new facility for the U.S. Open that, for the most part, relied on private financing. In other words, elections matter because the politics of stadium financing includes an array of options from which the voters can select.

We can persuade those we put in office that we prefer to invest in parks and playgrounds rather than luxury boxes. We can insist that high school sports are fully funded rather than extending public assistance to the minor leagues. We can ask why any public money should go to an immensely wealthy entertainment firm that has barely begun to explore the possibilities of partnerships or stock offerings for capital formation. We can compare Yankee Stadium with New York City schools to determine the meaning of obsolescence. We can look at children who live in substandard housing, and see if we can ask them to be patient while we rebuild or replace a sports palace.

Yankee Stadium is one of the extraordinary buildings that has defined the city, but the public interest requires that any future Stadium deal be submitted to a referendum so that the voters can review the decision made on their behalf. Such a check does not strip our elected officials of legitimate responsibility; it instead recognizes that the sports business is part of the entertainment industry, abounding with wealth and celebrity. Fair-minded public officials can be distracted in such circumstances, so direct popular review of stadium subsidies is a sensible feature of this particular economic development policy. In fairness, the public interest also requires that the Yankees and businesses like them be entitled to an expeditious review of all environmental, traffic, zoning and similar issues. A bad project should fail on the merits; a good one should not be ground to dust by administrative filibuster.

If the electorate decides that public subsidies for the Yankees and other sports franchises are unwarranted, the opportunity would present itself to change the stadium game in New York. The record indicates that the city's ownership of Yankee Stadium has come at the expense of more worthy candidates for public assistance and investment. Not even the business of major league baseball can claim that this particular firm requires a public subsidy to advance the larger commercial interests of the game.

The city should withdraw from the stadium game by selling the Stadium back to the Yankees or to another private party. Our public resources should be devoted to resolving conflict, promoting investments in the community that the market would miss, and caring for our neighbors when they cannot do so themselves. The city's ownership of Yankee Stadium fails those tests, and New Yorkers need to insist that their relationship with this great franchise be refashioned in a more sensible way. Despite the likely opposition of wealth and power to such a profound change, the city's true interest can prevail through a determined exercise of the public will.

Epilogue

Rudy Giuliani's mayoral romance with the Yankees had one last occasion. On December 28, 2001, three days before he left office, Giuliani announced new stadium deals for the Mets and Yankees that were projected to cost $1.6 billion for both facilities. He displayed models of the new ball parks, and he assured the assembled that his successor, Michael Bloomberg, and Governor George Pataki supported the projects.

The mayor's news conference lacked the cringe-inducing enthusiasm that usually attends stadium announcements. Public officials exchange vigorous handshakes with club owners and civic boosters. Banalities about "a home run for our community" or "the city is really big league now" are inevitable, yet they gush forth as if uttered for the first time. The collection of government officials and stadium lobbyists who have transferred the public treasury up will be called "a great team." But, barely a hundred days after the attacks of September 11, few people who attended the announcement were in a mood for false cheer.

Before he became America's Mayor, Rudy Giuliani was the First Fan. He had been as pumped as George Steinbrenner when the Yankees won the Series in 1996 near the end of his first term. It was the first title for the Yankees since 1978, their longest championship drought since they started collecting World Series banners in 1923. Joe Torre's team joined the conversation about greatest teams ever when they won three championships in a row from 1998 through 2000. In the Subway Series of 2000, Giuliani made no pretense of impartiality. He was pulling for the Yankees, and the Mets were on their own.

In 2001, the great team was aging, but they still won the American League East by 13.5 games over the Boston Red Sox. After September 11, Giuliani understood that the Yankees were one distinct, if limited, piece of New York City's recovery. When the playoffs began, he was not simply a mayor of a city with a team in contention like Oakland, Cleveland, and Seattle. He had become a national figure, the person who most publicly embodied the city's courage in bearing its grief and in its determination to find a way forward. No one thought that a World Series would erase the trauma of the terrorist attacks, but if the Yankees could make a run in post-season, baseball in the Bronx could offer a measure of encouragement to the struggling city.

For New York, the playoffs had a dismal start. The Yankees appeared to be overwhelmed in the American League Divisional Series when the Oakland A's won the first two games of the best of five series in Yankee Stadium. The Yankees fought back on the West Coast, winning the third game 1–0 on a home run by Jorge Posada, great pitching from Mike Mussina and Mariano Rivera, and a spectacular defensive assist from Derek Jeter. They evened the series in the fourth game 9–2, then won the final game back at the Stadium 5–3.

The second round of postseason, the American League Championship Series, was a rout. The Yankees found their stride, and took the first two games in Seattle against a Mariners team that had won a record 116 games that year. The teams returned to New York, where the Mariners won the third game. The Yankees came back and won the series by taking the fourth and fifth games to get to their fourth World Series in a row.

They faced the Arizona Diamondbacks, a four-year-old expansion team; but one with superb pitching in Curt Schilling and Randy Johnson and solid veterans like Luis Gonzalez, Mark Grace, and Craig Counsell. The Series opened in Phoenix, and the D-backs seemed to put an end to the dream of a fourth straight championship. Arizona won the opener 9–1, then shut out the Yankees 4–0 to go up two games to none.

Two nights later, on October 30, the teams played before a crowd in Yankee Stadium that was as emotional as any gathering at the Stadium at least since Lou Gehrig's farewell. President George Bush threw out the first pitch from the mound at the Stadium, a brave act that helped to reclaim the public square for a baseball game.

The Yankees had scored only one run in the two games in Arizona. They scored only two in this crucial third game, but Roger Clemens made them stand up. Clemens went seven innings, giving up just one run on three hits.

The next night the Yankees trailed by two runs in the bottom of the ninth. With two outs and Paul O'Neill on second, Tino Martinez tied the game with a home run to right-centerfield. In the bottom of the tenth, as the game passed midnight and the season moved into November, Derek Jeter hit a walkoff home run to tie the Series at two games.

On November 1, in the fifth game, the Yankees again trailed by two runs in the bottom of the ninth. Jorge Posada led off with a double. Byung-Hyun Kim, the first Korean to play in the World Series and the losing pitcher the night before, was on the mound again. He got the next two outs, but Scott Brosius hammered a home run to left to tie the game. The Yankees won in the bottom of the twelfth on a run-scoring single by Alfonso Soriano to draw to one victory from a dream championship.

Back in Phoenix, the Diamondbacks pounded the Yankees 15–2 behind Randy Johnson to force the Series to the limit. In the seventh game, the late-inning heroics were reserved for Arizona. Joe Torre turned the ball over to the brilliant Mariano Rivera in the eighth inning to hold a 2–1 lead. Rivera sailed through the eighth, but sloppy fielding, a hit batter, and a bloop single brought the Diamondbacks the World Series title.

The 2001 season would have been memorable under any other circumstances, but Giuliani had seen the Yankees battle in New York, winning all their games in the Stadium. They fought back when they were on the ropes, drew strength from a delirious crowd; and he saw how baseball could play a limited but important role in reviving his city. Securing new stadiums for the Yankees and Mets was an understandable focus of the mayor's last weeks in office. He could channel the city's emotions into a civic project that would be one part of the rebuilding effort.

At his press conference announcing the plans for new stadiums, Giuliani was genuinely enthused about the new ball parks. George Steinbrenner and other figures at the announcement seemed more subdued, as if they were attending out of respect for the mayor rather than in anticipation of a serious plan for new stadiums.As it turned out, the deals that Giuliani announced that day never had a chance.

Emotional intensity is not sufficient to bring home a public works project of the scale proposed for the new stadiums. As John Lindsay had demonstrated in the 1970s, persistence and control of the levers of municipal power were required to see a stadium built, and, without Giuliani in office, no one appeared ready to fill that vacuum.

Governor Pataki was on record as favoring spending that was limited to infrastructure. Mike Bloomberg was not even that committed. Where Giuliani embodied the powerful emotions of the 2001 season, Bloomberg represented the hard-headed financial analysis that would set New York's priorities. He skipped the news conference but declared earlier that day, "I have said that I think we should have great cultural and athletic facilities, and the issue is really can we afford them, and I will have to take a look at that down the road as the economy develops."[1]

Bloomberg made it down that road in a little over a week when he announced on January 7, 2002, "At the moment, everybody understands that given that the lack of housing, given the lack of school space, given the deficit in the operating budget, it is just not practical this year to go and build stadiums."[2] One week into his first term, and the new Yankee Stadium was dead.

Limited housing, failing schools and fiscal collapse had not prevented the city's takeover and renovation of Yankee Stadium twenty-five years before, but, at the moment, no New Yorker could be certain that the city was safe from another attack; nor did anyone have a compelling plan for recovery at Ground Zero. The stadiums would have to wait.

Less than five years after Bloomberg ended Giuliani's stadium dreams, the incumbent mayor joined George Steinbrenner and a collection of public officials and celebrities to turn the first spade of earth for a new Yankee Stadium to rise just north of the House that Ruth Built. The groundbreaking was held on August 16, 2006, the fifty-eighth anniversary of the Babe's death. The Stadium would be ready for Opening Day of the 2009 season.

The new Yankee Stadium promises to be an architectural marvel. Designed by Hellmuth, Obata and Kassabaum (HOK), it will restore the original façade of the 1923 building with the copper frieze returned to the top of the edifice. The Stadium will be open air with a capacity of 53,000 seats and sixty luxury boxes. Unlike the current Stadium, in the new facility the majority of seats will be in the lower level, closer to the field. The Stadium will include administrative offices for the Yankees, retail shops, and a 150-seat restaurant. The new facility promises to repeat what the 1923 building accomplished: to be an elegant stadium in a world of ball parks.

When it opened in Baltimore in 1992, Orioles Park at Camden Yards triggered the current generation of stadium design. Reverting to the neighborhood model of the World War I era, the newest ball parks stress a close proximity with the fans and idiosyncrasies in the contours of the field. They are a refreshing break from the cement donuts, the multi-purpose stadiums that so many cities built in the 1970s. Sometimes the retro look is terrific, as in Baltimore and San Francisco.

Other times it can have a contrived look that reminds us of the limitations of those early-twentieth-century structures. The new Yankee Stadium will be big and dramatic, the proper expression of this franchise.

For any team, the modern stadium is a marketing center in which the ball field is one part of the operation. Restaurants and memorabilia and clothing stores join other entertainment centers to supplement the original purpose of enjoying a game. These shops will have ample room to operate at the new Stadium. The historic dimensions of the Yankees' field will be retained, including the short porch in right field and Monument Valley in center, but the footprint of the Stadium itself will expand to accommodate the ancillary businesses of the modern game.

The importance of the Stadium design is underscored in the General Project Plan for the Yankee Stadium Redevelopment Civic Project. As it describes the limitations of the old Stadium, "The current Yankee Stadium faces physical, functional, and operational obsolescence issues."[3] The report specifies that seats and aisles are too narrow, that the upper deck is too steep and lacks sufficient bathrooms and concession stands, that kitchen space is too small, that clubhouse and press facilities are too cramped, and that on-site parking is insufficient.

The complaints are familiar. George Steinbrenner had been making them for a number of years. In 1993, when Steinbrenner returned from his second baseball suspension, he centered his demands for a new stadium on leaving the Bronx. He coveted Manhattan, specifically the area by the Jacob Javits Convention Center next to the West Side Highway. Steinbrenner charged that attendance in the Bronx was too low, then he would add a list of concerns that would give pause to anyone thinking about going to Yankee Stadium. Alternative sites were considered, from the New Jersey Meadowlands to the Yonkers Raceway, attracting support from almost no one except gullible mayors.

New York politics dictated that the Yankees belonged in the Bronx. Giuliani had been sympathetic to Steinbrenner's interest in a West Side Stadium, but Bloomberg had ideas of his own for the land next to the Javits Center. Bloomberg focused his administration on securing the

2012 Olympics, which would have included a new stadium at the West Side site, a stadium that would later be delivered to the New York Jets of the National Football League.

With the mayoral administration busy with the Olympics, the key governmental figures in the Yankees' future were the public officials in the Bronx. Once Steinbrenner accepted that his team was staying in the old neighborhood, complex financial arrangements, park acquisition, and other impediments to a new Stadium were managed at incredible speed. On June 15, 2005, the Yankees reached a Memorandum of Understanding (MOU) with the city and state. The agreement includes the following elements:

- a new stadium and related facilities, at an estimated cost of $1.2 billion, will be constructed immediately to the north of the existing Yankee Stadium;
- according to the Yankees website, the franchise will provide $800 million of that cost;
- four parking structures with a total of 4,735 spaces;
- the location of the new Stadium will require the taking of two local parks, McCombs Dam Park and part of John Mullaly Park;
- both the new Stadium and its site will be owned by the City of New York;
- the Stadium will be leased to the Yankees for a minimum of forty years up to a possible ninety-nine years.

The new Stadium will be a great commercial success for the franchise. It will have more amenities for the players. It will be far more comfortable for the fans, especially the fortunate ones in the luxury boxes. Less certain is whether the new Stadium is a good deal for the citizens and taxpayers of New York. In terms of the public interest, the city has never played the stadium game particularly well, and the latest bargain leaves questions that suggest that, once again, the Yankees and the politically connected have fared much better than their fellow New Yorkers.

Why is the deal so complex? To begin with, the agreement between the Yankees and the City of New York is complicated to a degree that makes a democratic discussion of the issues very difficult. The Memorandum of Understanding (MOU)

> sets forth certain understandings and agreements among New York State Urban Development Corporation d/b/a Empire State Development Corporation ("ESDC"), The City of New York (the "City"), and New York City Economic Development Corporation ("NYCEDC"), (ESDC, the City and NYDEDC, collectively, the "Public Parties") and the New York Yankees Limited Partnership, or one or more affiliated entities (collectively, the "Yankees"), with respect to (a) the design, development, construction, financing and operation of a new Yankee Stadium ("New Stadium") to serve as the home field for the New York Yankees professional baseball team ("Yankees Team"); (b) the design, development, construction and operation of certain parking garages to serve the New Stadium; (c) the construction of certain public infrastructure required to improve vehicular and pedestrian traffic in the vicinity of the New Stadium; (d) the design and development of park, recreational and other public space in the vicinity of the New Stadium, and (e) the renovation or demolition and re-use of the existing Yankee Stadium ("Old Stadium").[4]

So, the agreement between the city and the ball club breaks down into a collection of parties on each side. Several industrial development corporations operate in the city's name while the Yankees are both the Ballpark LLC and the franchise itself.

These various entities divide the responsibilities for acquiring public parks, designing the new Stadium and the parking structures, financing and constructing them, and, in the way of any major development project, navigating among the hurdles of SEQRA, ULURP, and PILOTs.[5]

The Yankees' Memorandum of Understanding and the General Project Plan are examples of a new model of stadium financing that purports to put a significant burden on the ball clubs. The new arrangements are characterized as partnerships. The public treasury and the sports franchise's own finances share the burdens of stadium construction and maintenance.

The Yankees website, for example, refers to "the $800 million the Yankees have fronted." That sounds simple enough. In an editorial about new stadiums for the Yankees and Mets, the *New York Times* was pleased that "the teams will pay for their new homes themselves."[6] The *Times* did note that some subsidies would help the teams, but the Memorandum of Understanding develops what the Yankees mean when they claim they will front $800 million.

First, the city will own the new stadium and its site just as it has since it acquired and renovated the current Stadium. The city will lease the new Stadium not directly to the Yankees but to an Industrial Development Agency (IDA) that will finance the new structure, then lease the new Stadium to the Ballpark LLC that will finally lease the new Stadium to the Yankees franchise.

The IDA will retire its bonds through payments in lieu of taxes (PILOT) that will be the responsibility of the Stadium LLC. Because the City owns both the new Stadium and its site, no property taxes will apply. The PILOT will be "equal to the full real estate taxes which the City would assess were the stadium Site and the New Stadium not exempt from such taxes."[7]

Who gains from this complexity? If the PILOT will be equal to real estate taxes, why not require the Yankees to finance the Stadium privately and pay taxes the same as most other businesses? That was the model that Jake Ruppert used when the original Stadium was built.

The benefit to the Yankees of the IDA is that it can offer tax-exempt bonds that pay a lower interest rate than the corporate bonds that the franchise itself could float. The IDA bonds are more attractive in the financial markets than, say hypothetical "Babe Ruth bonds" that would be backed by the Yankees, because the promise of repayment by almost any government entity in America is more certain than that of almost any private entity. The greater security means that the bonds can be issued at a lower interest rate, but the bonds are attractive even at a lower rate of return because the IDA can offer them exempt from local, state and federal taxes.

Of course, if the city, state, and national treasuries are denied those taxes, the money has to be made up somewhere. Good Jobs New York (GJNY) is a research center that focuses on public policies that appear to benefit prospering corporations. It has been the primary critic of the new Yankee Stadium deal.[8] Shifting the financial burden elsewhere in the community is counted by GJNY as a subsidy in the amount of over $120 million, one piece of a series of subsidies for the new Stadium that Good Jobs estimates adds up to over $663 million.[9]

A rousing conversation could examine whether the partnership between the Yankees and New York represents investments or more Stadium welfare, but an advanced degree in municipal finance might be necessary to participate in that conversation. The Jake Ruppert model of Stadium finance did not require that expertise, nor did the relatively straightforward public goods model that was used for the renovation of the 1970s. Those who do have the necessary background need to find a forum to make their views known. But in New York, that raises a second question about the new Stadium deal.

Who was represented in the processes that approved the new Stadium? The deal for the new Yankee Stadium had to win the approval of both the New York State Legislature and the New York City Council. On April 5, 2006, the City Council passed eleven land use items by votes of either 44–3 or 45–2. Earlier, the legislature had shown similar enthusiasm.

The Stadium had the support of what Good Jobs New York describes as "a stadium turnstile," a variation of the revolving door of people who work in government then use the knowledge gained in their public job to advance interests in the private sector. Because the administrative process can be so complex, having lobbyists who have worked in government agencies can be enormously useful in advancing a development project.

The Stadium deal also may have been helped by the return of a familiar New York institution. The *Times*'s account of the City Council vote explains that, "The stadium plan gained support in the Council in recent weeks after the Yankees reached an agreement with Bronx officials to contribute $50 million over 20 years to underwrite programs for Bronx community groups."[10] As practiced in the case of the new Stadium, the Bronx benefits directly through what is known as a "Community Benefit Agreement" (CBA).[11] Some of what the borough has been promised includes:

- the award of at least twenty-five percent of the construction contracts to Bronx Based Businesses qualified to perform the required responsibilities of which at least fifty percent would be qualified MWBLE (Minority Women-Owned and Local Business Enterprises);
- the employment of Bronx residents qualified to perform the required responsibilities equal to at least twenty-five percent of total job force;
- the employment of Bronx residents in post-construction new Yankee stadium operations, qualified to perform the required responsibilities, equal to at least twenty-five percent of the total new job force.

A Program Administrator is designated under the CBA to implement the program with an office budget of $450,000 during the construction of the project. George Washington Plunkitt of Tammany Hall could not have made a better deal.

The Yankees will spend $1,000,000 to promote job training in union apprenticeship programs. The franchise will also provide $800,000 "in cash grants to duly constituted Bronx resident not-for-profit institutions and community-based organizations." Another $100,000 worth of equipment and promotional merchandise will go "to duly constituted Bronx resident not-for-profit institutions, schools and youth and sports groups." Finally, fifteen thousand tickets worth an average of $25 apiece will go to those same groups and also to senior citizens. These tickets have a total value of $375,000.

In one of Plunkitt's descriptions of "honest graft," he maintained:

They didn't steal a dollar from the city treasury. They just seen their opportunities and took them. That is why, when a reform administration comes in and spends a half million dollars in tryin' to find the public robberies they talked about in the campaign, they don't find them.

The books always balance. The money in the city treasury is all right. Everything is all right. All they can show is that the Tammany heads of departments looked after their friends within the law, and gave them what opportunities they could to make honest graft.[12]

If the strategy succeeds, the Bronx will receive an important investment in its workforce. Stadiums are not known for providing long-term high-paying jobs, but, in this case, some Bronx workers could learn a trade and join a construction union. They would raise dramatically the standard of living of their families. As with Tammany, some poor people will receive an opportunity that previously had not been available.

Good Jobs New York asserts all kinds of shortcomings in the Yankee Stadium deal, but they also make the point that Plunkitt would recognize: "Our findings do not suggest any illegal behavior or conflicts of interest. But they do reveal a large, costly redevelopment project that was rushed through the public approval process without meaningful participation from the community or clearly defined benefits to residents and taxpayers."[13]

References to Tammany Hall and honest graft imply nefarious behavior, but every indication is that the process that led to the new Yankee Stadium has been entirely legal. Legal, but flawed. Sprinkling largesse about the Bronx to gain political support has been effective, and probably beneficial to some of the borough's poorer residents, but New York would benefit from a more open process that facilitates a discussion about the place of honest graft in the modern city.

As we considered in Chapter 9, some cities have taken the entire question of new sports stadiums out of esoteric administrative and legislative hearings and placed the matter before the voters through referenda. The electorates in Denver, Detroit. and Arlington, Texas, have approved new ball parks for the Rockies, Tigers, and Rangers. In the Bay Area, San Francisco and San Jose rejected a public stadium for the Giants on four occasions, and AT&T Park then was financed privately. New York could have a referendum on the Stadium deal, but the legislature would have to put the agreement on the ballot, the same legislature that transferred two parks in a matter of days.

As the New York process stands, the burden is on the public to penetrate the maze of legislative, executive, and judicial thickets to make their case. A referendum would shift the burden to the stadium boosters to justify their plans to the public.

An alternative to a comprehensive vote on the entire Stadium plan is a vote on the financing. When the state wants to raise capital for roads, schools, prisons, libraries, or certain other public purposes, it offers general obligation bonds. Under the New York State Constitution, general obligation bonds must be put on the ballot in the next general election. The electorate votes directly on the public good that the legislature has proposed.

The bonds that the Industrial Development Agency offers are not general obligation bonds, so they will not be subject to an electoral review. Of course, the legislature could amend the process to require a referendum, but the political culture of New York does not seem to consider democratic decision making to be a terribly high priority.

What are the civic values reflected in the Stadium deal? The General Project Plan dismissed a second renovation of the existing Yankee Stadium in part because the Yankees would lose a home field for the duration of the renovation, and that loss was described in the plan as representing "serious adverse financial consequences for the Yankees."[14] That last point should be considered in context.

In the April 19, 2007, issue of *Forbes* magazine, the Yankee franchise is estimated to be worth $1.2 billion. The next most thriving ball club is the New York Mets at $736 million. The Boston Red Sox are third at $724 million. The Los Angeles Dodgers and Chicago Cubs *combined* are slightly more prosperous than the Yankees. No other club is worth $500 million; more than half the franchises are worth less than $400 million; and seven of the thirty major league franchises have a current value of less than $300 million. Would "serious adverse financial consequences" mean that the Yankees would no longer be worth substantially more than the Kansas City Royals, the Pittsburgh Pirates, the Tampa Bay Rays, and the Florida Marlins *combined*?

Comparing the Yankees with other major league franchises establishes that there is no comparison. The Mets, Dodgers, Cubs, and Red Sox are very successful entertainment businesses in Major League Baseball (MLB). Along with the Yankees, they also play in the oldest ball parks or stadiums in the game. No doubt all of these franchises could increase revenues substantially by moving into the sports malls that include the modern major league baseball field. We have no reason to think that any of these clubs, let alone the Yankees, suffers commercially in its industry, but, in New York, public officials have made the Yankee fortune a civic priority.

The General Project Plan maintains: "The current Yankee Stadium faces physical, functional, and operational obsolescence issues."[15] The same thing could be said for much of the city's housing, hospitals, schools, subways, roadways, and other public goods. Bloomberg had made the same point in the first month of his administration when he blocked the Giuliani stadium plan.

Bloomberg cannot be faulted for indifference about schools and transportation. He has proposed bold action in both areas, but the efforts that have gone into fashioning the Yankee Stadium deal inevitably have come at the expense of other projects.

When the Stadium was renovated in the 1970s, the city ignored both the social collapse of the South Bronx and also the fiscal crisis that was overtaking New York. The civic priorities were thoroughly misplaced at that time, and the city suffered the consequences. Clear thinking is needed now even more than it was then, but public officials remain mesmerized by what they see as the plight of the Yankees, and the results this time could be catastrophic.

The new Yankee Stadium will be a dazzling cultural attraction. Its opening day and countless other games will draw the attention of the world. Tens of thousands of people will pack into it. Media from all over will highlight the Yankees' new home. In other words, it is exactly the kind of trophy that terrorists pursue relentlessly.

The Memorandum of Understanding mentions that if the Yankees fail to play their home games at the new Stadium, they will default on the agreement with the city. An exception is made for "certain *force majeur* events." The reference is to factors beyond control: a natural disaster, catastrophic accident, or terrorist attack.

New York should not let itself be paralyzed from necessary renewal because of threats from our enemies, but those threats are a compelling reason to make sure that the Yankees and the city are bearing their proper responsibilities. The Yankees can well afford the Stadium that rises in the Bronx, but the city cannot divert its attention from protecting the people who will enjoy that Stadium.

In a point made in Chapter 7, the money that the city has spent on stadiums is significant not only because of the money itself, but also because the money reflects less tangible resources. Time, meetings, reports, urgency—"The Boss really wants this one done"—persistence, imagination—these are all very difficult factors to measure, but they are critical to the success of any challenging project. These resources have been poured into helping the Yankees, a business that does not need help.

Using the enormous civic energy that has gone into serving the interests of the Yankees, what might public officials have done to make the city safer? How might the port have been better secured? The bridges and tunnels? What added protection against gas attacks on the subways? What greater security for the region's airports? The water supply? Natural gas lines? Wall Street? How much time, energy, imagination, and urgency have been diverted from protecting the city so that taxpayers could help the Yankees pay their bills?

The great personalities who play the New York Stadium Game eventually pass on. Jake Ruppert, Del Webb, Walter O'Malley, Robert Moses,

Bill Shea, and John Lindsay are all gone. What remains is how the game is played: In New York, a handful of men and women still decide how the city will allocate resources that now exceed a billion dollars per structure.

These small groups of the wealthy and powerful have served themselves well, at the expense of their fellow New Yorkers, and this indulgence of the rich and powerful is a delusion that the city can no longer afford.

Notes

Chapter 1

1. The *New York Times* was one of the papers that numbered the crowd at over 74,200, a figure that the Yankees had been offering. The actual count was still the largest attendance to that date for a baseball game.
2. *New York Evening Telegram*, April 18, 1923, p. 4.
3. *New York Times*, April 19, 1923, pp. 1 and 15.
4. Ibid., p. 15.
5. *New York Herald*, April 19, 1923, p. 17.
6. *New York Post*, April 18, 1923, p. 1.
7. See Steven A. Riess, "The Baseball Magnates and Urban Politics in The Progressive Era: 1895–1920," *The Journal of Sport History*, 1 (May 1974), esp. pp. 53–62.
8. William L. Riordan, *Plunkitt of Tammany Hall* (Mattituck, N.Y.: Amereon House; reissued 1982), p. 45.
9. See Reiss, op. cit.
10. See Steven A. Reiss, *Touching Base: Professional Baseball and American Culture in the Progressive Era*, rev. ed. (Chicago: University of Illinois Press, 1999), esp. pp. 69–83.
11. Riordan, p. 3.
12. Riordan, p. 4.
13. Riordan, p. 6.
14. Ann Douglas, *Terrible Honesty: Mongrel Manhattan in the 1920s* (New York: Noonday Press, 1995), p. 16.
15. Ibid., p. 65.
16. Robert Creamer, *Babe: The Legend Comes to Life* (New York: Simon & Schuster, 1974), pp. 219–20.

17. *New York Herald*, April 21, 1923, p. 10.

18. Gehrig himself enjoyed a memorable day. While the Yankees opened the Stadium, he pitched for the Columbia College Lions and struck out seventeen batters from Williams College.

19. *New York Tribune*, April 19, 1923, p. 13.

20. Ibid., p. 1.

21. *New York Herald*, April 21, 1923, p. 10.

22. *The Sporting News*, March 15, 1923, p. 1.

Chapter 2

1. See Michael Gershman, *Diamonds: The Evolution of the Ballpark* (New York: Houghton Mifflin, 1993), p. 59.

2. See M. R. Werner, *Tammany Hall* (New York: Doubleday, 1928), pp. 345–47.

3. See Albert G. Spalding, *Base Ball: America's National Game 1839–1915*, revised and re-edited by Samm Coombs and Bob West (San Francisco: Halo Press, 1991), p. 191.

4. Ibid., p. 192.

5. Werner, p. 372.

6. Werner, p. 404.

7. Werner, p. 462.

8. Werner, p. 496.

9. Frank Graham, *The New York Yankees: An Informal History* (New York: G.P. Putnam's Sons, 1943), p. 20.

10. Ibid.

11. *New York Times*, January 14, 1939, p. 14.

12. After winning five championships between 1903 and 1918, the Red Sox have managed to avoid winning another.

13. The scandal is ably covered in Eliot Asinof's *Eight Men Out: The Black Sox and the 1919 World Series* (New York: Henry Holt, 1963).

14. Graham, pp. 58–59.

15. See Harold Seymour, *Baseball: The Golden Age* (New York: Oxford University Press, 1971), pp. 270–71.

Chapter 3

1. *Bronx Home News*, April 19, 1923, p. 11.
2. Lloyd Ultan and Gary Hermalyn, *The Bronx in the Innocent Years 1890–1925*, 2nd ed. (New York: The Bronx County Historical Society, 1991), p. xi.
3. James Bryce, *The American Commonwealth*, Vol. II (London: Macmillan, 1889), p. 516.
4. See Jacob Riis, *How the Other Half Lives* (New York: Dover Publications, 1971).
5. *Marx and Engels: Basic Writings on Politics and Philosophy*, edited by Lewis S. Feuer (New York: Anchor Books, 1959), pp. 489–97.
6. See Neal Gabler, *Life the Movie: How Entertainment Conquered Reality* (New York: Alfred A. Knopf, 1998); see pp. 32–37.
7. Ibid., pp. 36–37.
8. M. R. Werner, *Tammany Hall* (New York: Doubleday, 1928), p. 304.
9. Gabler, pp. 37–38.
10. Feuer, pp. 457–58.
11. Riis, p. 88.
12. Gershman, Michael, *Diamonds: The Evolution of the Ballpark* (New York: Houghton Mifflin, 1993), p. 134.
13. The figures from the 1900 census indicate the imbalance:
   Manhattan—1,850,093
   Brooklyn—1,166,582
   Bronx—200,507
   Queens—152,999
   Staten Island—67,021
   See Ira Rosenwaike, *Population History of New York City* (Syracuse, N.Y.: Syracuse University Press, 1972), p. 58.
14. The exact figures are:
   Manhattan—2,284,103

Brooklyn—2,018,356
Bronx—732,016
Queens—469,042
Staten Island—116,531
See ibid., p.133.

15. Clifton Hood, *722 Miles: The Building of the Subways and How They Transformed New York* (Baltimore: Johns Hopkins University Press, 1993), p. 111.
16. Richard Plunz, *A History of Housing in New York City* (New York: Columbia University Press, 1990), p. 120.
17. Riis, p. 85.
18. Plunz, p. 132.
19. Ibid.
20. Ibid., p. 159.
21. Hood, p. 112.
22. Ibid., p. 110.
23. Ibid., p. 186.
24. Ibid., pp. 190–93.
25. Jane Salodof, in *New York Alive*, January/February 1990, p. 37.
26. Ibid., p. 38.
27. Ibid.
28. "Municipal Wholesale Terminal Markets and Their Relation to the Food Problem," Annual Report of the Department of Public Markets, p. 16. O'Malley's son, Walter, was the man who moved the Dodgers from Brooklyn to Los Angeles.
29. Ibid., p. 23.
30. Frederick Lewis Allen, *Only Yesterday: An Informal History of the Nineteen Twenties* (New York: Perennial Library, 1964), pp. 38–39.
31. *Subject—Investigation of Pro-British History Text-Books in Use in the Public Schools of this City*, Report from David Hirshfield to Mayor John Hylan, May 25, 1923, Hylan Papers, Municipal Archives, New York City.
32. Ibid., p. 14.

Chapter 4

1. *New York Times*, September 10, 1928, p. 1.
2. *New York Times*, May 20, 1929, p. 1.
3. *New York Times*, November 7, 1928, p. 25.
4. See Alan Boyer, "*The Great Gatsby*, the Black Sox, High Finance and American Law," in Spencer Weber Waller, Neil B. Cohen, and Paul Finkelman, *Baseball and the American Legal Mind* (New York: Garland, 1995), pp. 436–50.
5. See Oliver E. Allen, *The Tiger: The Rise and Fall of Tammany Hall* (New York: Addison-Wesley, 1993), chap. 9.
6. See Jordan Schwartz, *The New Dealers: Power Politics in the Age of Roosevelt* (New York: Alfred A. Knopf, 1993).
7. Jerry Mitchell, *The American Experiment with Government Corporations* (Armonk, N.Y.: M.E. Sharpe, 1999), p. 30.
8. Schwarz, p. xi.
9. See Marc Reisner, *Cadillac Desert: The American West and Its Disappearing Water* (New York: Penguin, 1993).
10. See Thomas Kessner, *Fiorello LaGuardia and the Making of Modern New York* (New York: McGraw-Hill, 1989), p. 294.
11. *New York Times*, September 10, 1931, p. 28.
12. *New York Times*, July 31, 1938, p. 1.
13. *New York Times*, November 5, 1948, p. 16.
14. Ibid., pp. 1, 3.
15. Ibid., p. 3.
16. Red Smith, *To Absent Friends* (New York: Atheneum, 1982), p. 11. Powell was one of baseball's numerous tragic figures. His major league career lasted eleven years, and he hit .435 in three World Series. He was also a brawler, and he ultimately shot himself to death at the age of forty while in police custody after being arrested for passing bad checks (*New York Times*, November 5, 1948, p. 16).
17. See Ray Robinson, *Iron Horse: Lou Gehrig in His Time* (New York: W.W. Norton, 1990), p. 244. Robinson also writes that Barrow in-

formed Eleanor Gehrig that her husband should get another job, cutting him off from the Yankees as his fatal illness was becoming known and his appreciation day was being planned. Mr. Robinson is also the author, with Christopher Jennison, of *Yankee Stadium: 75 Years of Drama, Glamor and Glory* (New York: Penguin Books, 1998). He also, with his wife, Phyllis, spent the better part of an entire day (March 24, 2000) discussing the themes in this book with the author.

Chapter 5

1. See Dan Warfield, *The Roaring Redhead: Larry MacPhail, Baseball's Great Innovator* (South Bend, Ind.: Diamond Communications, 1987).
2. Joe David Brown, "The Webb of Mystery," *Sports Illustrated*, February 29, 1960, p. 80.
3. Happy Chandler, with Vance Trimble, *Heroes, Plain Folks, and Skunks* (Chicago: Bonus Books, 1989), p. 217.
4. See Robert W. Creamer, *Stengel: His Life and Times* (New York: Simon & Schuster, 1984).
5. Brown, p. 74.
6. Ibid., p. 76.
7. Ibid., p. 77.
8. See Arelo Sederberg, Arelo and John F. Lawrence, "Del Webb, the Bashful Barnum," *Los Angeles Times*, "*West,*" September 14, 1969, p. 19.
9. Ibid.
10. Ibid.
11. Ibid., p. 17.
12. See "The Mobsters on Del Webb's Team," *New West*, April 11, 1977.
13. Letter to the author from Lewis D. Schiliro, Assistant Director in Charge, Federal Bureau of Investigation, U.S. Department of Justice, October 19, 1998.
14. Sederberg and Lawrence, p. 19.
15. *Los Angeles Times*, September 1, 1961, Pt. I, p. 22.

16. Arthur Mann, "How to Buy a Ball Club for Peanuts," *Saturday Evening Post*, April 9, 1955, reprinted in *Organized Professional Team Sports*, Hearings before the Antitrust Subcommittee of the Committee on the Judiciary, 85th Congress, 1st Sess., Part 2, 1957.

17. *Organized Professional Team Sports*, pp. 2133–34.

18. Ibid., pp. 2083–85.

19. Ibid., p. 2099.

20. Ibid.

21. Ibid.

22. Ibid.

23. Ibid.

24. Ibid.

25. Ibid.

26. Ibid., p. 2082.

27. Bowie Kuhn, *Hardball: The Education of a Baseball Commissioner* (New York: Times Books, 1987), p. 324.

Chapter 6

1. For the social significance of baseball's integration, see Jules Tygiel, *Baseball's Great Experiment* (New York: Oxford University Press, 1985).

2. For an assessment of the commercial implications of baseball's color barrier, see Neil J. Sullivan, "Baseball and Race: The Limits of Competition," *The Journal of Negro History*, Vol. 83, No. 3, 1998, pp. 168–77.

3. This chronicle of baseball's integration is drawn from Merl Kleinknecht, "Integration of Baseball after World War II," *Baseball Research Journal*, 1983, pp. 100–06.

4. Sullivan, p. 174.

5. See, for example, Robert Creamer, *Stengel: His Life and Times* (New York: Simon & Schuster, 1984), p. 282.

6. Ibid.

7. See Tony Kubek and Terry Pluto, *Sixty-One: The Team, the Record, the Men* (New York: Simon & Schuster, 1987), pp. 215–16.

8. Ibid., p. 216.

9. Ibid.

10. Ibid., p. 217.

11. Ira Rosenwaike, *Population History of New York City* (Syracuse, N.Y.: University of Syracuse Press, 1972). Figures appear on page 133.

12. See Jim Rooney, *Organizing the South Bronx* (Albany: State University of New York Press, 1995), esp. chap. 2.

13. Isa Kapp, "By the Waters of the Grand Concourse: Where Jewishness Is Free of Compulsion," *Commentary*, September 1949, pp. 269–73.

14. Ibid., p. 269.

15. Ibid.

16. Ibid., p. 270.

17. *New York Times*, July 21, 1966, p. 35.

18. Ibid.

19. Ibid.

20. Ibid.

21. Ibid.

22. Ibid., p. 39.

23. *New York Times*, August 13, 1972.

24. Ibid.

25. Constance Rosenblum, "A Street of Dreams," *New York Daily News*, Sunday News Magazine, April 6, 1980.

26. Ibid., p. 10.

27. Ibid., p. 20.

28. Ibid.

29. For a study of the Dodgers' move, see Neil J. Sullivan, *The Dodgers Move West* (New York: Oxford University Press, 1987).

30. Buzzie Bavasi with John Strege, *Off the Record* (Chicago: Contemporary Books, Inc., 1987), p. 77.

31. Peter Golenbock, *Bums* (New York: Putnam, 1984), p. 433.

32. Ibid.

33. Rosenwaike, op. cit.

34. William Julius Wilson, *The Declining Significance of Race*, 2nd ed. (Chicago: University of Chicago Press, 1980), p. 92.

35. Ibid., pp. 146–48.

Chapter 7

1. Letter from Michael Burke to John Lindsay, August 24, 1970, Lindsay Papers, Municipal Archives, New York City.

2. Ibid.

3. Ibid.

4. Ibid.

5. *New York Times*, April 5, 1971, p. 39.

6. *New York Times*, August 14, 1964, p. 18.

7. *New York Times*, August 15, 1964, p. 14.

8. *New York Times*, August 16, 1964, p. 2S.

9. Ibid.

10. Ibid.

11. *New York Times*, August 15, 1964, p. 14.

12. Ibid.

13. Ibid.

14. Ibid.

15. David Halberstam, *The Powers That Be* (New York: Alfred A. Knopf, 1979), p. 417.

16. Ibid., p. 418.

17. Leonard Wallace Robinson, "After the Yankees What? A TV Drama," *New York Times* Magazine, November 15, 1964, p. 52.

18. Ibid.

19. Ibid., p. 54.

20. David Halberstam, *October 1964* (New York: Fawcett Columbine, 1995), pp. 343–44.

21. Letter from Mike Burke to Richard Aurelio, October 2, 1970, Lindsay Papers, Municipal Archives, New York City.

22. Ibid.

23. Ibid.

24. For conferring equal representation on all five boroughs despite their wide differences in population, the Board was found to be unconstitutional for violating the so-called one man, one vote provision of the Fourteenth Amendment.

25. *New York Daily News*, March 28, 1971.

26. Ibid.

27. Letter from Michael Burke to John Lindsay, October 5, 1971, Municipal Archives, New York City.

28. Ibid.

29. Letter from Michael Burke to John Lindsay, November 5, 1971, Municipal Archives, New York City.

30. *New York Times*, November 23, 1971, p. 50.

31. *New York Daily News*, October 11, 1971.

32. *New York Times*, December 10, 1971, p. 1.

33. Ibid., p. 32.

34. *New York Times*, March 24, 1972, p. 1.

35. *New York Daily News*, September 9, 1971.

36. *New York Daily News*, April 6, 1973, p. 6C.

37. Ken Patton, City Planning Commission, October 13, 1971, Lindsay Papers, Municipal Archives, New York City.

38. Ibid.

39. Ibid.

40. *New York Times*, December 1, 1975, p. 1.

41. *New York Times*, December 1, 1975, p. 62.

42. Ibid.

43. *New York Times*, February 3, 1976, p. 63.

44. Ibid.

45. *New York Times*, December 1, 1975, p. 62.

Chapter 8

1. *New York Times*, January 4, 1973, p. 45.

2. *New York Times*, January 5, 1973, p. 23.

3. Ibid.

4. Ibid.

5. *New York Times*, January 4, 1973, p. 45.

6. Ibid.

7. Ibid.

8. *New York Times*, April 16, 1976, p. 21.

9. Oliver Allen, *New York, New York* (New York: Macmillan, 1990), p. 317.

10. Ken Auletta, *The Streets Were Paved with Gold* (New York: Vintage, 1980), p. 91.

11. Martin Shefter, *Political Crisis/Fiscal Crisis: The Collapse and Revival of New York City* (New York: Basic Books, 1987).

12. Ibid., p. 110.

13. Ibid., p. 117.

14. Auletta, p. 30.

15. Auletta, p. 58.

16. Alan Brinkley, *The End of Reform: New Deal Liberalism in Recession and War* (New York: Alfred A. Knopf, 1995).

17. Ibid., p. 269.

18. Marvin Miller, *A Whole Different Ball Game: The Sport and Business of Baseball* (New York: Birch Lane Press, 1991), p. 282.

19. Ed Koch, "Steinbrenner's Game Is Hardball," *New York Daily News*, May, 8, 1998.

20. Sam Howe Verhovek, "Yankees to Stay in New York City," *New York Times*, November 1, 1987, p. 49.

21. Sam Roberts, "It's Extra Innings for the Yankees and New York," *New York Times*, November 3, 1988, p. B1.

22. Anthony Baldo, "Secrets of the Front Office: What America's Pro Teams Are Worth," *Financial World*, July 9, 1991, pp. 42–43.

Chapter 9

1. Paul Schwartzman, "Yankees Boss Is Hot to Trot Outta Bronx," *New York Daily News*, June 17, 1993, p. 5.

2. Jim Dwyer, "Yankees Know How to Bill & Coo," *New York Daily News*, November 14, 1996.

3. Ibid.

4. Hellmuth, Obata, and Kassabaum, "Alternative Site Planning Report Volume Two: Yankee Stadium Alternative Site Assessment Study," March 1996, p. 4.

5. Richard Perez-Pena, "Stadium Plan Would Scuttle M.T.A. Hopes," *New York Times*, April 10, 1996, p. B1.

6. *New York Daily News*, May 8, 1998.

7. Richard Sandomir, "Experts Say Stadium Plan Would Cut Yankees' Take," *New York Times*, April 12, 1996, p. B1.

8. "The Perfect Pitch: The Bombers in the Bronx," a Report by Borough President Fernando Ferrer, p. 27.

9. *New York Post*, April 17, 1998, Bronx Borough President's Office.

10. *New York Daily News*, May 14, 1998.

11. Ibid.

12. Dean Chadwin, *Those Damn Yankees: The Secret Life of America's Greatest Franchise* (New York: Verso, 1999).

13. Ibid., p. 219.

14. *New York Times*, June 11, 1998, p. B5.

15. Peter Vallone, "New Stadium? Ask Taxpayers First," *New York Daily News*, April 23, 1998.

16. *New York Daily News*, July 12, 1988, p. 2.

17. Jim Dwyer, "Steinbrenner Can't Dodger City Memory," *New York Daily News*, July 12, 1998, pp. 2, 40.

18. Mike Lupica, "Boss' Scam Game," *New York Daily News*, July 12, 1998, p. 86.

19. Ibid.

20. Mike Lupica, "The Boss' New City Hall Underboss," *New York Daily News*, January 9, 2000.

21. Ibid.

22. Richard Sandomir, "Where Next Bronx Bombers? Steinbrenner Keeeps Saying He May Leave. He Hasn't. The Clock Ticks," *New York Times*, December 14, 1999, p. D1.

23. Luke Cyphers and Dave Goldiner, "The Boss of Yanks & Nets: Steinbrenner's Mammoth Merger," *New York Daily News*, February 26, 1999.

24. Sandomir, *New York Times*, December 14, 1999, p. D4.

25. Jim Dwyer, "It'll Be the House That Dupes Built," *New York Daily News*, December 9, 1999.

26. Ibid.

Chapter 10

1. Roger G. Noll and Andrew Zimbalist, eds., *Sports Jobs and Taxes: The Economic Impact of Sports Teams and Stadiums* (Washington, D.C.: The Brookings Institution, 1997).

2. Roger G. Noll and Andrew Zimbalist, "The Economic Impact of Sports Teams and Facilities," in Noll and Zimbalist, op cit., p. 56.

3. Ibid.

4. Ibid., p. 57.

5. Dennis Zimmerman, "Subsidizing Stadiums: Who Benefits? Who Pays?" in Noll and Zimbalist, op cit., pp. 142–43.

6. Robert A. Baade and Allen R. Sanderson, "The Employment Effect of Teams and Sports Facilities," in Noll and Zimbalist, op cit., p. 97.

7. James Quirk and Rodney D. Fort, *Pay Dirt: The Business of Professional Team Sports* (Princeton, N.J.: Princeton University Press, 1997), p. 174.

8. Mark S. Rosentraub, *Major League Lo$ers: The Real Cost of Sports and Who's Paying for It* (New York: Basic Books, 1997), p. 72.

9. Provided by Neil P. Harwayne, Deputy Superintendent of Operations, Board of Education of New York City, April 17, 2000.

10. Kenney Lucas and Paul Schwarzman, "City HS Football Field Isn't Level," *New York Daily News*, September 20, 1999, pp. 6–7.

11. Ibid., p. 7.

12. Milton and Rose Friedman, *Free to Choose* (New York: Avon Books, 1979), p. 98.

13. See Max Weber, *The Protestant Ethic and the Spirit of Capitalism* (New York: Prentice-Hall, 1980).

14. Carl E. Prince, *Brooklyn's Dodgers: The Bums, the Borough, and the Best of Baseball* (New York: Oxford University Press, 1995), p. 45.

15. William E. Leuchtenburg, *Franklin D. Roosevelt and the New Deal: 1932– 1940* (New York: Harper and Row, 1963), p. 119.

16. Ibid., p. 120.

17. Studs Terkel, *Hard Times: An Oral History of the Great Depression* (New York: Pantheon Books, 1986), p. 422.

18. Ibid., p. 425.

19. Jason De Parle, "What Welfare-to-Work Really Means," *New York Times Magazine*, December 20, 1998, p. 53.

20. Ibid.

21. Ibid., p. 54.

22. Ibid.

23. Noll and Zimbalist, op. cit., "Build the Stadium—Create the Jobs," p. 29.

24. "The Report of the Independent Members of the Commissioner's Blue Ribbon Panel on Baseball Economics," July 2000. *MLB Online.*

25. Ibid., p. 11.

26. Ibid., p. 13.

27. Ibid., p. 15.

28. Ibid., p. 17.

29. Philip Lentz, "Yanks Slam TV Home Run" *Crain's New York Business*, May 1–7, 2000, pp. 1, 41.

Epilogue

1. *New York Times*, December 29, 2001, p. A1.

2. Ibid., January 8, 2002, p. B3.

3. Yankee Stadium Redevelopment Civic Project, General Project Plan, January 18, 2006, p. 1.

4. New Yankee Stadium Project, June 15, 2005, pp. 1–2.

5. SEQRA is the State Environmental Quality Review Act; ULURP is the Uniform Land Use Review Procedure; and PILOTs are Payments in Lieu of Taxes.

6. *New York Times*, June 19, 2005.

7. Memorandum of Understanding, p. 7.

8. Their two major reports on the new Yankee Stadium are "Loot, Loot, Loot for the Home Team," February 2006; and "Insider Baseball: How Current and Former Public Officials Pitched a Community Shutout for the New York Yankees," July 2007.

9. "Insider Baseball," p. 5.

10. *New York Times*, April 6, 2006.

11. "Participation and Labor Force Mitigation and Community Benefits Program Related to the Construction of the New Yankee Stadium," April 2006.

12. William L. Riordan, *Plunkitt of Tammany Hall* (New York: Signet, 1995), p. 5.

13. "Insider Baseball," p. 2.

14. "General Project Plan," p. 2.

15. Ibid., p. 1.

Index